THE TYRANTS OF SYRACUSE: WAR IN ANCIENT SICILY

THE TYRANTS OF SYRACUSE: WAR IN ANCIENT SICILY

Volume II: 367–211 BC

by

Jeff Champion

Pen & Sword
MILITARY

First published in Great Britain in 2012 and reprinted in this format in 2021 by
PEN & SWORD MILITARY
An imprint of
Pen & Sword Books Ltd
47 Church Street
Barnsley
South Yorkshire
S70 2AS

ISBN 978 1 39901 318 5

Typeset in Sabon by
Concept, Huddersfield, West Yorkshire.

Printed and bound in England by
CPI Group (UK) Ltd, Croydon, CR0 4YY.

Pen & Sword Books Ltd incorporates the Imprints of Pen & Sword Aviation,
Pen & Sword Family History, Pen & Sword Maritime, Pen & Sword Military,
Pen & Sword Discovery, Wharncliffe Local History, Wharncliffe True Crime,
Wharncliffe Transport, Pen & Sword Select, Pen & Sword Military Classics,
Leo Cooper, The Praetorian Press, Remember When, Seaforth Publishing and
Frontline Publishing.

For a complete list of Pen & Sword titles please contact
PEN & SWORD BOOKS LIMITED
47 Church Street, Barnsley, South Yorkshire, S70 2AS, England
E-mail: enquiries@pen-and-sword.co.uk
Website: www.pen-and-sword.co.uk

Contents

Preface

In the early months of 405 the Syracusan assembly had been faced with a terrible crisis. In the preceding three years the Carthaginians, a Phoenician people who controlled the western end of Sicily, had broken the seventy years of peace and waged war on the Greeks of Sicily. Three major cities, Selinus, Himera and Akragas had been destroyed. Sicily was flooded with refugees. The Carthaginians were poised to attack the neighbouring city of Gela. The fifteen generals elected annually by the Syracusan people, the *demos*, had proven incapable of stopping the relentless Carthaginian advance.

In this moment of crisis, a young soldier named Dionysius stepped forward. He accused the generals of incompetence and treason. What Syracuse needed, he claimed, was strong and effective military leadership. If the people should vote for him to be *strategos autocrator* – a general with full powers, a temporary dictator – he would put an end to the Carthaginian threat.

In this moment of desperation, Dionysius' proposal struck a chord with many in the assembly. The last time the Carthaginians had invaded Greek Sicily, in 480, they had been soundly beaten by Gelon, the first tyrant of Syracuse. Gelon was remembered as the saviour of Greek civilisation from a barbarian invasion. Few recalled that he had also overthrown the first Syracusan democracy and destroyed several Greek cities in his rise to power. The assembly voted to give Dionysius the powers he sought. Most probably believed that this would be a short-term expediency and once the barbarian threat was removed, things would return to normal; few would have believed that they had voted away their democracy for two generations.

Dionysius would use his position and the legendary wealth of Syracuse to seize power as tyrant and to build a dynasty. The island of Ortygia would be separated from the rest of Syracuse and turned into a private fortress. From here Dionysius and later tyrants used their mercenaries and informers to terrorize the Syracusan people into submission.

For the duration of his reign, Dionysius would campaign intermittently against the Carthaginians and, by the end of his life he had created an empire that included most of the Greek cities of Sicily and southern Italy. Syracuse would become the most powerful city in the Greek world, its alliance sought by the traditional leading cities of Athens and Sparta. This had come, however, at a terrible cost: during his reign Dionysius had destroyed almost as many Greek cities as had the Carthaginians.

By the time of his death in 367, Dionysius' rule was unchallenged. Those Syracusans who thought that his death would end the tyranny and allow Syracuse to return to a constitutional government were to be heartily disappointed: the tyranny would pass seamlessly to his son, also named Dionysius.

In passing on the tyranny onto his son, Dionysius renewed a harsh political legacy that had begun over a century earlier. For the first three centuries after their foundations, the Greek cities of Sicily had followed a political path common to many Greek cities: an aristocratic government which was overthrown by tyrants, who were then in turn driven out by the people. The first tyrant of Syracuse, Gelon, the victor of Himera, had also created a dynasty but his brother, Thrasybulus, was eventually driven out of Syracuse in 466 and a democracy was installed.

The Syracusan democracy would thrive for sixty years. A period considered as a golden age by later Sicilians, such as the historian Diodorus.[1] This was the government that had been overthrown by Dionysius. Long periods of tyranny had not been the usual form of government for the Greek cities outside of Sicily for over a century; other states had endured tyrants but would eventually drive them out and return to more representative governments. The Syracusan *demos* would share this desire for a freer political system, yet they would be constantly thwarted by the rise of new tyrants.

This volume attempts to produce an easily accessible, narrative history of the events from the death of Dionysius the Elder until the capture of Syracuse by the Romans. As was the case in the first volume, the coverage of events in this book will be uneven, as a result of the patchy nature of the surviving ancient sources. This book can be loosely be divided into three sections: the struggles of the Syracusan people, led at times by Dion and Timoleon, to overthrow the tyranny of Dionysius the Younger (367–336); the collapse of Timoleon's political settlement and the tyranny of Agathocles (336–289); and the rule of Hieron II and the intervention of Rome into the affairs of Sicily (276–212). The period between the death of Agathocles' and the rise of Hieron was one of chaos, broken only by the brief intervention into Sicilian affairs by the brilliant, but mercurial, Pyrrhus of Epirus.

The first part will be dominated by the careers of Dion and Timoleon, due largely to the survival of Plutarch's biographies.[2] Care must be taken using these works, however, as Plutarch was strongly biased in favour of his two heroes at the expense of the Syracusan *demos*. Fortunately his narrative can be balanced with the more sober account of Diodorus.

For the career of Agathocles we are largely dependant on the writings of Diodorus. The last decade of his career falls into that period where Diodorus' history has largely been lost and it is necessary to supplement those surviving fragments with the derivative work of Justin.[3] Justin's work is useful as it is full of colourful anecdotes of people, yet he was extraordinarily careless in his method of composition and has a poor reputation as an historian. This gives rise to a saying in my old Classics Departments (designed to get students to read the ancient authors rather than modern historians), that: any ancient source is more useful than the best modern opinion, even Justin.

The rule of Hieron and the invasion of the Romans are covered in some detail by both Polybius and Livy.[4] Both were, however, more concerned with describing the rise of Rome rather than events in Sicily. This perhaps leaves us with a somewhat distorted record of events, particularly regarding the internal politics of Syracuse in its final years after the death of Hieron.

I have generally used the Latin forms of personal names as I believe that these are better known. For geographical names I have been less consistent, freely mixing both Latin, Greek and modern forms. Where known, modern place names will appear in brackets after the first instance of the ancient name. Throughout the work I will use the terms Sicilian and Italian to refer exclusively to the Greek populations of those regions. All dates, unless otherwise noted, are BC.

In the first volume of this work Dionysius the Elder was known simply as Dionysius and his son as Dionysius the Younger. For simplicity's sake I will reverse that method in this book and use Dionysius to refer to Dionysius the Younger, while designating his father as Dionysius the Elder.

I would like to thank the following for their assistance in research and composition: Andrew Card, Geoff Devitt, Julie Rose and Geoff Tindall. For help in other ways I would also like to thank: Tony Pontikos, Vince Rispoli and David Waugh.

Last, but most importantly I would like to thank my wife Janine for her constant support. Over the last four years she allowed me to hijack large parts of her first European holidays to search for obscure battlefields and sites, often in some less than salubrious locations. It is a standing joke that at least once a trip I will take her for a long walk through a wasteland. Fortunately the good has outweighed the bad, as we have visited such wonderful places as Taormina, Agrigento, Selinus, Motya, Erice, Himera, the Aeolian Islands, Carthage, Kerkouane and, of course, the amazing city of Syracuse.

Plates

Maps

List of Maps

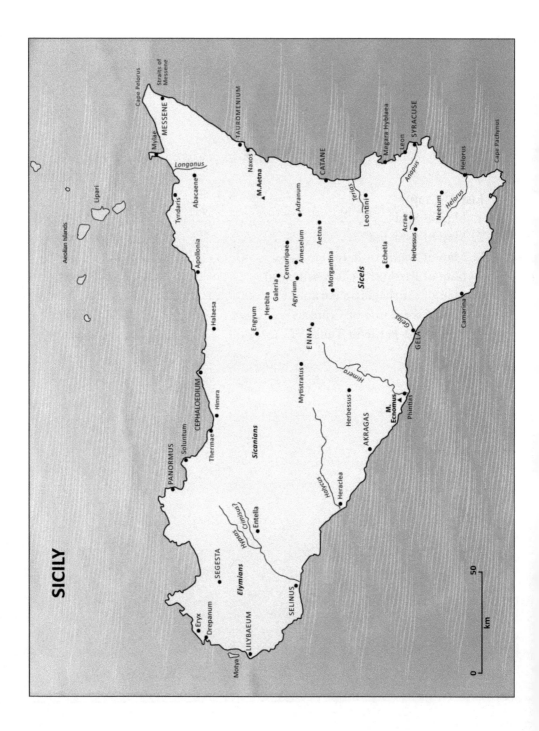

SICILY

Aeolian Islands

Lipari

Cape Pelorus
Straits of Messene
MESSENE
Mylae
TAUROMENIUM
Longanus
Naxos
M.Aetna
Abacaene
Tyndaris
CATANE
Apollonia
Adranum
Terias
Ameselum
M.Aetna
Aetna
Leontini
Megara Hyblaea
Leon
SYRACUSE
Centuripae
Agyrium
Morgantina
Acrae
Herbessus
Anapus
Cape Pachynus
Helorus
Neetum
Helorus
Galeria
Herbita
Echetla
Sicels
Halaesa
Engyum
ENNA
Camarina
Cephaloedium
Himera
Mytistratus
Gelas
GELA
Sicanians
Thermae
Himera
Soluntum
Herbessus
Phintias
M. Ecnomus
PANORMUS
Halycus
Heraclea
AKRAGAS
Hypsas
Chimsus?
Entella
Segesta
Elymians
SELINUS
Eryx
Drepanum
LILYBAEUM
Motya

0   50
km

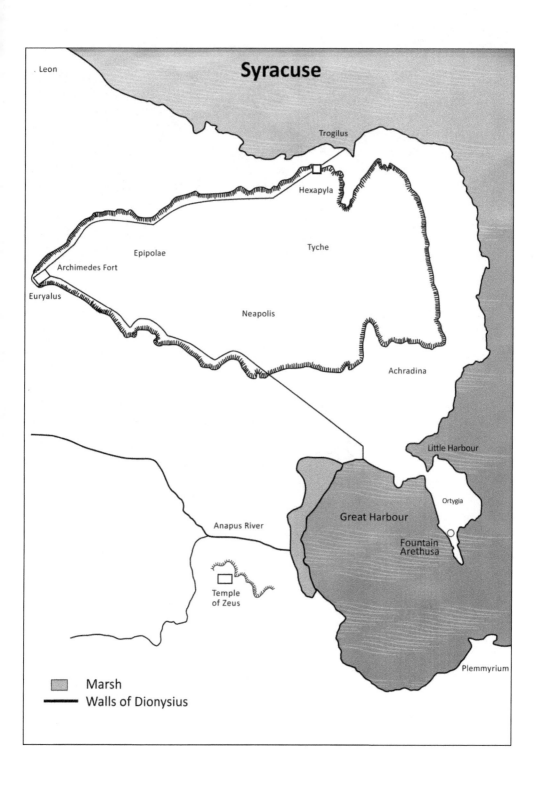

Syracuse

Leon

Trogilus

Hexapyla

Tyche

Epipolae

Archimedes Fort

Euryalus

Neapolis

Achradina

Little Harbour

Ortygia

Great Harbour

Anapus River

Fountain
Arethusa

Temple
of Zeus

Plemmyrium

Marsh

Walls of Dionysius

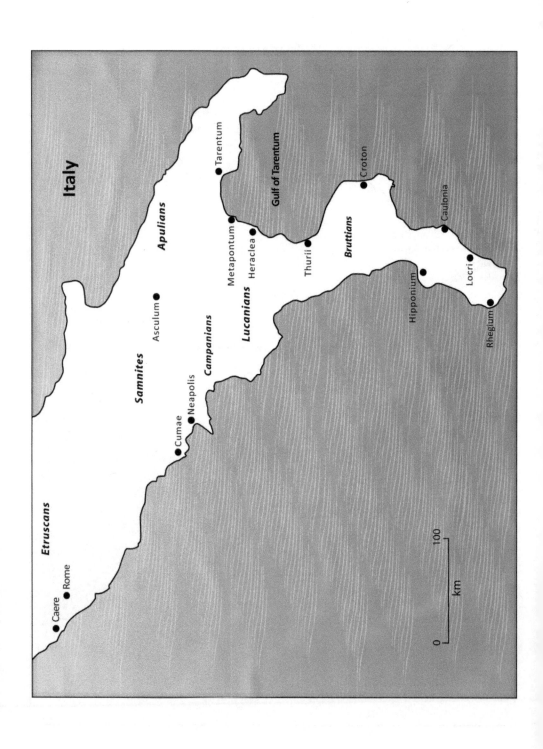

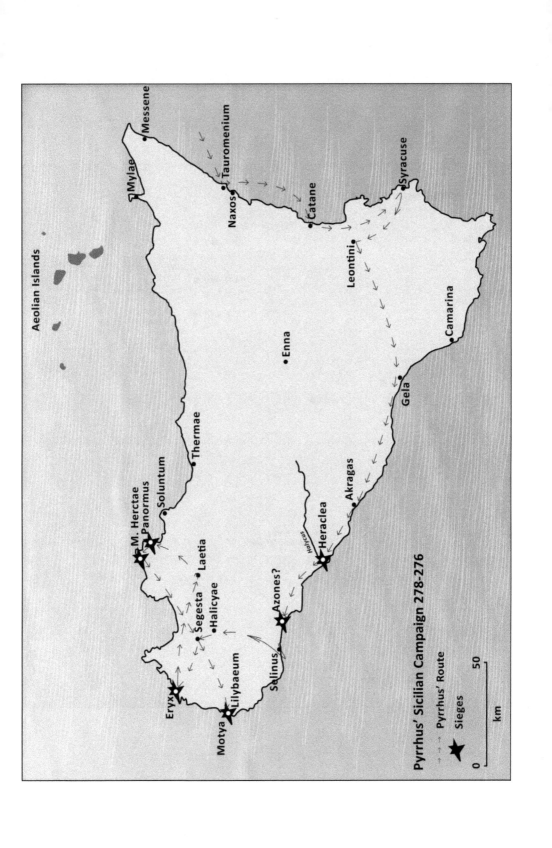

Aeolian Islands

Messene
Mylae
Tauromenium
Naxos
Catane
Leontini
Syracuse
Camarina
Enna
Gela
Thermae
Soluntum
M. Herctae
Panormus
Segesta
Laetia
Halicyae
Akragas
Heraclea
Halycus
Azones?
Eryx
Motya
Lilybaeum
Selinus

Pyrrhus' Sicilian Campaign 278-276

→→→ Pyrrhus' Route
★ Sieges

0   50
km

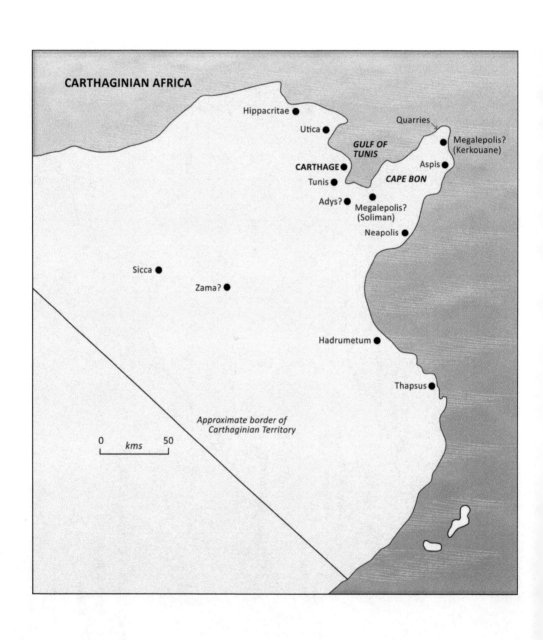

CARTHAGINIAN AFRICA

Hippacritae ●

Quarries

Utica ●

GULF OF
TUNIS

Megalepolis?
(Kerkouane) ●

CARTHAGE ●

Aspis ●

CAPE BON

Tunis ●

Adys? ●

Megalepolis?
(Soliman) ●

Neapolis ●

Sicca ●

Zama? ●

Hadrumetum ●

Thapsus ●

Approximate border of
Carthaginian Territory

0   kms   50

Battle of Crimisus River   Initial Deployment

Crimisus River

1 Greek Cavalry initial
attack on chariots
2 Greek Cavalry withdraw
to flanks

Carthaginian Infantry

Carthaginian Chariots

⚔ 1

⫷⫷ 2   Greek Cavalry   2 ⫸⫸

Hills

Timoleon
Greek Infantry

Battle of Crimisus River   First Greek Attack

Crimisus River

1 Greek Infantry attack and
defeat Carthaginian Infantry
2 Carthaginian vanguard flees

Carthaginian
Mercenary
Infantry

⫷⫷ 2   2 ⫸⫸

Carthaginian
Chariots ?

Carthaginian Infantry

Carthaginian
Chariots ?

⚔ 1

Timoleon
Greek Infantry

Battle of Crimisus River   Second Greek Attack

Crimisus River

1 Aided by thunderstrom
Greek final assault routs
Carthaginian army

Thunderstorm

Carthaginian
Mercenary
Infantry

⚔ 1

Timoleon
Greek Infantry

Battle of Tunis   First Carthaginian Attacks

1 Carthaginican chariots attack, some break through Greek line.
2 Carthaginian cavalry attack and are driven off.

Bomilcar's Infantry advancing to battlefield

Lake of Tunis

Sacred Band	Carthaginian Infantry
Hanno	

Carthaginian Cavalry

2

Carthaginian Chariots

1

Greek Slingers and Archers

Agathocles	Other Infantry	Syracusans	Greek Mercenaries	Etrusan, Samnite and Gallish Mercenaries
Disguised Sailors				

Battle of Tunis   Hanno's Infantry Attack

1 Greek light infantry deal with surviving chariots?
2 Hanno attacks Greeks but is defeated and killed
3 Bomilcar's infantry attempt to withdraw but panic and flee

3

Bomilcar's Infantry

Lake of Tunis

Sacred Band	Carthaginian Infantry
Hanno	

2

Agathocles	Other Infantry	Syracusans	Greek Mercenaries	Etrusan, Samnite and Gallish Mercenaries

1

Greek Slingers, Archers and Sailors

Chapter 1

The Succession of Dionysius the Younger

Being conscious that he was surpassed by Dion in ability, influence, and in the affection of the people, and fearing that, if he kept Dion with him, he might give him some opportunity of overthrowing him, he gave him a trireme to sail to Corinth, declaring that he did so for both their sakes.

Nepos, *Dion* 4

In the early weeks of 367, Dionysius the Elder died peacefully in his bed. This quiet passing away was much to the disgust of ancient writers, who had hoped that the gods would punish him for his crimes with a lingering and painful death. He had ruled Syracuse as tyrant for 38 years; according to the ancient writers he left an empire 'bound fast by adamantine chains.'[1]

The empire that Dionysius the Elder had created was centred on Syracuse, which he had made into the largest and most powerful of Greek cities. The Athenian philosopher Plato claims that Dionysius' control of Sicily was such that he 'had gathered the whole of Sicily into a single city.'[2] This is largely rhetoric, as the Carthaginians controlled many of the Sicilian cities, but probably reflects the control that Dionysius exerted over the Greek cities of eastern Sicily, many of which had been implanted with large populations of his former mercenaries. Plato's statement is also an attack on Dionysius' policy of destroying Greek cities and forcibly relocating their populations to Syracuse. By these means Syracuse's population had swollen until its territory contained possibly as many as 500,000 inhabitants. The city had become a fortress, being enclosed within 27km of fortifications. It was renowned in ancient times for its extraordinary wealth. In addition, Syracuse controlled the Greek cities of southern Italy, from Rhegium to Croton.

During his reign Dionysius the Elder had married twice and produced four sons, two from each wife. Multiple sons were always a cause for conflict over the succession and could lead to murder and civil war following the death of a ruler. Dionysius the Elder is reputed to have excluded his sons from political responsibility during his life due to a paranoid fear that they would become his rivals and assassins. There was, therefore, no pre-determined successor. Primogeniture was usual but not always practised, especially when there was more than one mother. A later ruler of Syracuse, Pyrrhus of Epirus, would describe this reality. When asked by one of his three sons, all by different mothers, who should inherit the throne, he replied, 'to the one of you who keeps his sword the sharpest.'[3] This was the famous curse of Oedipus, that thrones should be won by the sword and not inherited by order of birth.

The court of Dionysius the Elder was no different and the conflict over the succession began as soon as he suffered his fatal illness. The court was split into two factions. His oldest son, Dionysius, was the son of a non-Syracusan mother, Doris, from the Italian city of Locri. Dionysius the Elder's other wife, Aristomache, was a native Syracusan; she and her brother, Dion, were from a leading aristocratic and very wealthy family. Dion was brother-in-law to Dionysius, having married his niece, Arete, the daughter of Aristomache. In the days before the tyrant's death Dion attempted to have his nephews (and brothers-in-law), Hipparinus and Nysaeus, recognized as the heirs to the tyranny.

The year following Dionysius the Elder's death would be dominated by the rivalry between Dionysius and Dion. We have two main ancient accounts of this struggle, those of Plutarch and Diodorus, of which Plutarch's is the most detailed. Using Plutarch as an historical source is not, however, without its pitfalls. Plutarch freely admits that he is a biographer not an historian and his main interest is the character of his subjects. As he confesses:

> I always cherish in my soul the records of the noblest and most estimable characters, to repel and put far from me whatever base, malicious, or ignoble suggestion my enforced associations may intrude upon me, calmly and dispassionately turning my thoughts away from them to the fairest of my examples.[4]

In *Dion* he appears to have taken this tendency to excess. When reading Plutarch's account of this power struggle the undoubted favour shown by the author towards Dion is obvious. He begins his biography as he intends to continue. According to Plutarch, Dion's life demonstrated 'that wisdom and justice must be united with power and good fortune if public careers are to take on beauty as well as grandeur.'[5] Furthermore Dion was 'of a lofty character, magnanimous, and manly.'[6] When it came to military matters 'Dion was a consummate general; where he himself made the plans, he achieved the best results, and where failure was due to others, he restored and bettered the situation.'[7]

The only criticisms Plutarch levels at Dion are that:

His character had naturally a certain majesty, together with a harsh-
ness that repelled intercourse and was hard to deal with ... but many
also who were intimate with him and many who loved the simplicity
and nobility of his disposition, were apt to find fault with the manner
of his intercourse with men, on the ground that he dealt with those
who sought his aid more rudely and harshly than was needful in
public life.[8]

In contrast to his hero, Plutarch describes his opponent Dionysius as a man
of no worth or ability, 'despised by every one of his associates, devoted as
he was to wine, dice, and women.'[9] Plutarch did not limit his criticisms to
Dionysius but also poured scorn on Dion's democratic allies. They were
politically inept and ungrateful as they 'stumbled in their undertakings, and
yet hated Dion, who, like a physician, wished to subject the city to a strict
and temperate regimen.'[10] In battle they are undisciplined and cowardly,
constantly having to be saved from their own folly by Dion. Plutarch
reserves his worst condemnations for Heracleides, a fellow exile of Dion
who later turns on him and joins the democrats. Heracleides' main purpose
in the narrative appears to be to allow Plutarch to contrast his villainy to the
virtues of his hero. Dion is described as being 'superior to Heracleides, not
so much in power and wisdom, as in goodness and justice; for therein lay
real superiority, whereas 'envy led Heracleides to be faithless and base.[11]

Fortunately, as a counter to Plutarch's portrayals, we also have Diodorus'
account, although it is less complete. Dion is praised, but less profusely,
as a man who had a 'nobility of spirit', 'a great proficiency in philosophy
and, in matter of courage and skill in the art of war, far surpassed the other
Syracusans of his time.'[12] In Diodorus' history the Syracusan citizens usually
fight bravely and show political judgement. Heracleides is not criticized at
all but is praised because the Syracusans 'believed that he would never aim
at tyrannical power.'[13] For these reasons, Diodorus' more sober account,
where it exists, will generally be preferred to that of Plutarch. In addition
to the two main sources there also survives a brief biography of Dion by
Cornelius Nepos, and sections of Justin's history.[14]

Dion was born about 410 and was in his early forties at the time of
Dionysius the Elder's death. He was a student and friend of Plato, and
therefore supposedly an enemy of both tyranny and democracy. This made
him a hero to the ancient authors, most of whom shared his aristocratic
background and politics. It is also claimed that he was Plato's lover, but
unless he was sent to Athens as a child this would appear to be unlikely. He
was already in his twenties at the time of Plato's first visit to Syracuse and
homosexual relationships between adult-male citizens were frowned upon.
Sex was very much about power in ancient Greece and it was assumed that

in homosexual relationships one partner played a passive role and therefore unmanned himself. Any openly sexual relationship with Plato as an adult would have left Dion open to ridicule and damaged his political career.

Despite his dedication to Plato's philosophy, Dion had been one of the previous tyrant's most powerful advisors. Nepos excuses this, claiming that this was largely done to protect his family: 'for though the cruelty of Dionysius offended him, yet he was desirous that he should be secure because of his family connexion with himself, and still more for the sake of his own relatives.'[15]

Dionysius was younger than Dion, about 30-years-old at the time of his father's death. Plutarch gives a very unflattering portrait of the oldest son and presumed heir. His father, fearing a rival, had kept 'him closely shut up at home ... and in ignorance of affairs' As a result he was seen' to be dwarfed and deformed in character from his lack of education.'[16] Dionysius the Elder's exclusion of his sons from government affairs and the paranoid atmosphere at his court had a negative effect on their characters. All were renowned for their heavy drinking and licentious behaviour. Justin gives us a very unappealing description of Dionysius' physical features and character, claiming that he: 'fell into indolence, and contracted, from excessive indulgence at table, great corpulence of body, and a disease in his eyes, so that he could not bear the sunshine, or dust, or even the brightness of ordinary daylight.'[17]

Despite his supposed ignorance of affairs, Dionysius appears to have been the master of the situation. He outmanoeuvred his uncle by convincing the doctor to administer a strong sedative to his father, preventing Dion from talking to the tyrant and obtaining a decision in favour of his nephews. After the death of his father, Dionysius called a session of the Syracusan assembly and 'having buried his father with magnificent obsequies in the citadel by the gates called royal, he made secure for himself the administration of the government.'[18] He had skilfully sidelined Dion, and his half-brothers, seizing the tyranny for himself.

Those among the Syracusan *demos* who had hoped for an end to the tyranny and a return to democracy were sadly disappointed. The new tyrant appears to have kept the loyalty of enough of his father's mercenaries and courtiers to ensure his succession. From the tyrant's stronghold on the fortified island of Ortygia he was able to enforce the continued subservience of the population. Despite this position of strength, Dionysius 'applied himself first to gain the favour of his subjects' and 'therefore released 3,000 prisoners from the gaols, remitted the people the taxes for three years, and sought the affection of all by whatever blandishments he could use.'[19]

The most immediate problem that the new tyrant had to face was the threat of war with Carthage. His father had concluded a treaty with the Carthaginians shortly before his death. This peace would probably have been signed in his father's name and, if so, the Carthaginians could have claimed that it had been voided by his death. They had ended 368 with a series of victories over the Greeks and may have felt that the succession crisis in Syracuse was an opportune time to renew the war.

This emergency was the main item of discussion at the first conference of the new tyrant and his advisors. Plutarch claims that Dion dominated the meeting speaking 'upon the needs of the situation in such a manner that his wisdom made all the rest appear children, and his boldness of speech made them seem mere slaves of tyranny, who were wont to give their counsels timorously and ignobly to gratify the young man.'[20] He offered to go to Carthage personally to negotiate a new peace. Dion had previously been used as an ambassador to negotiate a treaty with the Carthaginians, who 'never regarded any man that spoke the Greek tongue with more admiration.'[21] Somewhat imprudently he sent a letter to the Carthaginians in which he advised them to always include him in any negotiations as 'he would help them to arrange everything securely.'[22]

Dionysius shrewdly decided not to send his main domestic rival to confer with his foremost external enemy. Nevertheless, Dionysius managed to renew the peace with the Carthaginians and it would continue for the duration of his reign. Although the details are not recorded it was most likely on the same terms as those of his father: the Carthaginians would control all of Sicily west of the Halycus River, including the Greek cities of Selinus and Heraclea; the other Greek cities, east of this line and outside of Syracusan territory, would remain neutral.

Conducting a war was always the largest of an ancient city's expenses and Dionysius the Elder had been notorious for the heavy taxation he had imposed to fund his many campaigns. It was by making peace with Carthage that Dionysius was able to attempt to buy further favour among his new subjects by repealing taxes for three years. In the early years of his reign Dionysius' rule is recorded as being very mild. Plutarch alleges, however, that his mildness was a result of his 'sundry amours, idle amusements with wine and women, and other unseemly pastimes. In this way the tyranny, being softened, like iron in the fire, appeared to its subjects to be kindly, and gradually remitted its excessive cruelty, though its edge was blunted not so much by any clemency in the sovereign as by his love of ease.'[23]

What does appear likely is that Dionysius was initially unsure of his position. He therefore courted the favour of the Syracusans and included the powerful Dion among his closest advisors. The stated purpose of the tyranny had, however, always been to command the armies of Syracuse and to liberate the Greek cities from Carthaginian control. During this period of peace the new tyrant had little to occupy his time and abandoned himself to a life of luxury and hedonism, including indulging in a 'drinking bout for ninety consecutive days from its beginning, and that during this time the court gave no access or admission to men or matters of consequence.'[24]

Dion, in common with his teacher Plato, appears to have been a bit of a prig and disapproved of the luxury and hedonism of the court, 'having set his affection on virtue in preference to pleasure and self-indulgence.'[25] Plato, during his first visit to Syracuse, had loudly pronounced his disapproval of the extravagance he had found in the wealthy cities of Italy and Sicily, claiming that this was the reason for their political instability. Dion's constant lectures of disapproval and his powerful position were greatly resented by Dionysius' other advisors. Plutarch states that this rivalry was a result of 'the difference between his way of life and theirs, and in his refusal to mingle with others.'[26] More realistically he also alleges that they feared Dion was continuing to use his wealth and power to subvert Dionysius' rule in order to replace him with his nephews.

Dion had previously brought Plato to the court of Dionysius the Elder, but the philosopher had fallen out with the tyrant and nearly ended up being sold into slavery. Dion believed that if he could persuade Plato to return to Syracuse, Plato could convince Dionysius 'to become his disciple, in order that his character might be regulated by the principles of virtue, and that he might be conformed to that divinest and most beautiful model of all being, in obedience to whose direction the universe issues from disorder into order.' Such an education would help curb Dionysius' excesses, for unlike his ruthless father, he 'did not belong to the worst class of tyrants.'[27] Dion believed that if forced to live under a tyrant then the most expedient course of action was to convert him to philosophy.

Although it is beyond the scope of this work, and the capability of the author, to fully discuss the entirety of Plato's philosophy, some discussion of his political theories is necessary. Plato, perhaps as a result of the execution of his teacher Socrates by the Athenian democracy, was obsessed with the concept of justice; he believed that society must be governed in a just way. Plato was also fixated on being able to define exactly concepts such as justice and virtue. He argued that unless a ruler had a perfect understanding of justice then he could not implement it; only philosophers had the education necessary to comprehend justice. As Plato wrote 'to men like him, I said, when perfected by years and education, and to these only you will entrust the State.'[28] As a result it was necessary that society be governed by philosophers.

Plato's argument asserted that rulers needed to be experts in their field, just as doctors, sea-captains, artisans or farmers were. An ideal society would therefore be one where everyone did the job for which they had both the training and the aptitude. Plato, therefore, envisioned that the ideal society would have a rigid caste system. Justice would be based on this division of labour, with every citizen doing that for which they were most suited. At the top would be the philosophers, either as a ruling council or in the person of a philosopher-king. Next would be the guardians who would defend the society and enforce its laws. The bottom classes would be the tradesmen, farmers and labourers, those who did all the actual work.

In order to have the lower classes accept their position, Plato proposed an elaborate system of indoctrination from birth, selective breeding of the population and the taking away of children from the parents to be raised by the state. These ideas were based on an idealized view of Spartan society. None would have been out of place in some of the worst totalitarian regimes of the modern era.

Modern admirers of Plato's undoubted contribution to philosophy are often embarrassed by such arguments, admitting that if he did indeed mean them to be taken literally, 'then he deserves all the obloquy which has been heaped on him'. They generally argue along the lines that he did not mean for *The Republic* 'to be taken as a blue-print for a real-life polity' but merely 'to cast light on the nature of justice in the soul.'[29]

Unfortunately for this idealized view of Plato's teachings, in a later work, *Statesman*, he spells out exactly how such a regime should deal with dissent:

> With a view to the public good they purge the State by killing some, or exiling some; whether they reduce the size of the body corporate by sending out from the hive swarms of citizens, or, by introducing persons from without, increase it; while they act according to the rules of wisdom and justice, and use their power with a view to the general security and improvement, the city over which they rule, and which has these characteristics, may be described as the only true State.[30]

When asked about this, Plato's hero Socrates responds by saying, 'I agree, stranger, in the greater part of what you say; but as to their ruling without laws – the expression has a harsh sound.'[31] Not that it is wrong, only that it sounds harsh. In reality, Plato, through his mouthpiece Socrates, was advocating exactly the same policies of repression that had been carried out by the tyrants of Sicily. This, it should be kept in mind, was the ideological underpinnings of the sort of state Dion wished to introduce into Syracuse. To the average citizen of Syracuse it might have been difficult to discern the difference between a philosopher-king and a tyrant.

It should also be noted that Plutarch's description of events in Syracuse, and his admiration of Dion, were also influenced by his own political views and admiration of Plato. He believed that in deciding their form of government, any sensible man would 'would follow Plato's advice and choose no other than monarchy, the only one which is able to sustain that top note of virtue.'[32]

Another of the causes of Plutarch's bias was his choice of Timonades as his major source for the period after Dion's return to Syracuse and his conflict with the democratic forces in the city. Timonades was a fellow student of Dion at Plato's Academy in Athens during Dion's exile. He accompanied Dion to Syracuse for the campaign against Dionysius and was therefore an eye-witness to these events. As a source, Timonades was undoubtedly favourable towards Dion and hostile to his democratic opponents. This leads Porter to argue in his commentary on *Dion* that:

> It is not surprising that Plutarch, with his admiration for Plato, his predilection for Monarchy and his somewhat limited conception of the duty of a biographer, should have based his account of the crucial years of Dion's life on the narrative of one of Dion's partisans ignoring what the historians had urged in criticism of Dion or in defence of his democratic opponents.[33]

Eventually Dion convinced Plato to return to Syracuse. Plato stated that his reason for returning was that 'if ever anyone was to try to carry out in practice my ideas about laws and constitutions, now was the time for making the attempt.'[34] Plutarch puts it more succinctly, claiming that Plato returned 'out of shame more than anything else, lest men should think him nothing but theory and unwilling to take any action.'[35] It is necessary here to include a note of caution. Although most historians accept the historicity of Plato's visits to the court of Dionysius the Younger and the authenticity of at least some of his *Letters*, there is a small but convinced minority who claim that they are fictitious.

Although the battle for succession had been won by Dionysius, his supporters realized that with Plato's invitation a new fight had begun. This new battle would be over who would influence the tyrant and his policies.

Chapter 2

Dionysius and Plato

Plato, however, had so much influence over Dionysius by his authority, and produced such an effect on him by his eloquence, that he persuaded him to put an end to his tyranny, and to restore liberty to the Syracusans.

Nepos, *Dion* 3

The invitation of Plato to Syracuse provoked Dion's enemies to persuade Dionysius to recall his father's supporter Philistus, 'a man versed in letters and acquainted with the ways of tyrants, that they might have in him a counterpoise to Plato and philosophy'.[1] Philistus had been one of Dionysius the Elder's earliest and staunchest supporters. He later fell out with him, supposedly over marriage intrigues, but possibly because he had participated in a plot to replace the tyrant with his brother Leptines. Philistus had been exiled to Adria in Italy where he wrote a history of Sicily. He was accused by other ancient authors of using his writings to glorify Dionysius the Elder.

As soon as Philistus returned he began to intrigue against Dion. He accused him of plotting with Heracleides, the commander of the garrison of Ortygia, to overthrow the tyranny. There was probably some basis to these accusations. Plutarch states that Dion first hoped to win Dionysius over to the teachings of Plato but if this attempt failed he would help restore the democracy, 'not that he approved of democracy, but thought it better than tyranny in lack of a sound and healthy aristocracy'.[2] In other words, Dion was really a supporter of oligarchy but had decided that even a democracy would be better than the continued rule of Dionysius.

It was into this highly charged political atmosphere that Plato finally arrived in Syracuse in late 367. At first all went well and the study of philosophy and science suddenly became fashionable amongst the elite of the city. 'There was also something like a general rush for letters and philosophy, and the palace was filled with dust, as they say, owing to the multitude of geometricians there.'[3] The latter was the result of their method of drawing sketches in the sand. The presence of the already famous Plato certainly encouraged other philosophers to come to the Syracusan court.

Dionysius, whose rule had been remarkably benign up to this point, was supposed to have dropped hints that he might relinquish his position and put an end to the tyranny. The faction around Philistus was horrified, as they 'thought that time and familiarity would render Plato's influence almost irresistible, if now, after a brief intimacy, he had so altered and transformed the sentiments of the youthful prince.'[4] They increased their attacks on Dion, repeating their accusations that he planned to replace Dionysius with his nephews. The nationalist card was also played: they accused Plato of being an agent of the Athenians, trying to conquer Syracuse with words after their two previous invasions of Sicily had failed miserably.

Philistus and his supporters succeeded in arousing Dionysius' suspicions. The final blow to Dion's reputation came when they obtained the letter he had written to the Carthaginians. There are three different versions of the account of Dion's expulsion. Plutarch claims that this evidence finally convinced Dionysius that Dion was in actuality plotting against him. Three months after Plato's arrival Dionysius confronted Dion with the letter and refused to listen to any defence. Dion was placed on board a ship and without delay exiled to Italy. Nepos states that Dionysius realized the two could not co-exist peacefully in the same city and sent Dion directly to Corinth for his own protection. Diodorus records that Dionysius, fearing that Dion was powerful enough to overthrow him, 'decided to get him out of the way by arresting him on a charge involving the death penalty.' Dion managed to escape to Greece along with his brother Megacles.[5]

Dion's exile caused considerable consternation in Syracuse amongst the tyrant's advisors who were not part of Philistus' faction. They feared they too could be summarily dismissed, or worse, at Dionysius' whim. The women of the court, including Dionysius' wife and half-sister, Sophrosyne, were also supporters of Dion. The democratic faction was encouraged by the thought that the ruling elite were fighting among themselves and were 'cheered by the expectation of a revolution and a speedy change in the government.'[6] Taken aback by these responses, Dionysius did a political back-flip, claiming that Dion had not been exiled but merely sent on a diplomatic mission to Italy. He continued the fiction by allowing Dion to continue to draw on income from his estates in Sicily.

With Plato's star pupil now removed, Dionysius began to behave towards the philosopher like a spoiled child. He forced him to move to the acropolis and gave him a 'guard of honour'; in effect Plato was now a prisoner of the tyrant. Dionysius was reputedly so smitten that he desired that 'he alone should have his love returned by Plato and be admired beyond all others, and he was ready to entrust Plato with the administration of the tyranny if only he would not set his friendship for Dion above that which he had for him.'[7]

Whether or not Dionysius was serious in his offers was never determined. In 365, the Lucanians, a people of southern Italy, attacked Dionysius' territories in Italy. He was compelled to fulfil his position of general and take command of the Syracusan forces. Diodorus records that Dionysius 'pursued war listlessly for some time against the Lucanians and then, in the latest battles having had the advantage, he gladly brought to a close the war against them.'[8] In fact this was a very real achievement, as the Lucanians had become a serious threat to the Greek cities of Italy. It was no doubt downplayed by the ancient authors in order to maintain their portrayal of Dionysius as weak and ineffective. Dionysius remained involved in Italy after the war. He founded two cities in Apulia to combat piracy in the area and to secure Syracuse's sea route to Greece. These foundations were a continuation of his father's policy of protecting the crossing to Greece by planting colonies around the Adriatic Sea.

Once he had completed his Italian expedition Dionysius returned to Syracuse in either 364 or 363. Here he renewed his infatuation with philosophy. Diodorus accuses him of:

> Having given himself over to a peaceful existence, he relieved the soldiers of their drills in warfare and though he had succeeded to the greatest of the realms in Europe, the tyranny that was said by his father to be bound fast by adamantine chains, yet, strange to say, he lost it all by his pusillanimity.[9]

Justin may record a different version of these years of Dionysius' rule. He claims that Dionysius, after applying 'himself first to gain the favour of his subjects' then showed his true nature putting to death both his enemies and his supporters: 'not filling the gaols, like his father, with prisoners, but the whole city with dead bodies. Hence he became not more contemptible than hateful to every one.[10]

It appears that Dionysius had abandoned his early policy of benign rule and followed the example of his father, ruling by terrorizing any opposition through the use of his mercenaries and informers. Large numbers of the latter are recorded as being hunted down and murdered after his fall. Nepos claims that it was due to the influence of Philistus that Dionysius 'began to grow somewhat more cruel.'[11]

Dionysius' change of heart might have been the result of reports coming to him from Greece. Before leaving for Italy, Dionysius had released Plato and allowed him to return to Athens, provided he promise that he would not act against the tyrant. Dion, still in exile, joined Plato at his school, The Academy, in Athens. While there, Plato attempted to improve Dion's image of being arrogant and rude, telling him that they were not very useful traits in a politician, especially one trying to build an opposition to a tyranny. It is perhaps during this period that Dion was won over completely to Plato's political philosophy, abandoning his preference for oligarchy and supporting the concept of the rule of philosopher-kings.

Dion spent much of his time in exile visiting various cities, attempting to promote his own cause and to obtain backing for an overthrow of Dionysius. The Spartans were impressed enough to make him a citizen. All this did not go unnoticed in Syracuse and, in an effort to curtail Dion's activities, Dionysius stopped sending him the income from his estates and took it for himself. Nor did Dion's campaign meet with much real support in Greece. Many cities were willing to vote him various honours but none was willing to directly confront the power of Syracuse. Sparta was allied with Dionysius who had supplied them with ships for their continuing war against Thebes.

Despite filling his court with philosophers Dionysius could not be satisfied until he had convinced Plato to return to Syracuse. At first Plato was not interested, but Dionysius 'like a tyrant, was always extravagant in his desires and headstrong in all that he undertook.'[12] He decided to use both inducements and threats to persuade Plato to return. Dionysius sent a letter to Plato claiming that if he would 'come now in the first place, Dion's affairs will be dealt with in whatever way you yourself desire ... but if not, none of Dion's affairs will have results in accordance with your wishes.'[13]

Plato later claimed that his friends 'were literally pushing me out with their urgent entreaties, it was the same old tale – that I must not betray Dion.'[14] With great reluctance Plato eventually agreed to return to Syracuse, saying that he 'came for the third time to the straits of Scylla, that he might once more measure back his way to fell Charybdis.'[15] On his arrival in 361 he was dismayed to learn that Dionysius had not invited him to return in order to learn from him but rather to display his own supposed grasp of philosophy. Plato claims that the tyrant had written 'what professes to be his own handbook, very different, so he says, from the doctrines which he heard from me; but of its contents I know nothing.'[16]

Despite this, at first all went well between the tyrant and the philosopher. Plato expressed the hope that 'a young man, quick to learn, hearing talk of the great truths of philosophy, should feel a craving for the higher life.'[17] This bonhomie soon vanished when Plato insisted on bringing up the topic of Dion's recall. Dionysius, in a fit of pique, took his revenge, finally selling Dion's estates and keeping the money for himself.

Dionysius, perhaps as a last ditch effort to impress Plato, chose this moment to cut the pay of his mercenaries. This provoked a mutiny which forced the tyrant to back down and revoke the measure. Their commander, Heracleides, was accused of inciting the revolt and fled to Greece. Dionysius then began to suspect that Plato might be involved in undermining his position. He placed Plato under arrest and handed him over to the custody of his mercenaries. These men hated Plato, believing that he was the architect of their pay cut. They also believed that he had advised the tyrant to dismiss them completely.

Now no longer trying to impress Plato, Dionysius vented his full wrath against Dion. In an act of spite, Dionysius forced his half-sister, Arete, to divorce Dion, and married her to one of his friends, Timocrates. The loss of his estates, and the calculated insult of the divorce, convinced Dion that it was time to abandon philosophy and overthrow Dionysius by force. His supporters in Syracuse encouraged him with reports that the people were willing to revolt, claiming that he had only to appear and the people of Syracuse would flock to him.

Eventually Dionysius, influenced by the pleas of other philosophers agreed to release Plato. This was a relief to Plato who described how: 'I had the good fortune to return safely; and for this I must, next to the God, thank Dionysius, because, though many wished to make an end of me, he prevented them and paid some proper respect to my situation.'[18]

Plato returned to Greece in 360 where he met Dion at the Olympic Games. Dion had already determined to overthrow Dionysius by force and sought Plato's support. Plato gave his blessing to the quest and told Dion that his 'aspiration however was the same that I should say my own or that of any other right-minded man ought to be.' He refused to go on the grounds that he was too old for such ventures and that he had been a guest of the tyrant and owed him a debt for allowing him to leave Syracuse without harm. He did, however, tell Dion 'that he might call my friends to his aid, if they wished.'[19] With Plato's support, a number of the other members of The Academy, including Timonades, did agree to join their friend on his mission.

Deciding on a military expedition was one thing, organizing it another. Individuals would support him but no state was willing to risk war with Syracuse. It was no wonder that they baulked at attacking the tyrant. According to both Aelian and Diodorus the tyrant's forces were enormous:

> four hundred ships of war, infantry numbering nearly 100,000, 10,000 horse, and as great a store of arms, food, and money as one in all probability possessed who had to maintain lavishly the aforesaid forces; and, apart from all we have mentioned, had a city which was the largest of the cities of Hellas, and harbours and docks and fortified citadels that were impregnable, and, besides, a great number of powerful allies.[20]

These figures, if accurately recorded, would be the paper strength of all the forces available for military service throughout Dionysius' domains. It would be unlikely that both the money and organisational capacity would ever exist to raise such an enormous force.

The bias in the sources against Dionysius makes it difficult to determine exactly why he was so unpopular. Early in his reign reportedly his rule had been relatively mild. He had campaigned successfully in Italy and secured ten years of peace against the Carthaginians which had allowed Syracuse to recover its strength and prosperity. The very success of the peace may have been a major cause of his unpopularity. His father had come to power on the promise of liberating the Greek cities from the Carthaginians. The original title of the tyrant was *strategos autocrator*, general with all power. During a period of prolonged peace the Syracusans no doubt asked themselves why they should have to pay for the tyrant's 10,000 mercenaries 400 warships and his luxurious court. Others may have asked now that he had such impressive forces, why did he not fulfil his role and liberate the Greek cities from Carthaginian control. It is also possible that he was hated by many simply for being a dictator.

Dion was also joined at Corinth by Heracleides and the two began to secretly gather the forces necessary for the invasion. But as Nepos states: 'they made but little progress; for a tyranny of many years' standing was thought to be of great strength, and for that reason few were induced to join in so perilous an undertaking.'[21] During this period Heracleides argued with Dion and left him to recruit his own expedition. Plutarch blames this on the defects in his character but, as subsequent events would show, it was more likely an argument over the political future of Syracuse.

It took three years before Dion was finally able to gather together even a modest sized force of 1,000 mercenaries. The Syracusan exiles, when they saw the size of his army, abandoned him. Only 30 out of a total of 1,000 joined. When the mercenaries heard that they were to attack Syracuse they too nearly deserted. Dion managed, however, to talk them round. They nearly revolted again when on the eve of their departure from Greece an eclipse of the moon occurred – usually believed to be an omen of disaster. Fortunately Dion's seer declared that it was a good omen for the expedition as it foretold the eclipse of a great power: the tyranny of Dionysius. More favourable omens followed and, with the apparent blessing of the gods, the flotilla set sail for Sicily.

Chapter 3

The Return of Dion

Miltas the seer stood up amongst them and bade them be of good cheer and expect the best results; for the divine powers indicated an eclipse of something that was now resplendent; but nothing was more resplendent than the tyranny of Dionysius, and it was the radiance of this which they would extinguish as soon as they reached Sicily.

Plutarch, *Dion* 24

The date of Dion's departure to Sicily can be accurately dated to August of 357, due to the recording of a lunar eclipse. Despite the magnitude of the task, Dion's fleet was small, amounting to only three merchant vessels and two thirty-oared galleys. As well as his mercenaries, Dion's ships carried 5,000 shields and other weapons in order to arm any supporters.

The standard Greek infantryman of this time was a hoplite, a man wealthy enough to provide his own arms. His basic equipment was a stabbing spear nearly three metres long, and a shield about a metre wide. Anyone who could afford it would add a helmet. A wealthier man might augment his defensive equipment with a breastplate and greaves but these were relatively rare. The ownership of a spear and a shield was the minimum necessary requirement to serve in the line of battle. Even a hoplite shield was, however, a considerable expense, beyond the means of the poorer citizens. When a state, or in this case Dion, wished to increase its number of hoplites it would do so by providing the poor with a shield.

The hoplite formed up in a close-order formation known as a phalanx. The hoplites would often be shoulder to shoulder, usually around eight ranks deep, with their shields touching. They would maintain a solid line as they advanced, rather than running out from the ranks to seek individual foes. The shield was considered the most important piece of equipment as it protected not only oneself but one's neighbours and thereby presented an unbroken line of shields to the enemy. Although it is not certain, the evidence suggests that the Carthaginians adopted the same equipment and tactics for their citizen and Libyan infantry.

Learning that Philistus was campaigning in southern Italy with a fleet, Dion decided to risk the dangerous passage to Sicily via the open sea. Ancient warships were built for speed and were not very seaworthy if the weather turned bad. As a consequence captains preferred to hug the coast, both for safety and to secure provisions, especially water. Dion's fleet was fortunate as it had good weather for the twelve days of their voyage and the merchant ships were able to carry enough provisions for the small force. They made landfall at Cape Pachynus, the most south-eastern point of Sicily.

Their pilot advised that they disembark here as the seas were always treacherous along the southern coast of the island. Dion was unwilling to land so close to Syracuse and disregarded the advice, ordering the voyage to continue. As feared, the fleet was caught in a storm, driven further south to the coast of Africa and narrowly avoided shipwreck. Eventually the winds changed and they were able to reach Sicily.

Here Dion was able to make use of his contacts among the Carthaginians. He sailed to the Greek city of Heraclea, which had been ceded to the Carthaginians by the treaty signed in 368. The Carthaginian commander of the garrison, Synalus, was a friend of Dion but, not knowing who was leading the expedition, tried to prevent the landing. Dion's mercenaries put the Carthaginians to flight, although at his orders they killed none. The two friends then met and Synalus provided Dion with supplies.

It was just this sort of close relationship between the wealthy Greeks of Sicily and their Carthaginian counterparts that left them open to accusations of treachery. The elder Dionysius had used these suspicions to denounce his fellow generals and obtain the emergency powers that had allowed him to create his tyranny. His son had used them to justify his exile of Dion.

So far Dion's desperate expedition had succeeded from a combination of skill, good timing and luck. It was about to receive its biggest piece of luck. Unaware of Dion's venture, Dionysius had left Syracuse to campaign in Italy with a fleet of eighty ships. Unlike Dion, Dionysius' fortune on this occasion was wretched. When later asked by the Macedonian king Philip II what he had inherited from his father, Dionysius ruefully replied, 'everything else, but not the luck by which he obtained those possessions and kept them.'[1] Taking advantage of the tyrant's absence, Dion was able to march his small force directly against Syracuse, gathering reinforcements as he went.

News of Dion's advance quickly reached Syracuse and a messenger was immediately dispatched to recall Dionysius. Timocrates, Dionysius' governor in Syracuse, took steps to crush any dissent within the city. Dionysius' bad luck is supposed to have continued when the letters the messenger was carrying were stolen. Plutarch records a story that the courier had packed some meat in with them and they were stolen by a hungry fox while he slept. The man, not unnaturally, vanished rather than face the tyrant empty handed. Even if elements of the story are true, a more cynical reporter might suspect the messenger of being bribed, rather than believe this ancient version of the 'dog ate my homework' excuse.

Whatever the reason, there was a delay before Dionysius received the news. Meanwhile many of the rural population of Syracuse had joined the rebellion. The Campanian mercenaries of the tyrant, who had been given lands and citizenship in other Sicilian cities, were fed reports that Dion would first attack their cities and as a result they deserted Syracuse. Upon learning of the success of his stratagem, Dion advanced from Acrae to a position 3km to the southwest of the city, on the Anapus River. Here he sacrificed and prayed to the rising sun. Once again his seers declared the omens to be favourable.

Dion's original 1,000 had been joined by another 20,000 men. Most came from the Syracusan countryside but others had poured in from all over Sicily and Italy. Morale was high and they advanced rapidly on the city, 'exhorting one another with joyful shouts to win their liberty.'[2] As they approached Syracuse, its inhabitants joined the revolt. Their first targets were the supporters of the tyranny, particular the informers who were universally despised. They were hunted down and mercilessly beaten to death. The rapid advance had caught Timocrates in the city and he was cut off from the fortress of Ortygia by the mob. He was forced to flee Syracuse, leaving the garrison without a commander at this crucial time.

Finally Dion entered the city in triumph

leading the way himself in brilliant armour, with his brother Megacles on one side of him, and on the other, Callippus the Athenian, both crowned with garlands. A hundred of his mercenaries followed Dion as a body-guard, and his officers led the rest in good order, the Syracusans looking on and welcoming as it were a sacred religious procession for the return of liberty and democracy into the city, after an absence of forty-eight years.[3]

After entering the city he announced to the enthusiastic crowds that the Syracusans and all other Sicilians were to be free from tyranny. The people, believing themselves to be free at last, responded by showering him with flowers and honoured him as if he were divine. An impromptu assembly was held in which the people appointed Dion, and his brother Megacles, to be generals with absolute power and voted them bodyguards. The Syracusans' joy and gratitude appears to have overruled their judgment on this occasion, as this position of *strategos autocrator* and the possession of a bodyguard were common precursors for the seizure of power as a tyrant. At Dion's request – perhaps in an attempt to distance himself from any hint of tyranny – another twenty generals were elected. Of these, half were chosen from the exiles who had returned with Dion, giving him a majority of his supporters on the board of generals.

Dion had delivered his speech from a sun-dial that had been set up by Dionysius. His ever-optimistic seers announced this was yet another good omen, as a monument of the tyrant lie under his feet. This time, however, they hedged their enthusiasm with the caveat that the sun-dial might predict a rapid change of fortune. After this Dion captured the Epipolae and freed the citizens imprisoned in the quarries. The accounts of the first few days of the liberation of the city support the argument that Dionysius had abandoned his more benign rule and reverted to his father's methods of oppression: utilizing mercenaries and informers, and imprisoning opponents.

More Syracusans flocked to Dion and he is reported to have commanded 50,000 men. Most of them would have been poorly armed, as Dionysius and his father, not trusting their subjects, had a policy of disarming their hoplites when they returned from campaign and storing their arms on the acropolis. Others were labourers, too poor to own arms. On the seventh day after his arrival in the city, the extra arms arrived from Heraclea and were distributed among the citizens. The Syracusans quickly built a siege-wall to cut off the island of Ortygia from the rest of the city. At this point the rebellion appeared to be going well; only the capture of the leaderless stronghold of Ortygia remained to be completed. It was on this same day, however, that the doubts of the seers were realized. Dionysius returned to Syracuse with his fleet and landed at Ortygia.

After arriving in Syracuse, Dionysius sent envoys to negotiate in secret with his former counsellor. Dion insisted, however, that all negotiations be carried out in public 'with the Syracusans, on the ground that they were a free people.'[4] The tyrant offered to return the levying of taxes and control of military service to the assembly. These important powers of a free city had both been appropriated by his father.

This offer was rejected by the Syracusans who believed that they had already won back these rights by their own efforts. Dion replied that if Dionysius renounced the tyranny he would grant him immunity from prosecution and negotiate a reasonable settlement for him. An embassy was sent to Ortygia to discuss terms and reported back that Dionysius was ready to relinquish his position for his own sake, not because of any demands of Dion. A truce was agreed to while terms were discussed. The delay was merely a ruse by the tyrant as he had already determined to launch an attack on the city.

The next morning Dionysius plied his barbarian mercenaries with wine. They were probably Gauls and Spaniards as most of his Campanians had deserted. Gauls were notorious throughout antiquity for their excessive consumption of alcohol, especially before battle. Dionysius ordered them to attack the siege-wall cutting off the island. The attack was unexpected and caught the Syracusan guards, never noted for their discipline, by surprise.

Plutarch claims that chaos prevailed as the Syracusan citizens panicked and fled the onslaught. Dion's mercenaries rushed to assist but were held back by the mob of fugitives. Dion, unable to have his orders heard in the tumult, placed himself at the front of his troops and, leading by example, charged the enemy. Plutarch, however, never wastes an opportunity to deride the Syracusans in order to promote his hero Dion at their expense. Diodorus, by contrast, blames the initial surprise on Dion for 'being unexpectedly tricked by the violation of the truce.' He further claims that 'the Syracusans, by the hope of freedom, were wrought up to a high pitch of rivalry' and fought with great courage.[5]

The fighting was heavy and as Dion was recognized by the enemy, the conflict centred on his person. Dion was wounded in the arm by a javelin and fell to the ground. Both the Gauls and Spanish fought by first throwing spears and then charging in to fight at close quarters with their swords. By now the Greek hoplites had managed to recover from their confusion and form their close-packed phalanx formation. The peninsula adjoining Ortygia is at this point about 300m wide. As the fighting was occurring in a confined space, 'as if in a stadium,' this formation was unstoppable. Diodorus describes how the Syracusan phalanx gave them the advantage in the battle:

Many fell, and not a few were wounded, receiving all the blows in front; for on the one hand those in the front rank courageously met death defending the rest, and those arrayed behind them covering them with their shields as they fell and holding firm in the desperate peril took the most dangerous risks to win the victory.'[6]

The Syracusans routed the mercenaries and drove them back onto Ortygia. Eight hundred of the mercenaries were killed in the action. Dionysius, in order to maintain the loyalty of the survivors, gave the dead expensive funerals and distributed large amounts of money to the rest. The Syracusans were elated with their victory and, in the traditional Greek manner, set up a trophy decorated with the arms of the defeated to celebrate it at the point where they had first routed the enemy. The Syracusans honoured Dion with a wreath of gold and rewarded his mercenaries with a grant of money, the equivalent of about two weeks pay.

Dionysius continued to send embassies to the Syracusans to discuss a settlement but Dion kept putting them off while he strengthened his siegeworks around the island. Once these were finished he repeated that there was only one possible settlement, that Dionysius should resign his position as tyrant although he would be given certain privileges. This was unacceptable to Dionysius as he believed that he still held a position of strength as long as he retained Ortygia and could receive support from his empire in Italy.

During these exchanges of embassies, Dionysius sent letters to Dion from his captive family. One was supposedly from his son, Hipparinus, but was really a forgery from Dionysius. Dion unwisely opened it in public. It was a calculated piece of propaganda, designed to

> bring odium on Dion. For there were reminders of his zealous services in behalf of the tyranny, and threats against the persons of his dearest ones, his sister, children, and wife; there were also dire injunctions coupled with lamentations, and, what affected him most of all, a demand that he should not abolish, but assume, the tyranny; that he should not give liberty to men who hated him and would never forget their wrongs, but take the power himself, and thereby assure his friends and kindred of their safety.[7]

Dionysius was trying to divide and rule, by causing Dion's democratic allies to mistrust him. Such reminders of his past strengthened the suspicion among the democrats of Syracuse that Dion still had ambitions of imposing either himself, or his nephew, as a new tyrant.

With Ortygia now besieged the war became a matter of raid and counter-raid. Dionysius decided to use his fleet to ravage the Syracusan coastal regions. His main weakness was a shortage of food on the island so he dispatched a merchant fleet to buy grain. The smaller Syracusan fleet retaliated, sending out raiders who managed to capture many of the supply vessels.

As the siege dragged on over the winter and into the next year, Dionysius received further set-backs when the tribes of southern Italy took advantage of his absence to launch attacks on the Greek cities of his empire. In Lucania there gathered a large force of destitute men and escaped slaves, both most likely the victims of the earlier wars of the Syracusan tyrants. They managed to capture a number of Dionysius' cities, including Hipponium and Thurii. The new conquerors organized themselves in a federation and were known as the Bruttians, possibly from the local word for runaway slaves.

Dionysius decided on further attacks to distract the besiegers. He sent Philistus to Rhegium to gather a force of over 500 cavalry and 2,000 infantry. The target was the city of Leontini, to the northwest of Syracuse, which had rebelled from Dionysius. Philistus launched a surprise night attack and captured a foothold within the walls. The Syracusans rushed a relief expedition to the city and they succeeded in driving the invaders out.

As the siege dragged on the distrust felt towards Dion continued to grow among the Syracusans. His enemies blamed him for the failure to capture Ortygia and mistrusted his continued negotiations with Dionysius. It was at this time that Heracleides arrived in Syracuse with a fleet of twenty war-ships and 1,500 soldiers. Plutarch comments on his arrival by beginning his assassination of his character, describing him as: 'a man of military capacity and well known for the commands which he had held under the tyrants, but irresolute, fickle, and least to be relied upon as partner in an enterprise involving power and glory.'[8] Diodorus, by contrast, describes him as 'a man of very great distinction and considered worthy of the position, he was chosen admiral by the Syracusans'.[9]

Heracleides, who had already fallen out with Dion prior to his return, threw his lot in with the democrats and 'having a certain natural gift of persuading and moving a populace' won them over 'all the more easily because they were repelled by the gravity of Dion.'[10] The people held an assembly without the permission of their generals and voted to give Heracleides command of the fleet. Dion was outraged at this violation of his privileges as *strategos autocrator* and threatened to resign. The Syracusans conceded the point with bad grace and reluctantly revoked the appointment. Dion, his sense of self-importance now assuaged, called a new assembly, re-appointed Heracleides to the command of the fleet, and gave him a bodyguard.

Heracleides backed Dion in public but in secret he continued to support the democrats. Dion found himself in a difficult situation, for if he

> advised to let Dionysius leave the citadel under a truce, he would be charged with sparing and preserving him; and for, wishing to give no offence, he simply continued the siege, it would be said that he was protracting the war, in order that he might the longer be in command and overawe the citizens.[11]

The most prominent opponent of Dion was a man named Sosis who claimed in the assembly that the Syracusans 'had merely exchanged a stupid and drunken tyrant for a watchful and sober master.'[12] The following day Sosis used the old trick of pretending he had been attacked by Dion's mercenaries and accusing him of the assault before the people. Those who were suspicious of Dion's motives were ready to believe such charges. Sosis appears, however, to have been extremely careless in his preparations and his trickery was soon exposed. He was condemned to death by the assembly. The whole episode does, however, demonstrate the level of distrust that existed between the supporters of Dion and the democrats. It was an uneasy alliance built on the premise that my enemy's enemy is my friend.

After his defeat at Leontini, Philistus returned to Italy and fitted out sixty triremes to reinforce Ortygia. On his return to Sicily he was intercepted by Heracleides and a Syracusan fleet of similar size. Heracleides outmanoeuvred and surrounded Philistus' fleet. The Syracusans were keen to capture Philistus alive but, fearing that he would be tortured after capture, he committed suicide. The Syracusans, denied their vengeance, sated their hatred of the tyrant's supporters on his body. They 'dragged it through the whole city, and cast it forth unburied.'[13] Plutarch has a different version of Philistus' fate, claiming that he was taken alive and:

> The Syracusans, to begin with, stripped off his breast-plate and exposed his body, naked, to insult and abuse, although he was now an old man; then, that they cut off his head, and gave his body to the boys of the city, with orders to drag it through Achradina and throw it into the stone quarries. And Timaeus, enlarging upon these indignities, says that the boys tied a rope to the lame leg of the dead Philistus and dragged his body through the city, while all the Syracusans mocked and jeered as they saw drawn about by the leg the man who had said to Dionysius [the Elder] that he must not run away from his tyranny on a swift horse, but wait until he was dragged from it by the leg.[14]

The victory at sea increased the confidence of the democrats and their resentment of Dion and his mercenaries. The fleet, always the service of the poorest classes, the 'sailor rabble', was renowned in ancient Greece for its pro-democratic politics. The sailors believed that it was the fleet that was doing all the serious fighting and the mercenaries were now an unnecessary expense. The more politically astute would have hoped that they could rid the city of Dion's private army.

With the defeat of Philistus, Dionysius' situation had become desperate. In a last-ditch effort to hold on to power, he approached Dion and made a proposal to share the tyranny with him. When this was rejected he finally offered to surrender Ortygia to him, including his mercenaries and five months pay for them. Dionysius would then retire and live on the revenues of the estates he held in Italy. Acceptance of Dionysius' offer would have put Dion in a strong position to seize the tyranny for himself. Either because of his honour or because he suspected another trap, Dion refused to deal with Dionysius and directed him to approach the assembly. The Syracusans, now confident of total victory, wished to capture Dionysius alive. They refused his terms. This was a poor decision, as an untaken Ortygia remained a constant threat to the city and allowed Dion a pretext to keep his body-guard of mercenaries within the city's walls.

Dionysius handed over command of the island to his eldest son, Apollocrates. Then, taking advantage of a favourable wind, he eluded Heracleides' fleet and escaped to Italy. Heracleides' failure was denounced by the citizens who now remembered that he too had been a former servant of the tyrant. During the summer of 356 the most extreme faction of the democrats managed to gain control of the assembly. They passed that most revolutionary of legislation: a redistribution of land, 'urging that liberty was based on equality, and slavery on the poverty of those who had naught.'[15]

The disgraced Heracleides saw his chance to make a come-back and threw his lot in with the radicals. He encouraged them to vote to end payment to Dion's mercenaries and to elect new generals. These measures were a direct challenge to both Dion and the aristocrats of Syracuse, whose wealth and position depended on their ownership of their large estates and their domination of the politically important posts of general.

Throughout this work the term faction will be used for convenience's sake when describing the political groupings around powerful politicians. These groups should in no way be seen as organized, disciplined political parties in the modern sense. Ancient Greek politics was all about individuals and the competition between them. Leading politicians were always rich because only such individuals had the time to involve themselves fully in politics. Only the wealthy could make the ostentatious displays that made them both prominent and popular by funding religious festivals, plays, warships or public works. Much of a leader's following would be personal – friends and family – who would attach themselves for what they could get out of the association. As Waterfield so astutely observes: 'politicians did at least pretend to have altruistic motives but favouritism was openly acknowledged and was not generally thought immoral.'[16]

This type of support was not always sufficient, and the ambitious politician would often have to win a majority in the assembly by proposing legislation that would favour the democracy and the poor. By these methods a large following could be won to support a particular programme, but it was never a permanent construct. It was this need to win the support of the common people, by definition the uneducated, that led to the contempt for democracy felt by philosophers such as Plato and Aristotle. At the most extreme end of Greek politics were the demands for the cancellation of debts and the redistribution of land.

The new regime had an inauspicious start. Although it was mid-summer, an unseasonal thunderstorm occurred which was seen as an evil portent. As a result the vote for new generals was not taken and the assembly was suspended for fifteen days. It should be noted that the priests who interpreted such omens would have been aristocrats and may have had political motives for their pronouncement. New generals, including Heracleides, were eventually elected despite further bad omens. Plutarch derides the Syracusans for turning against their former saviour Dion, claiming that:

After their long sickness of tyranny, and to act the part of independence out of season, they stumbled in their undertakings, and yet hated Dion, who, like a physician, wished to subject the city to a strict and temperate regimen … but since no entreaties could stay the onset of the multitudes, and the city, like a ship at sea, was at the mercy of the blasts of its demagogues.[17]

Here Plutarch is closely following a metaphor of Plato, in which he compares a ruler to a physician who purges the body for its own good. Purge here appears to have the same political meaning as it does in English. The Syracusan democrats feared that Dion was preparing to use his bodyguard to carry out his own purge, overthrowing the democracy and introducing a narrow oligarchy or a new tyrant in the guise of a philosopher king.

Chapter 4

The Overthrow of Dionysius and the Rule of Dion

Dion could not endure this opposition patiently, but retorted with that verse of Homer in the second book of the Iliad, in which is this sentiment, 'That a state cannot be managed well by the government of many.' Much ill feeling, on the part of the people, followed this remark; for he appeared to have let it escape him that he wished everything to be under his own authority.

Nepos, *Dion* 6

The new democracy was threatened on two sides. There was their open enemy, the garrison of the tyrant occupying Ortygia and closer to home were the 3,000 mercenaries of Dion. They were an ongoing problem for the new government, who had no money with which to pay them. The mercenaries were offered citizenship in an attempt to both compensate them and to win them over, but they angrily rejected the offer and remained loyal to Dion. They asked him to lead them in a revolt against the *demos* 'and to take vengeance upon the Syracusans as a common enemy.'[1]

At first Dion refused, but as the people became openly hostile, he agreed to escape the city. The mercenaries attempted to escort him out of the gates, abusing the people as they went. The Syracusans, not wishing to have a private army loose in the countryside, openly turned on Dion. Made confident by the small numbers of their enemy, they attacked, hoping to kill them before they escaped the city.

Dion at first attempted to win back the support of the citizens, reminding them that the tyrant still held Ortygia. The people's blood was up, however, and class struggle – *stasis* – once it had broken out inside a Greek city could be murderous. Dion still hoped to avoid bloodshed and ordered his mercenaries to charge the citizens but not strike unless attacked. The demonstration had its desired effect. The people, probably not fully armed and faced by the charge of Dion's veterans, fled. Dion was able to make his escape out of the city and march toward the neighbouring city of Leontini. The failure of the drawn-out siege of Ortygia had caused the democrats to suspect the motives of Dion and his wealthy supporters. From a purely strategic perspective it was, nonetheless, unwise for the democrats to have launched their coup before Ortygia had been captured.

Some of the new generals saw the threat posed by Dion's escape. They ordered the citizens to arm themselves properly and set out in pursuit of Dion. The pursuing cavalry caught Dion as he was preparing to cross a river and began to skirmish with his troops. This time Dion was less forgiving; he turned his forces around and ordered them to attack in earnest. They routed the Syracusans and inflicted heavy losses on them. Possibly the fleeing cavalry had disordered the infantry marching behind them, preventing them from forming up. It is also possible that the aristocratic cavalry were only half-hearted in their attack. Many were spared and taken prisoner when they claimed to be Dion's supporters. These Dion set free without ransom, no doubt to maintain his support base within the city.

Leontini had a long history of harbouring opponents of various Syracusan governments and being used as a base for guerrilla warfare against the city. It was long coveted by the Syracusans and had fallen in out of their control over the preceding centuries. Leontini's citizens, many of whom were settled ex-mercenaries of the tyrants, welcomed Dion and granted citizenship to his troops. The Syracusans sent an embassy to Leontini denouncing Dion but were told to mind their own affairs.

Despite this setback, the Syracusans continued the siege of Ortygia and reduced the tyrant's forces to the point of starvation. They were on the verge of surrendering the citadel when, at the proverbial last minute, a supply squadron entered the Great Harbour and anchored at Ortygia. This was commanded by Nypsius, a Campanian mercenary and 'a man who excelled in valour and in sagacity of generalship.'[2] The Syracusans responded to the threat: they manned all their triremes and attacked the enemy while they were still unloading. The attack caught the tyrant's forces by surprise and the Syracusans destroyed or captured many ships. Nonetheless, the damage had already been done and enough supplies had been landed to allow Nypsius to convince the mercenaries to continue the fight.

The limited success went to the Syracusans' heads and overcame their caution. They celebrated their victory with magnificent sacrifices to the Gods followed by an all-night party. Their elected generals were not confident enough to enforce discipline and hence the guards on the siege-works also joined in the festivities. Although the citizen hoplites of Syracuse usually fought with courage, their lack of discipline was always a problem for their leaders.

Nypsius, observing 'that the guards through contempt and drunkenness had betaken themselves to sleep,'[3] decided that there was an opportunity to attack the siege-lines. He quickly seized the fortifications and killed any remaining guards. The mercenaries, 10,000 in total, then formed up and easily defeated those Syracusans who rushed against them. Nypsius gave his troops license to sack and murder at will. The Syracusans, still arriving piece-meal, attempted to block the narrow alleys. Fighting continued throughout the night with both sides 'slaying one another at random in the darkness, and every quarter teemed with dead.' Despite the resistance, a large part of the city was sacked, 'its men being slain, its walls torn down, and its women and children dragged shrieking to the acropolis.'[4]

When daylight broke the Syracusans saw the extent of the disaster. In their desperation they decided to send a delegation of his former friends to Dion to beg for assistance. The embassy assumed the traditional pose of supplicants, grasping his knees while repenting their past actions and begging for help. Meanwhile the mercenaries of Dionysius had retired to Ortygia. With the immediate threat now gone, the radical democrats now repented their approach to Dion, urging the citizens to bar him from the city and to win their liberty by their own swords. A new messenger was sent to Dion to tell him that he was no longer welcome. At the same time, 'others from the horsemen and more reputable citizens,'[5] that is the wealthy, sent their own message urging him to return.

As night approached the democrats took possession of the gates, deter-mined to keep Dion out of the city. The disunity among the Syracusans allowed Nypsius to once again attack the city. He sent out his mercenaries who quickly seized the entire siege-wall. Then they began to sack the city with even greater ferocity. Dionysius had 'despaired of his cause and fiercely hated the Syracusans, he wished to make their city as it were a tomb for his falling tyranny.'[6] The foreign mercenaries were given orders to murder the population at will and to burn the city. This they did with great enthusiasm. The Syracusans fled in panic, although many were caught and slaughtered, or died in the flames.

Once again the Syracusans changed their mind and begged Dion to advance with all haste; even his opponent Heracleides pleaded that he come. Dion received the news of the new attack while still 12km from the city. He pushed his men hard over the last part of the march, sending his light-armed troops ahead. Once he arrived at the city, Dion formed up his troops along with those Syracusans who had managed to escape with their arms. He divided his troops into multiple columns and attacked through all the available gates. They caught the jubilant mercenaries of the tyrant while still in the act of looting and killed 4,000 of them. The rest managed to flee back to the safety of Ortygia.

Dion now set about saving the city by organizing the fire-fighting efforts. Most of the democratic leaders used this time to escape the city but Heracleides surrendered himself to Dion. His supporters urged him to execute him and rid the city of 'the hunt for mob-favour, which, no less than tyranny, was a raging distemper.'[7] Dion instead took the opportunity to make everybody aware of his self-professed virtue, announcing that as a student of Plato he had learned self-mastery and how to be merciful. He then claimed that such studies had made him 'superior to Heracleides, not so much in power and wisdom, as in goodness and justice; for therein lay real superiority; whereas successes in war, even though they had to be shared with no man, must at least be shared with fortune.'[8]

After pardoning Heracleides, Dion rebuilt the siege-works and again cut off Ortygia from the land. Once he had buried the dead, ransomed the prisoners and set up a trophy to his victory, Dion called an assembly. Here Heracleides proposed that Dion be made the sole *strategos autocrator* and be given command of both the army and the fleet. The wealthiest class, the aristocratic cavalry, supported the motion but the poor and the sailors opposed it. They demanded that Heracleides remain in control of the fleet. Despite his failures, they considered him to be more answerable to the people than Dion.

Dion yielded to the assembly and re-appointed Heracleides as admiral. The people then pressed that their legislation for the redistribution of land to be implemented. Forgiving an old friend may have been acceptable behaviour for a student of Plato but giving away one's wealth to the uneducated masses certainly was not. Dion used his new powers to repeal the laws, making him even more unpopular among the poor.

Heracleides was ordered to take the fleet to Messene (Messina), probably to prevent further reinforcements arriving for Dionysius. It is also likely that Dion gave the command, at least partially, in order to get Heracleides and his supporters amongst the sailor rabble out of the city. Once outside of Dion's presence Heracleides again began to plot against him. He repeated the accusations that Dion was trying to make himself tyrant. Meanwhile Heracleides was accused by his enemies of plotting with Dionysius. Dion's supporters in Syracuse admonished him for returning Heracleides to a position of power.

Meanwhile a force of Dionysius', under the command of a Spartan, Pharax, landed in the south of Sicily near Akragas. The Spartans were strong supporters of the tyrannies of both Dionysius and his father. Dion decided to ignore Pharax until the greater threat of Ortygia had been captured. Heracleides and the sailors repeated the accusation that he was trying to prolong the war in order to maintain his power. This was an allegation often directed at the previous tyrant, Dionysius the Elder.

As prior events in the assembly have shown, Dion's position in Syracuse does not appear strong enough to completely ignore the will of the people. Reluctantly he was forced to march against Pharax, taking the rest of the fleet with him. In the first encounter he suffered a minor defeat. Plutarch claims that the defeat was due more to 'seditious disorders'[9] within the army than to the enemy. As the army was mostly made up of the wealthy hoplite class, this would indicate that they too were turning against their commander. Dion prepared the Syracusans for a second battle but on the night before he received news that Heracleides, reputedly in league with Pharax, was sailing for Syracuse. Heracleides' plan was to seize the city and once again exile Dion.

Dion moved quickly. He took with him his strongest supporters, the cavalry, and rode all night for the city, covering the 140km before mid-morning the next day. Dion just managed to beat the fleet into the city. Heracleides returned to sea, probably going back to Messene. Here he met with another Spartan, Gaesylus, who claimed that he had been sent to take command of the Sicilians. The precedent for Sparta sending commanders had begun with Gylippus, who had successfully commanded the Syracusans in their defeat of the Athenian invasion sixty years earlier. Heracleides, desperate for an ally, 'gladly took up this man, attached him to himself like an amulet, as it were, against the influence of Dion, and showed him to his confederates; then, secretly sending a herald to Syracuse, he ordered the citizens to receive their Spartan commander.'[10]

Dion refused Gaesylus admission into the city, claiming that 'the Syracusans had commanders enough, and that if their situation absolutely required a Spartan also, he himself was the man, since he had been made a citizen of Sparta.'[11] Dion once again pardoned Heracleides. His position in the assembly and the fleet must have been so strong that Dion had little choice other than to provoke a civil war. He did, however, force Heracleides to make solemn oaths to support him. Dion also disbanded the fleet, using the excuse that it was of no further use and cost too much to maintain. The real reason may have been to eliminate a source of organized and armed support for Heracleides.

Dion now pressed the siege of Ortygia with vigour. Provisions began to fail on the island and the mercenaries became rebellious. Apollocrates was finally forced to come to terms. He surrendered the citadel and all its arms to Dion while he and his family were allowed to sail away in five triremes. The surrender caused massive celebrations in the city and the whole population turned out to witness

> the rising of the sun upon a free Syracuse. For since, among the illustrations men give of the mutations of fortune, the expulsion of Dionysius is still to this day the strongest and plainest, what joy must we suppose those men themselves then felt, and how great a pride, who, with the fewest resources, overthrew the greatest tyranny that ever was![12]

The gates of the fortress were flung open and Dion was reunited with his family. His sister and son ran to meet him but his wife, Arete, followed in tears, unsure of how to meet her husband after she had been forced to live with another man. She had no need to fear as Dion burst into tears and embraced her, telling her to take their son to his house.

The overthrow of the tyranny brought great fame to Dion, who was widely regarded by many Greeks as the greatest man alive. Plato wrote to him telling him that the eyes of the world were upon him. Dion, for his part, worried about what his fellow philosophers would think of him. He continued to treat the Syracusans with his customary lack of tact. Dion was determined to follow his philosophy and 'to curb the Syracusans, who were given to excessive license and luxury.'[13]

The defeat of the tyranny was, however, only a beginning to the solution of Syracuse's political problems. Heracleides again set himself up as the leader of the opposition and publicly avoided Dion. As a dedicated follower of Plato, Dion was determined to 'put a curb upon unmixed democracy in Syracuse, regarding it as not a civil polity, but rather, in the words of Plato, a "bazaar of polities".' His plan was to impose a government based on the Sparta model: 'wherein an aristocracy should preside, and administer the most important affairs; for he saw that the Corinthians had a polity which leaned towards oligarchy, and that they transacted little public business in their assembly of the people.'[14] Just what Dion's position was in these years is not recorded but most likely he held onto his position of *strategos autocrator*, in effect tyrant. He also refused to destroy the stronghold and symbol of the tyranny, the citadel on Ortygia, despite the demands of the Syracusan people.

The Spartan form of government was much admired by the aristocrats among the Greeks who claimed that it mixed the best of all forms of governments. It was in fact a very narrow oligarchy. Traditionally, legislative power lay exclusively in the hands of the *gerousia*, a council of thirty members, the two kings and twenty-eight elders appointed for life. Their decisions would be announced to an assembly of the Spartans, in effect wealthy land-holders, who could only show assent or dissent. At some stage another group of magistrates came into being, the *Ephors*. Originally their role was to supervise the Spartan kings but they gradually assumed more and more power. By the end of the fifth century they were the dominant political force in Sparta, with Xenophon comparing their power to that of tyrants. They were elected annually by the assembly for a term of one year and for this reason writers such as Aristotle claimed they were the main democratic component of Sparta's constitution.[15] Such claims ignore the fact that they were elected solely by the assembly of wealthy landowners, however; in all aspects of Sparta's constitution the poor were completely excluded. This was the real reason that the Spartan constitution was so admired by the oligarchs in other Greek cities.

Heracleides soon began to criticize Dion on a number of issues: his failure to destroy the tyrant's fortress of Ortygia, his refusal to allow the destruction of Dionysius the Elder's tomb and his use of foreign advisors from oligarchic Corinth in framing his proposed constitution. Despite his supposed virtue and belief in justice, Dion now showed himself to be just as ruthless as his predecessors. He ordered the murder of his chief rival, Heracleides. According to Nepos, after the murder Dion began to act like the worst of tyrants:

> This act struck extreme terror into every one; for nobody, after Heracleides was killed, considered himself safe. Dion, when his adversary was removed, distributed among his soldiers, with greater freedom, the property of those whom he knew to have been unfavourable to him. But after this division had taken place, money, as his daily expenses grew very great, began to fail him; nor was there anything on which he could lay his hands but the property of his friends; a circumstance which was attended with this effect, that while he gained the soldiery, he lost the aristocracy. At this state of things he was overcome with anxiety, and, being unaccustomed to be ill spoken of, he could not patiently endure that a bad opinion of him should be entertained by those by whose praises he had just before been extolled to the skies. The common people, however, when the feelings of the soldiers were rendered unfavourable towards him, spoke with less restraint, and said that 'he was a tyrant not to be endured.'[16]

The democrats were not done with, however, and looked about for a weapon to use against the new tyrant. It soon appeared in the form of Callippus, an Athenian who had come to Syracuse as one of Dion's mercenaries and therefore had been awarded citizenship. Callippus had fought bravely in the war against the tyranny, was trusted by Dion and popular among the other mercenaries. In fact, Dion was using him as an informer to spy on any malcontents among the mercenaries. Callippus was now recruited by the democrats, reputedly for twenty talents of silver,[17] to murder Dion. Using his position he was able to identify and recruit those mercenaries willing to help carry out the assassination.

The period leading up to the attack was one of tragedy for Dion. His son, who had been corrupted by living at the court of the tyrant, fell – or possibly jumped – from the roof of their home and was killed. Callipus decided it was time to act while Dion was distracted by his grief. Dion was also supposed to have been suffering from guilt over the murder of Heracleides. The women of Dion's family heard rumours of Callipus' plot. To defuse suspicion Callipus swore a most sacred oath to the goddesses of the underworld, Demeter and Peresphone.

Despite his oaths, Callipus decided to strike on the very day of the goddesses' festival. The assassins struck while Dion was celebrating at home with friends. They entered the house unarmed and then had accomplices outside barricade the doors and windows. They fell on Dion and tried to strangle him but he fought back. His friends, however, abandoned him, hoping to save their own skins. Eventually, one of the attackers was handed a sword from those outside and cut Dion's throat while the others held him powerless 'as if he had been a victim at the altar'.[18] His sister and pregnant wife were cast into prison, where his wife later gave birth to a son. They survived possibly because Callipus was soon beset with problems of his own. Dion's rule of the city had lasted less than three years.

Nepos claims that as soon as Dion's murder became

> publicly known, the feeling of the populace was wonderfully altered, for those who had called him a tyrant while he was alive, called him now the deliverer of his country and the expeller of a tyrant. So suddenly had pity succeeded to hatred, that they wished to redeem him from Acheron, if they could, with their own blood. He was therefore honoured with a sepulchral monument in the city, in the most frequented part of it, after having been interred at the public expense.[19]

This change of heart was unlikely to have occurred as immediately as Nepos claims. Callipus was initially praised as a tyrannicide, an appellation of honour, before he seized power in the city. This reversal of policy probably occurred thirteen months later, after Callippus had been driven from the city and Dion's partisans returned to power. It is also in contrast to Nepos' description of Dion's increasingly repressive behaviour. Perhaps memories of Dion's rule softened during the chaos that would follow his death.

After the overthrow of Callipus, the Syracusans released Dion's sister, wife and new son into the care of one of his Syracusan friends, Hicetas. He promised to send them to Dion's friends in the Peloponnesus. Unfortunately for them, Hicetas too harboured political ambitions and decided they were too much of a threat. He paid the sailors to murder them during the voyage. They threw them overboard, either alive or after cutting their throats.[20] Dion's return to Syracuse, which had begun so promisingly, had ultimately ended with his own murder and the destruction of his family. The only consolation the ancient writers could find was that the killers, Callippus and Hicetas, would both be murdered in their turn and divine justice seen to be done.

Chapter 5

The Years of Chaos and the Return of Dionysius

In Sicily the Syracusans, who were engaged in civil strife and were forced to live as slaves under many varied tyrannies.

Diodorus 19.65

After the murder of Dion, Callippus was celebrated in Syracuse as having delivered the city from tyranny. Callippus was supreme in Syracuse but, rather than restore the democracy as hoped, he is recorded as seizing power and becoming yet another tyrant. Callippus is described as 'a pupil of Plato, having been a companion and fellow-pupil of Dion.'[1] Plato, horrified by his actions, disowned him and claimed that he 'had become intimately acquainted with him, not as a fellow pupil in philosophy, but in consequence of initiation into the mysteries and the recurrent comradeship which this brought.'[2]

As Dion's murderer, the ancient writers were universally hostile to Callippus and out to blacken his name. There are some indications that he may have governed by being the most influential politician among the democrats rather than a genuine tyrant. He was renowned as an orator, a skill essential in such a role; after his departure from Syracuse he is recorded as bringing autonomy to the people of Rhegium, not an action usually associated with a tyrant.

This is, nonetheless, pure speculation. All sides of Greek politics supposedly detested tyranny, but it appears that in their desperation, both extremes of the political divide were willing to put their faith in powerful individuals in order to defeat their political opponents. Few would have supported the re-introduction of the tyranny but, as the rise of Dionysius the Elder had shown, once a strong man had gained control of the city, provided he had sufficient military force in the form of a mercenary garrison, he could be difficult to remove. The failure of Dion to tear down the citadel on Ortygia had allowed further tyrants to continue to use it as a base from which they could terrorize the city into submission. The need of the new tyrants to pay their mercenaries would have contributed to the impoverishment of the city over the coming decade. Dionysius the Elder had paid his mercenaries at double the usual rate to ensure their loyalty during his rise to power. Other tyrants most likely followed his example.

Whatever his new position, Callippus' rise to power was strongly opposed by the aristocratic supporters of Dion and *stasis* once again broke out in the city. Callippus and his supporters won the ensuing struggle and forced their enemies to flee to Leontini. It may have been as a result of this conflict that Callippus seized power as a tyrant. At Leontini the rebels were joined by Hipparinus, one of the nephews of Dion and a son of the Dionysius the Elder.

Callippus led Syracuse for only thirteen months before, much to the satisfaction of the ancient writers, the gods took their revenge for his impiety. He led an expedition against the city of Catane (Catania) to drive out mercenaries loyal to the house of Dionysius. While Callippus was away from the city, Hipparinus took advantage of his absence. Learning that only a small garrison remained in the city, he

> decided to march from Leontini with a body of troops, and attack Syracuse, after dispatching some envoys to the city, with orders to slay the guards. After carrying out these orders, they opened the gates. Hipparinus entered with his mercenaries, and made himself master of Syracuse.[3]

From the nature of his coup it must be assumed that Hipparinus had supporters in the city who kept him well informed and let his troops into the city.

Callippus was now reduced to the role of a freebooter, wandering Sicily with an army of mercenaries looking for a city to occupy. He was defeated at Messene where many of his followers were killed. He then crossed into Italy and captured Rhegium from a garrison of Dionysius. The city was probably only a shell of its former self, having been destroyed by Dionysius the Elder back in 388 and turned into a private estate of the tyrant. Dionysius had restored a section of the city and renamed it Phoebia. This was done in honour of Apollo (Phoebus) as Dionysius claimed to be the son of Apollo and his mother Doris. Like many with regal aspirations, Dionysius had disowned his mortal father and claimed divine ancestors. After expelling Dionysius' garrison Callippus recalled the original population, gave them back their autonomy and possibly restored the democracy – the Rhegians are later described as taking decisions in an assembly. Eventually Callippus could no longer pay his mercenaries. They turned on him and supposedly murdered him with the same sword that they had used to murder Dion.

It was possibly Hipparinus, rather than Callipus, who released Dion's sister (his mother), wife (his sister) and new son into the care of an old friend, Hicetas. Hipparinus ruled Syracuse for just two years, from 352 until 351. Little is known about his rule except that, like his half-brother, he was held in contempt by his subjects for his drunkenness and hated for being yet another tyrant. He was assassinated in 351 and was succeeded as tyrant by his younger brother, Nysaeus. Nysaeus ruled for four years until 346. Again not much is recorded of Nysaeus' reign other than his love of drinking and his notorious reputation for sexual excess. One would like to think the murders of Dion's family were committed after the downfall of both Hipparinus and Nysaeus, when Hicetas had become a candidate for the tyranny himself, but this cannot be certain. The death of Dion's son would have been welcomed by the two tyrants but implication in the murder of their mother and sister would have been abhorred as a terrible sacrilege by the Greeks.

The decade since Dionysius' overthrow had seen the city racked by civil war as various individuals, whom Plato describes as 'men of insatiable cravings and empty heads'[4] fought for control of the city. Although personal ambition had much to do with these conflicts, there may also have been an element of class struggle involved. Dion and his nephews Hipparinus and Nysaeus seem to have been supported largely by the aristocratic elite, whereas their rival Callippus had the backing of the democrats and most likely the poor.

During his ten year exile from Syracuse, Dionysius had based himself in the Italian city of Locri, which was the home of his mother and a traditional ally of Syracuse. At first Dionysius was welcomed by the people, although they may have had no choice as the city had been captured and garrisoned by his father. Dionysius occupied the acropolis of the city and began to reign as tyrant. He soon became hated by his subjects as he ruled them with utmost cruelty and licentiousness. His behaviour towards the women of the city was scandalous. Dionysius 'sent for all the maidens of the Locrians in turn; and then rolled about naked, with them naked also, on this layer of flowers, omitting no circumstance of infamy.'[5] Justin adds further crimes, claiming that he took advantage of an old religious festival to prostitute the woman of the city, and when they came to obey his summons stripped them of their finery and 'tortured to make them discover their husbands' wealth.'[6]

Despite his behaviour Dionysius still appears to have had supporters in Syracuse, probably among the opponents of the aristocratic faction. Although we cannot be certain of Dionysius' politics, his father had a reputation as a demagogue. Dionysius may have still been popular among his father's main supporters: the ex-mercenaries and refugees who had been given citizenship, along with those poor who had benefited from his limited land reforms. In 346 Dionysius returned to Syracuse with both a fleet and a force of mercenaries and took the city by surprise. Again a number of

Syracusans, consisting mostly of the nobility who feared reprisal, fled the city to take refuge at Leontini. This city had fallen under the rule of Hicetas.

During the previous decade of his exile the power of Syracuse had declined dramatically. The constant changes in government had all but destroyed Dionysius the Elder's empire. Most of the cities of eastern Sicily had shaken off Syracusan control only to fall under the rule of their own petty tyrants. Syracuse's population had shrunk dramatically as many abandoned the city to avoid the constant purges that followed each change of tyrant. Plutarch describes the situation that confronted Dionysius on his return:

> The city, therefore, was continually exchanging one tyrant for another, and owing to a multitude of ills was almost abandoned, while as for the rest of Sicily, part of it was ruined and already wholly without inhabitants by reason of the wars, and most of the cities were occupied by Barbarians of mixed races and soldiers out of employment, who readily consented to the successive changes in the despotic power.[7]

While Dionysius was absent from their city, the citizens of Locri took the opportunity to drive out his garrison and restore their freedom. They then vented their anger against the former tyrant by taking revenge on his family. Their vengeance was particularly brutal, as after they

> got his wife and children into their power, prostituted them in the public roads with great insult, sparing them no kind of degradation. And when they had wreaked their vengeance upon them, they thrust needles under the nails of their fingers, and put them to death with torture. And when they were dead, they pounded their bones in mortars, and having cut up and distributed the rest of their flesh, they imprecated curses on all who did not eat of it; and in accordance with this unholy imprecation, they put their flesh into the mills with the flour, that it might be eaten by all those who made bread. And all the other parts they sunk in the sea.[8]

The fate of his family did little to improve the temperament of Dionysius who appears to have lost all sense of moderation. It was maybe at this point that he carried out the purge recorded by Justin, murdering: 'not only the relatives of his brothers, but his brothers themselves; so that he left to those, to whom he owed a share of power, not even a share of life, and commenced cruelty upon his kindred before he exercised it upon strangers.'[9]

It is perhaps during this period that Dionysius' most famous act of psychological terror occurred, the legendary 'Sword of Damocles.' When one of Dionysius' courtiers, Damocles, admired the tyrant's power and wealth, he was asked: 'Damocles, as this kind of life pleases you, to have a taste of it yourself, and to make a trial of the good fortune that attends me?' Damocles replied that he 'should like it extremely.' Dionysius then placed Damocles on a golden couch surrounded by servants and the best foods. Above his head, however, was a sword suspended by a single horse-hair, threatening at any moment to fall and slay him. Damocles could no longer enjoy the luxuries and begged to be returned to his usual station. The moral of the story was supposed to have been that 'there can be no happiness for one who is under constant apprehensions.'[10]

Increasing numbers of Syracusans fled to join Hicetas at Leontini and 'put themselves under his protection, and chose him their general for the war; not that he was better than any acknowledged tyrant, but because they had no other refuge, and felt confidence in one who was a Syracusan by birth.'[11] Despite Hicetas' supposed crimes it appears that once again many Syracusans believed that anyone was better than Dionysius.

The Carthaginians had stood aloof from the struggles of the Greek cities of Sicily for the past twenty years other than to provide tacit support to Dion. Traditionally their most powerful enemies among the Greeks had been the tyrants, particularly those of Syracuse: Gelon and Dionysius the Elder. Diodorus describes them as now 'renouncing their opposition to tyrants.'[12] Their previous opposition was probably a policy of supporting whatever weakened the tyrants of Syracuse but did not lead to outright war.

Hicetas, in his desire to take Syracuse for himself, had secretly betrayed his allies and 'since he had made a tyranny for himself, and not the freedom of Syracuse, his sole object in taking the field, had already held secret conferences with the Carthaginians.' This was done in the hope that: 'he might more easily turn the control of affairs into the hands of the Carthaginians and use these invaders as allies and helpers in a struggle against the Syracusans or against Dionysius.'[13] His approach to the Carthaginians was probably seen by them as a golden opportunity to reduce, or remove, the threat of the tyrants of Syracuse by placing a puppet ruler in the city dependent upon their support. The Persian Empire had long used this method to control the Greek cities of Asia.

The Carthaginians sent a well supplied and equipped expedition to Sicily under the command of Hanno. The invasion force consisted of 150 warships, 50,000 infantry and 300 chariots. They began their campaign by besieging Entella, a city in central Sicily which had been previously captured by Campanian mercenaries from its original Elymian occupants. The Elymians were traditional allies of Carthage and this campaign, which appears at first sight to have been an unnecessary diversion, was most likely designed to punish the Campanians.

When the Syracusan exiles in Leontini learned of the Carthaginian expedition they feared that the Sicilians, in their disunited state, would not be able to oppose this new threat. Nor would they be able to recover Syracuse while threatened by the Carthaginians operating to their rear. In their desperation they sent an embassy to their mother city of Corinth requesting assistance to help overthrow the tyranny before it was too late. Hicetas pretended to support the embassy but had already made his secret alliance with the Carthaginians.

That the Syracusan exiles should seek help from Corinth was not un-expected. Syracuse had been founded by colonists from Corinth and the relationship between mother cities and their colonies was usually close, involving religious obligations on the part of the colonies. This did not, how-ever, always ensure strong political ties, as the constant conflict between Corinth and one of its other colonies, Corcyra demonstrates. Syracuse had also destroyed one of its colonies, Camarina, nonetheless the relationship between Syracuse and Corinth does appear to have been initially strong. As far back as the early fifth century Corinth had intervened diplomatically on behalf of Syracuse against the tyrant Hippocrates of Gela. Corinth had also been instrumental in obtaining Spartan support for Syracuse against the Athenian invasion of 415. After the defeat of the Athenians, relations between the two appear to have become more distant as Syracuse allied itself with Sparta. The Syracusans had sent aid to Sparta while it was at war with the Corinthians.

Notwithstanding their strained relations, the request was also somewhat unusual as Corinth at this time was a declining power. Despite being on the winning side in the Peloponnesian War it had suffered badly during the conflict and won few of the rewards of victory. In the following ongoing wars between Sparta and Thebes, *stasis* had broken out between the pro and anti-Spartan factions in the city. As Corinth switched alliances depend-ing on who held power, its territory became a battlefield and it had been repeatedly ravaged by both sides. After adopting a role largely of neutrality after 365, Corinth began to recover but 'remained only a shadow of what she had been before the Peloponnesian War.'[14]

While this request was being discussed, Hicetas decided to forestall any possible interference from Corinth and seize Syracuse for himself. Hicetas was, at this time, described as the most powerful of the Sicilian tyrants 'and possessed a force that was able to cope with that of Dionysius.'[15] The total size of his forces is not recorded but we know that at one stage Hicetas commanded 5,000 select troops while still able to leave a force large enough to besiege Dionysius' forces in Ortygia.

The extent of Dionysius' forces is also not recorded in the sources. The traditional figure for the tyrant's garrison was 10,000 mercenaries but his empire was now a fraction of its former size. A year later the garrison consisted of only 2,000 men but this was after the loss in battle of 3,000 troops. Whether Dionysius could rely on the Syracusan citizen levies at this time is questionable. In any event, given the reduced state of Syracuse's wealth and population, and the desertions to Hicetas, this could not have been a substantial number. From the sources it is clear that both sides would have been able to field in excess of 5,000 troops, perhaps as many as 10,000, but Hicetas' force was slightly larger.

Hicetas marched on Syracuse and set up his camp at the Temple of Zeus. This temple occupied the only hill to the south of the city and dominated the coastal plain. Hicetas then began his siege but achieved little against the powerful walls that Dionysius the Elder had built. In the normal way of Greek warfare – and politics – he most likely hoped that a rising against Dionysius would hand the city over to him. The hoped for rebellion did not come and Hicetas was forced to retreat due to lack of provisions.

Dionysius saw his chance and pursued the retreating army. He launched an immediate attack on Hicetas' rearguard. Hicetas, however, proved to be the superior commander. He turned his army, formed it up for battle and attacked his pursuers, who were most likely disorganized by their rapid pursuit. His troops easily broke Dionysius' army which fled, leaving 3,000 dead on the field. Hicetas immediately followed up his victory, pursuing Dionysius' troops and entering the city before the walls could be manned (presumably Dionysius had stripped much of his garrison for the attack). Hicetas gained control of the entire city outside of Ortygia. Once again Syracuse was divided between two hostile forces and Dionysius was under siege in his island fortress.

One argument put forward for the persistence of tyranny in Syracuse was the need for effective military leadership against the various foreign enemies of the Greeks, the Carthaginians and later the Mamertines and Romans. The failure of the democracy to save Akragas was certainly the catalyst for the rise of Dionysius the Elder and the return of tyranny to Syracuse.

Although undoubtedly an important cause, events of the twenty years after the death of Dionysius demonstrate that this was not the only factor at play. The Carthaginians had kept the peace, yet the last decade of this period had seen no less than five changes of tyrant. The period had ended with Syracuse divided between rival claimants to the tyranny, with Hicetas seeking aid from the hated Carthaginians.

Another constant issue was the political struggle between rich and poor, democrat and oligarch, always endemic in the Greek cities. Ten years after Dionysius the Elder's death the *demos* had risen up against his son and, with the assistance of a private army led by the exiled Dion, driven the tyrant out of the city, besieging him within the walls of Ortygia. Almost immediately the rebels would split along political lines due to the chasm between rich and poor.

It is possible, therefore, to see different tyrants as representatives of conflicting political factions and assign populist or oligarchic support to their seizures of power. Gelon had crushed the first Syracusan democracy; Dion was a follower of Plato and an opponent of democracy; Callipus had murdered Dion on behalf of the radical democrats. Only in a few cases, however, can the political programmes of the tyrants be discerned with any confidence.

Another factor – one easy to overlook – was the overweening ambition of many individual politicians. Ancient Greek society was intensely competitive, even extending to cultural events where the audience would vote for, and award prizes to, their favourite plays. Pre-eminence over one's peers was always the goal of the ambitious. This lust for glory was freely admitted by the Athenian mercenary general, Xenophon: when he sought the sole command of an army: 'Xenophon partly would have liked to do so, in the belief that by so doing he would win to himself a higher repute in the esteem of his friends, and that his name would be reported to the city written large.'[16] Politics was one of the most important arenas in which one could compete to obtain fame. In such struggles family ties, friendship and the promise of favouritism were often more important than any political platform. The enormous wealth of the Greeks of Sicily allowed such individuals to continue their quest for power outside of the assembly by raising private armies of mercenaries.

Like many people before and since, when faced by a crisis, military or political, the Syracusans would look for decisive leadership. Many would have looked around the city at the statues of Gelon and decided that another strong individual could once again save them. At such times it was never difficult to find an ambitious politician ready to put himself forward.

At the time of the fighting between Hicetas and Dionysius, the Corinthians had met to discuss sending assistance to the Syracusan exiles. Somewhat surprisingly, they reversed their earlier policy and voted in favour of launching an expedition to overthrow Dionysius. Plutarch describes the motives for their apparent change of heart:

> But when the embassy arrived, the Corinthians, since they were wont to be ever solicitous for their colonial cities and for Syracuse in particular, and since by good fortune there was nothing in Greece at that time to disturb them, but they were enjoying peace and leisure, voted readily to give the assistance desired.[17]

It is at this point that Plutarch's next hero in the history of Syracuse appears, Timoleon of Corinth, is selected to lead a small expedition to Syracuse.

Chapter 6
Timoleon Arrives in Sicily

Among these were Timoleon the Corinthian and Aemilius Paulus,
whose Lives I have now undertaken to lay before my readers; the men
were alike not only in the good principles which they adopted, but also
in the good fortune which they enjoyed in their conduct of affairs.

Plutarch, *Timoleon* Preface

If Plutarch had taken to excess his tendency to record the noblest deeds of
his subjects and ignore the ignoble in *Dion*, he overindulges to the fullest in
Timoleon. Timoleon is described in endless superlatives as a man completely honourable in all his actions, always correct in his decisions and,
most importantly, blessed by the gods. Only once does Plutarch criticize
Timoleon, for failing to prevent the execution of Hicetas' wife and children
by the vengeful Syracusans. Plutarch describes this as 'to have been the most
displeasing thing in Timoleon's career'[1] This event is portrayed, however,
as a sin of neglect rather than the result of any malice on the part of his hero.

The *Life* is itself very colourless. There are few of the anecdotes or
speeches that bring Plutarch's other characters so much to life. The moralist
in Plutarch portrays Timoleon as the favourite of the gods, particularly
Fortune, predestined to bring justice to the evil tyrants of Sicily. As Talbert,
in his commentary on *Timoleon*, so astutely observes: 'there is hardly any
relief afforded from the unceasing chorus of indiscriminate praise, either by
the charming personal details which Plutarch introduces so ably elsewhere,
or by faults or emotions.' He further adds that 'Plutarch's portrait has
impressed men of all ages ... but it is not the portrait of a man.'[2]

Although Plutarch cites a number of sources for *Timoleon*, modern
scholars tend to believe that he used two extensively. The first is supposed
to be an unknown biography from Aristotle's school of philosophy which
would have been interested in the ethical dilemmas of Timoleon's life. This
proposition is, however, merely learned speculation. More certain is that
Plutarch made much use of the Sicilian historian Timaeus. Other historians
in antiquity roundly criticized Timaeus' portrayal of Timoleon as being

uncritical and obsequious. Polybius is particularly savage in his lengthy attack, describing Timaeus as an 'ignoramus' who 'makes Timoleon greater than the most illustrious gods.'[3]

There are two other major sources for Timoleon's life and campaigns in Sicily, those of Nepos and Diodorus. Nepos' *Timoleon* is mostly a shorter version of Plutarch's and is generally considered to be based on the same sources. Diodorus' narrative is again a more temperate account, in which Timoleon is praised but not so extensively. He also describes some incidents that are discreditable to Timoleon. Diodorus' account is at times so dissimilar that it is generally considered he relied mainly on different source material to that of Plutarch. That Diodorus' version of events is different is not surprising, as he was attempting to write a general history of events in Sicily rather than a biography.

Again, as he does with Dion, Plutarch introduces a villain in order to further emphasize the virtues of his hero. On this occasion the villain is Hicetas, the tyrant of Leontini and the murderer of Dion's family. Plutarch's list of Hicetas' crimes and shortcomings is lengthy: he is described as evil, seeking power for its own sake, envious, at times cowardly, and treacherous. Above all it is his betrayal of Syracuse to the hated Carthaginians that is most to be despised. Neither of our other main sources portrays Hicetas in this way. Diodorus simply calls him the most powerful tyrant in Sicily. Nepos limits himself to echoing one of Plutarch's criticisms, claiming that Hicetas did not fight Dionysius 'from hatred of tyranny, but from a desire for it.'[4] It would appear that Plutarch, as with the case of Heracleides, has produced a straw man who exists to contrast with, and therefore highlight, the virtues of his hero.

Beyond this, however, Plutarch is contemptuous of all the Sicilian leaders except for Dion and Timoleon, claiming that of: 'the Greek leaders and generals who took part in Sicilian affairs during the time of Timoleon, not one was free from corruption except Dion.'[5] Although Plutarch's *Lives* are the most extensive source material for this period of Syracusan history, he is a problematic source when used in isolation. Any historian attempting a reconstruction of events based solely on Plutarch's narratives would do well to keep the warning of the eminent historian Brian Bosworth firmly in mind: 'heaven help you if your evidence is the *Lives* and the *Lives* alone.'[6] It is for these reasons that the following narrative will again rely largely on Diodorus' account wherever possible.

Timoleon was born in Corinth in about 411, the second son of one of the leading aristocratic families. Nothing is recorded about his early life except that in a battle fought against the city of Argos he had saved the life of his elder brother, Timophanes, by holding: 'his shield over him as he lay on the ground, and after receiving many javelins and many hand to hand blows upon his person and his armour, at last succeeded in repulsing the enemy.'[7] This act made him a war-hero and gave him a reputation for personal bravery.

At some time around 366, Corinth raised a force of 400 mercenaries to provide the city with a permanent military force. Xenophon states that this detachment was recruited for purely military reasons. Aristotle claims, however, that the oligarchs raised it 'because, not being able to trust the people, the oligarchs are compelled to hire mercenaries, and the general who is in command of them often ends in becoming a tyrant.'[8] The Corinthians chose Timophanes to command this detachment and soon learnt the truth of Aristotle's assertion. Like many others holding such an office Timophanes used the force of mercenaries to overthrow the existing government and to seize power. Although an aristocrat himself, and part of the oligarchy, Timophanes: 'without regard for honour and justice, at once took measures to bring the city under his own power, and after putting to death without a trial great numbers of the leading citizens, declared himself tyrant.'[9]

Timoleon opposed his brother's tyranny and attempted to dissuade him from his actions, but to no avail. He decided on more drastic action and plotted to assassinate his brother. There are three surviving accounts of the murder. Plutarch describes that along with two friends Timoleon confronted his brother and, after reason again failed, he: 'stood weeping with muffled head, while the other two, drawing their swords, speedily despatched him.'[10] Nepos largely supports Plutarch but further distances Timoleon from the deed: 'he himself not only did not put his hand to the work, but would not even look upon his brother's blood; for, until the deed was done, he kept himself at a distance on the watch, lest any of his brother's guards should come to his aid.'[11] Diodorus, who is less interested in protecting Timoleon's reputation, implies that Timoleon did the deed himself, putting 'him to death as he was promenading in the market-place.'[12] Diodorus places these events in 346/5, just before Timoleon's departure to Syracuse, and appears to have conflated events for dramatic effect. Based on the evidence of Xenophon and Aristotle, it is better on this occasion to prefer the chronology of Plutarch and date the assassination to about 365.

Tyrannicides were always greatly admired in ancient Greek society but any honour that may have accrued to Timoleon was tempered by the fact that the tyrant he had assassinated was his own brother. These conflicting attitudes caused great dissension in Corinth as: 'one side claimed that as the perpetrator of a kin-murder Timoleon should receive the punishment prescribed by the laws, whereas the other party asserted just the opposite, that they should applaud him as a tyrannicide.'[13] As Timoleon survived the episode it would appear that he must have been acquitted. His own mother was less forgiving and disowned him, refusing him entry into her house. Timoleon's guilt seems to have brought on a bout of severe depression. As a result he withdrew from public affairs and retired to the countryside, 'wandering in great distress of mind among the most desolate parts of the country.'[14]

Timoleon had remained absent from public affairs for twenty years when the request for assistance against Dionysius came from the Syracusan exiles and his appointment is therefore remarkable. Again there are different versions of his appointment to the command. Diodorus simply states that he was appointed by the ruling oligarchic council (*gerousia*). Plutarch, intent on promoting Timoleon's anti-tyrannical credentials, states that:

> One of the common people rose to his feet and nominated Timoleon the son of Timodemus, although he no longer took part in public business, and had no expectation or purpose of doing so; but some god, as it would seem, put it into the man's mind to nominate him, such was the kindliness of Fortune that shone forth at once upon his election, and such the grace that attended his subsequent actions and adorned his virtues.[15]

On this occasion it is best to accept Diodorus as all the surviving evidence suggest that Corinth was an oligarchy at this time. Plutarch himself states that Corinth had been an oligarchy only a decade earlier. It is generally assumed that Plutarch's implication that Corinth was a democracy is an attempt to 'create the impression that Timoleon was a popular choice for the mission of liberating Syracuse.'[16]

The selection of Timoleon at first appears surprising if he had been absent from affairs for twenty years, although Diodorus describes his early career as one of a 'man of highest prestige amongst his fellow citizens for bravery and sagacity as a general.'[17] Plutarch attributes it to divine intervention. He does, however, record one other possible motive. One of the leaders of Corinth was supposed to have bid him farewell by claiming that if he were successful 'we shall think of thee as a tyrannicide; but if poorly, as a fratricide.'[18] In other words, he was a disposable commodity and his presence in the city would not be missed.

While the expedition was being prepared, a message was brought to the Corinthians from Hicetas exposing his treacherous dealings with the Carthaginians. He informed them that his new allies had forbidden the Corinthian expedition and would destroy it if it attempted to reach Sicily. The letter supposedly incited the Corinthians to greater action and united the city behind the venture.

Perhaps as a result of this unity, the omens were universally good. In Corinth the priestesses of Peresphone, and her mother Demeter, dreamt that they had heard the goddesses say that they would accompany the expedition to Sicily. The island was particularly sacred to Peresphone as it was the place of her rape by Hades and later given to her as a wedding present. The Corinthians equipped two sacred triremes and named them after the goddesses. Timoleon travelled to the sacred oracle at Delphi and while he was there a votive crown from a statue of Nike (Victory) fell upon his head. When, in the summer of 344, the fleet sailed from the city they enjoyed a favourable wind and a heavenly light show. The soothsayers declared that the gods had undoubtedly blessed the undertaking.

Despite the enthusiasm for the expedition the force was small; just ten warships and 700 mercenaries. The mercenaries were also a disreputable lot as most had previously served the Phocians, who had plundered the temple at Delphi to pay their wages. As such they were considered to be cursed by most Greeks. Talbert proposes plausibly that the cash-strapped Corinthians were forced to hire such desperate men as they could not afford to fully pay others. An ancient Greek soldier's pay was made up of two parts: payment for service *(misthos)* and provisions. The first was always paid in cash and the latter could be given as food or paid in cash. By the fourth century payment cash was also the norm for the latter. As Timoleon was unable to pay the *misthos*, the mercenaries were promised full payment from any booty that was won during the campaign.[19]

The sending of such a small expedition, consisting of so many participants who were shunned and therefore expendable, implies that the Corinthians were not confident of success. As with the earlier sending of the Spartan general Gylippus to Syracuse to command against the Athenians, the impact that Timoleon's leadership would have was far greater than the Corinthians, or anyone else, could have predicted.

After leaving Corinth the fleet put in at Metapontum, on the southern coast of Italy. Here Timoleon was met by ambassadors from both Carthage and Rhegium. The Carthaginians warned him not to come to Sicily, while the Rhegians offered to join him as allies. Encouraged by the offer of assistance, Timoleon defied the Carthaginians and set sail for Rhegium. Here he received news that Hicetas had captured Syracuse three days earlier.

The Carthaginians had sent twenty triremes to Rhegium, transporting a delegation from their ally Hicetas. The envoys demanded that Timoleon should send his expedition back to Greece but if he wished he could continue onto Sicily alone and join Hicetas as a counsellor. Timoleon and his officers, viewing the ships of the hated foreigners, were 'indignant at the insult put upon them, and were all of them filled with rage at Hicetas ... on the one hand for his treachery, and to the Carthaginians on the other for making him tyrant.'[20]

Timoleon, outnumbered by the ships of the Carthaginians, replied that he would concede to their demands but first wished to inform his new allies, the Rhegians. In reality, Timoleon had no intention of retreating but had contrived with the Rhegians that they distract the Carthaginians while he evaded the blockade. The Rhegians called an assembly and deliberately delivered long speeches. Meanwhile all the Corinthians except Timoleon manned their vessels and nine of the ships put out to sea. As soon as he had heard that they were gone, Timoleon slipped out of the assembly and sailed away in the last ship.

The Carthaginians, realizing that they had been deceived, set out in pursuit but were unable to overtake the Greeks. Timoleon landed in Sicily at Tauromemium (Taormina). The city was governed by Andromachus, the father of the historian Timaeus, who welcomed Timoleon as he had long been a supporter of the Syracusan opponents of Dionysius and 'was also known to be always averse and hostile to tyrants.'[21] Andromachus is sometimes referred to as the tyrant of the city but both Diodorus and Plutarch describe him as *hegemon*, leader. Given that Timoleon did not later depose him along with the other tyrants it is more likely that he was the dominant politician within a constitutional government.

The Carthaginians arrived soon after and threatened to destroy Tauromenium. Andromachus met their threats with derision and ordered them to either depart or be attacked. He then persuaded the citizens to allow Timoleon to use the city as a base and supplied him with a detachment of soldiers.

Not all the Greeks of Sicily were as welcoming as Andromachus. The Sicilians remembered how others had come from Greece, Callippus in particular, who 'while declaring that they came to secure the freedom of Sicily and wished to overthrow its tyrants, made the calamities of Sicily under her tyrants seem as gold in comparison.' Many feared that Timoleon 'would be no whit better than those who had preceded him, but that the same sophistries and lures were come to them again.'[22] Others were dismayed by the small size of his force. All rejected his appeals for assistance, except for the small city of Adranum which lay inland to the north of Catane. Its population was politically divided, with some supporting Hicetas and others Timoleon. As was the way in such conflicts, each faction was willing to invite outsiders into their city to assist in their struggle.

Both generals decided to intervene in Adranum. Hicetas advanced on the city with 5,000 of his best troops, leaving the rest to continue the siege of Ortygia. Timoleon's force now numbered 1,000. Despite being badly outnumbered, he decided to fight as his supplies were short and the mercenaries still had not been paid. He badly needed a victory in order to win plunder and boost the morale of the expedition.

Timoleon's intelligence appears to have been better than that of his rival. Learning that Hicetas was also approaching Adranum he force-marched his army on the second day after leaving Tauromenium, covering the 60km in less than two days. Given the distance covered, Timoleon must have used the longer inland route around Mount Aetna rather than the shorter coastal route. Most likely he did not want to be trapped along the narrow coastal road between the army of Hicetas and the fleet of the Carthaginians.

Timoleon arrived at the outskirts of Adranum in the late afternoon. Once again Timoleon's intelligence was superior: he learned that Hicetas' force had only just arrived and was making camp. Timoleon's subordinates halted the vanguard, prepared to make camp and feed the army in preparation for a battle the next day. Timoleon saw, however, a great opportunity and implored his soldiers to form up and attack immediately while the enemy was unprepared. He took up his arms and led his army rapidly over the 6km to the enemy camp. Hicetas' men were busy pitching camp and in total disarray when Timoleon's troops hit them. Most fled without fighting, but 300 were killed and 600 were captured, along with all the baggage.

The pro-Timoleon faction within Adranum threw open their gates and welcomed Timoleon into the city. Plutarch, ever ready to find divine sanction for Timoleon's crusade, records how the people of Adranum told him that at the start of the battle the doors of their temple had flown open and the spear of the god trembled. He goes on to claim that: 'these prodigies, as it would seem, were a sign not only of the victory which was then won, but also of the achievements succeeding them, to which that struggle afforded a propitious beginning.'[23] More practically, with this victory Timoleon had, at least for the moment, solved his supply problems and given legitimacy to his campaign.

Chapter 7

The Final Overthrow of Dionysius the Younger

For his fame not only filled at once all Sicily and Italy, but within a few
days Greece echoed with his great success, so that the city of Corinth,
which was in doubt whether his armament had got across the sea,
heard at one and the same time that it had safely crossed, and that
it was victorious. So prosperous was the course of his enterprises,
and such was the speed with which Fortune crowned the beauty of
his achievements.

Plutarch, *Timoleon* 21

Up to this point our two main sources largely agree in their description
of events, but after Timoleon's victory at Adranum they diverge widely.
Diodorus records that: 'capping this manoeuvre with another, he proceeded
forthwith to Syracuse. Covering the distance at full speed, he fell on the city
without warning, having made better time than those who were routed and
fleeing.'[1] Once there, he seized a portion of the city and a three way struggle
for control of Syracuse followed. The final surrender of Dionysius does not
occur until a year later. Plutarch records a more prolonged period before
Timoleon finally arrived at Syracuse. He describes a number of cities allying
themselves with Timoleon and Dionysius surrendering Ortygia to Timoleon
before he marched on the city. In Plutarch's account Dionysius' surrender
takes place only fifty days after Timoleon's arrival in Sicily. The struggle
for Syracuse is then a two way fight between Hicetas and his Carthaginian
allies, and Timoleon, which lasts for an undisclosed amount of time.

The two accounts have caused much debate in academic circles with
some writers favouring one side or the other, and others trying to reconcile
the two versions. The two most accessible accounts in English are those
of Westlake and Talbert. Westlake largely dismisses Diodorus' account as
being implausible. He argues that Timoleon could not have force-marched
his exhausted army to Syracuse quickly enough to have surprised Hicetas'
garrison and that his army was too small to have captured, and held, part
of the city. He does, however, accept Diodorus' dating of Timoleon's final

seizure of the city. Westlake therefore attempts to reconcile Plutarch's account with Diodorus' time frame. He does this by the convoluted method of making Dionysius' surrender of Ortygia to Timoleon as conditional, with the tyrant living in Timoleon's camp and treating him as a mercenary commander until he is finally forced to abdicate a year later.[2]

Talbert accepts that Westlake's first two objections to Diodorus' account 'are reasonable, but they do not decisively demonstrate the falsehood of the narrative.'[3] He does, however, point out the unlikelihood of Timoleon making any sort of alliance with Dionysius at this time, as his 'Sicilian allies will have been suspicious of any negotiations with Dionysius.'[4] Nor would the presence of the tyrant in his camp have been acceptable. Talbert mounts a convincing defence for the plausibility of Diodorus', by arguing that Timoleon could easily have rested his army for one day and then covered the 85km to the city inside two days. Such rapid marches were a hallmark of Timoleon's generalship and not unprecedented. Hicetas' army, demoralized and lacking in supply, most likely retreated back to Leontini and would have been in no position to block Timoleon's march.

Plutarch is notorious for twisting chronology in order to make his narratives more dramatic. It is possible that here he has removed Dionysius from the conflict prematurely in order to highlight the struggle between his hero Timoleon and his villain Hicetas. For these reasons Diodorus' chronology will be followed, albeit with some reservation.[5]

Once Timoleon had entered the city, 'great confusion reigned in Syracuse, where Dionysius held the Island, Hicetas Achradina and Neapolis, and Timoleon the rest of the city.'[6] The city, so often divided between two opposing camps, was now split into three. It is possible that Hicetas' reduced garrison, consisting of his poorest troops without their leader, was unwilling to oppose Timoleon's victorious army until the situation had clarified.

Meanwhile Hicetas had been in contact with his Carthaginian allies and they sent him a force reputedly numbering 150 triremes and 50,000 soldiers commanded by Mago.[7] Here Plutarch openly displays his abhorrence of Hicetas' alliance with the barbarians, decrying that: 'never before in all their countless wars in Sicily had the Carthaginians succeeded in taking Syracuse; but now Hicetas admitted them and handed over to them the city, and men saw that it was a barbarian camp.'[8]

At first the great size of the Carthaginian force was supposed to have caused dismay amongst Timoleon and his men but their spirits were soon revived when they, in turn, received reinforcements. Mamercus, the tyrant of Catane, joined Timoleon and brought with him a considerable army. Mamercus was a Campanian and former mercenary of Dionysius. A number of the garrisons of the outlying Syracusan forts also declared for Timoleon.

Timoleon's force was, nonetheless, still heavily outnumbered. Hicetas and the Carthaginians placed his foothold in Syracuse under siege. Syracuse was a large city by ancient standards and its fortifications had expanded as the city grew, thus sections of the city would have been separated from one another by the surviving older walls. Where these did not exist, barricades could easily be thrown up to block the narrow streets.

At some stage Timoleon himself withdrew from the city and returned to his base at Adranum, perhaps to unite with his new allies. Here Hicetas made an attempt to assassinate him because Timoleon 'at no time kept a guard in array about his person, and at this time in particular, owing to his trust in their god, he was altogether without anxiety or suspicion'. As the two assassins approached Timoleon in a temple, one was struck down by a bystander who recognized him as the murderer of his father. The surviving assassin clung to the altar and obtained mercy from his proposed victim. That Hicetas would attempt to assassinate Timoleon is credible. Plutarch, however, records the incident to support his theme of Timoleon as 'one who had come under divine guidance to avenge the wrongs of Sicily.'[9]

Meanwhile Hicetas and his Carthaginian allies were pressing Timoleon's troops in Syracuse. Using their naval supremacy they placed his garrison under blockade and cut off their food supplies. The garrison was constantly harassed 'and they were forever dividing up their forces in skirmishes and battles around the walls, and in repelling all sorts of engines and every species of siege warfare.'[10]

Timoleon responded by sending his garrison food from Catane in small fishing boats. They would take advantage of any bad weather to sneak through the blockading triremes, which would become scattered in the rough seas. Learning of this, Mago and Hicetas determined to take Catane and put an end to this supply route. They took a task force consisting of their best ships and troops and sailed for Catane. The Corinthian commander of Timoleon's garrison in Syracuse observed that in the absence of their generals the remaining enemy was keeping a careless watch. He launched a surprise sortie on the besiegers and took them unawares. The attack was a success and managed to capture the important area of Achradina, which lay alongside Ortygia. The attack also secured large amounts of booty, grain and money, easing the pressure on Timoleon's garrison.

Mago and Hicetas were approaching Catane when a messenger overtook them and told them of the capture of Achradina. Perplexed by the news, they appear to have lost their nerve and immediately returned to Syracuse without attacking Catane. As Plutarch scathingly observes they had 'neither taken the city against which they went forth, nor kept the one they had.'[11]

At this time Timoleon received a further boost to his cause. The Corinthians, excited by his earlier successes, had dispatched reinforcements of ten ships, 2,000 hoplites and 200 cavalry. At first the Corinthians had been delayed in Italy by a detachment of the Carthaginian fleet until it was forced to take shelter due to a storm. The squall abruptly abated and the Greeks, taking advantage of the Carthaginian absence 'speedily manned the ferry-boats and fishing craft which they found at hand, put off, and made their way across to Sicily, with such safety and in so great a calm that their horses also swam along by the side of the boats and were towed by the reins.' To make such a crossing the Greeks must have landed somewhere near Messene but this was also the obvious place for the Carthaginians to have sought shelter as the city had gone over to their side. If so it is difficult to believe that the Greeks could have crossed in the presence of a hostile fleet. In this passage Plutarch tells a far-fetched tale of the Carthaginian commander having deserting his post in order to sail to Syracuse and there pretend to have defeated the Corinthians. It was 'while he was thus babbling and playing the trickster'[12] that the Corinthians crossed. Although difficult to believe, the absence of the Carthaginian fleet at Messene does give some credibility to this tale.

Now reinforced by the Corinthians, Timoleon decided that it was time to settle matters in Syracuse. He gathered an army of 4,000 men and marched on the city. At the approach of Timoleon's force, Mago is supposed to have become 'suspicious of treachery,' due to the fraternization of the Greek troops of both sides, not uncommon during a long siege. One of the Corinthians is supposed to have asked Hicetas' men why

> you, who are Greeks, are eager to barbarize a city of such great size and furnished with such great advantages, thus settling Carthaginians, who are the basest and bloodiest of men, nearer to us, when you ought to pray for many Sicilies to lie as a barrier between Greece and them? Or do you suppose that they have collected an army and are come hither from the pillars of Heracles and the Atlantic sea in order to risk their lives in behalf of the dynasty of Hicetas? He, if he reasoned like a true leader, would not be casting out his kindred people, nor would he be leading against his country her natural enemies, but would be enjoying a befitting amount of honour and power, with the consent of Timoleon and the Corinthians.[13]

All these are reasonable questions for a Greek to ask and many of Hicetas' men must have shared such misgivings. No doubt aware of such sympathies among his Greek allies, Mago, who 'had long wanted a pretext for going away,' decided to abandon both the city and his ally. Hicetas begged him to remain, pointing out how superior they were to the enemy in numbers. Mago is supposed to have retorted that they 'were more inferior to Timoleon in bravery and good fortune … and weighing anchor at once, sailed off to Libya, thus letting Sicily slip out of his hands disgracefully and for no reason that man could suggest.'[14] Diodorus has Mago retreating to the Epicraty, the Carthaginian region of Sicily. The Carthaginians obviously agreed with Plutarch's assessment as, soon after, Mago committed suicide, probably to avoid the execution that was the usual Carthaginian reward for failed generals. Nonetheless, determined to display their displeasure they 'impaled his dead body, in their rage at his conduct of the expedition.'[15]

As Plutarch states, the abrupt departure of Mago's force was a disgrace and a terrible betrayal of both his ally and his city. Modern historians have similarly denounced his retreat as cowardly and tried to deduce the reasons for it. One theory is that Mago was forced to abandon Syracuse in order to return to Carthage to put down an attempted coup by another military commander. The sparse evidence for this coup does place the event sometime during the reign of Philip of Macedon (359–336).[16] Mago's suicide, more likely the action of a defeated commander than a political saviour, argues strongly against this theory.

Both Talbert and Westlake argue in favour of the reasons given by Plutarch. Westlake claims that there had always been unease between the allies as both 'intended to make use of the other in his own interests.'[17] He asserts that Timoleon played on these suspicions and ordered his troops to fraternize with those of Hicetas. The constant small victories of Timoleon, culminating in the debacle of the march to Catane, intensified Mago's fears and he decided to cut his losses and abandon his ally. Talbert largely agrees but emphasizes the 'illogicality of Mago's decision' claimed by the sources and concludes that 'Mago does seem to have been a weak commander.'[18]

With Hicetas now abandoned by his allies, Timoleon finally felt strong enough to attack his fortifications within Syracuse:

> The attack was made in all three places at once, and the troops of Hicetas were overwhelmed and took to flight. That the city was taken by storm and fell quickly into their hands after the enemy had been driven out, it is right to ascribe to the bravery of the soldiers and the ability of their general; but that not one of the Corinthians was killed or even wounded.[19]

This lack of fight by Hicetas' troops has also puzzled modern historians especially as Plutarch had earlier described how: 'Hicetas was still eager for battle and would not let go his hold upon the city, but clung to the parts of it in his possession, which were strong and dangerous to attack.'[20] Diodorus' brief account does little to shed light on events, merely stating that 'Hicetas was left isolated while Timoleon victoriously occupied Syracuse.'[21] There are various explanations put forward to explain the lack of fight put up by Hicetas' men. One is that his mercenaries were totally demoralized and surrendered or fled without a fight. This is unlikely, as most appear to have rejoined Hicetus who is described soon after as has having a substantial army. Another is that Plutarch simply exaggerated the lack of fighting to once again boost the divine good fortune of his hero. Westlake proposes that Timoleon made a secret deal whereby they would make a pretence of fighting to save both their reputations while not weakening their forces.

Hicetas could then retire to secure Leontini with his large army intact and Timoleon concentrate on capturing the rest of Syracuse.[22]

If we accept Diodorus' outline of events, another question that arises is what was Dionysius doing while the other protagonists were fighting for control of the city? It may be that Diodorus simply chose to omit these details from his brief account. A more likely reason is that Dionysius, with his tiny garrison of only 2,000 troops, deliberately chose to do nothing, hoping that his enemies would seriously weaken or destroy one another. With the retreat of the Carthaginian fleet he must have felt a glimmer of hope. This hope was destroyed by Hicetas' precipitous withdrawal, and Dionysius was left to face a siege by the united forces of Timoleon and the Syracusans. Diodorus portrays the final, pathetic end of the tyrant:

> Thus, through cowardice and meanness, he lost that celebrated tyranny which had been, as people said, bound with fetters of steel, and spent the remaining years of his life in poverty at Corinth, furnishing in his life and misfortune an example to all who vaunt themselves unwisely on their successes. He who had possessed four hundred triremes arrived shortly after in Corinth in a small tub of a freighter, conspicuously displaying the enormity of the change in his fortunes.[23]

Diodorus' brief account infers that Dionysius' surrender came soon after the defeat of Hicetas but he does place it in a different chapter, after noting the change of year, so it may have dragged-on for some months. The fall of Dionysius from tyrant of the most powerful Greek city to refugee was one that delighted the ancient authors who were always looking for evidence of divine justice. Justin records in gloating detail how Dionysius lived a life of dissolution before being forced by poverty to adopt

> the profession of a schoolmaster, and taught children in the open streets, either that he might continually be seen in public by those who feared him, or might be more readily despised by those who did not fear him ... Yet amidst all these arts of dissimulation, he was accused of aspiring to the sovereignty, and was left at liberty only because he was despised.[24]

By contrast, Plutarch vividly describes the nobility of Timoleon's first act after expelling the tyrant:

> When he had become master of the citadel, he did not repeat the experience of Dion, nor did he spare the place on account of the beauty and great cost of its architecture, but guarding against the suspicions which had brought calumny and then destruction upon his predecessor, he made proclamation that all Syracusans who wished should come

with implements of iron and help in the demolition of the tyrants' bulwarks. And when they had all come up, considering that day with its proclamation to be a most secure beginning of freedom, they overthrew and demolished, not only the citadel, but also the palaces and the tombs of the tyrants. Then, as soon as he had levelled off the place, Timoleon built the courts of justice there, thus gratifying the citizens by making their democracy triumphant over tyranny.[25]

This action was a powerful symbol that not only had the old tyranny been overthrown but that Timoleon had no ambitions to seize the tyranny for himself. As revolutionaries throughout the ages have found, however, destroying an old regime is only the beginning; creating a new administration can be even more difficult. Both Plutarch and Diodorus' claim that the new government was a democracy and the new laws paid special attention to establishing equality. Democracy in the ancient world could, however, take many forms; the possible nature of the future government of Syracuse will be discussed later.

Although the sources do not record what position, if any, Timoleon may have held in the new government, if any, that of commander in chief, *strategos autocrator*, is by far the most likely. It is possible that, for a time at least, the situation in the city was similar to that after Dion's arrival, with a radical democracy and a *strategos autocrator* co-existing uneasily. This office must have been granted to Timoleon by a vote by the Syracusan assembly after the removal of Hicetas from the city. It was a vote of the assembly that had elevated Dionysius the Elder to this rank, confirmed the succession of his son and granted it to Dion. The first and third votes were taken voluntarily due to the crises of war, the second taken under duress. The election of Timoleon was also a voluntary decision. Timoleon's destruction of the fortifications would have removed many of the accusations and suspicions of tyranny that had dogged Dion after his removal of Dionysius.

The liberation of Syracuse was a remarkable achievement that echoed, not only around Sicily, but soon spread to the entire Greek world. For Timoleon it was only a beginning. He still hoped to accomplish the liberation of all the Greek cities of Sicily from their tyrannies and to rid them of the Carthaginian menace.

Chapter 8

The Battle of Crimisus River

Timoleon, after defeating Hicetas, put to flight a vast army of the
Carthaginians on the river Crimisus, and obliged those who had now
for several years maintained their ground in Sicily, to be satisfied if they
were allowed to retain Africa.

Nepos, *Timoleon* 2

Before Timoleon could embark on his crusade to liberate the Greeks of
Sicily there was still work to done be in Syracuse. Fifteen years of civil war
had reduced the city to a shadow of its former wealth and power. Large
parts of the city were so depopulated that they had returned to pasture and
were being used to graze horses. Other cities of Sicily had suffered similar
fates and some were reputedly overrun with wildlife.

Timoleon and the Syracusans sent letters to Corinth requesting them to
send colonists to Sicily. The Corinthians passed on the invitation, spreading
the word at the sacred games in Greece and sending messages to the Greeks
of the islands and Asia. The call was met with great enthusiasm. Sicily was
renowned for its wealth and the wars and civil strife of the Greek cities
ensured that there were always plenty of stateless, landless, or adventurous
people looking for a new start. Ten thousand prospective colonists gathered
in Corinth and set sail for Syracuse. The Syracusans gave grants of land to
the new arrivals and sold to them the abandoned houses within the city.

Once the process of recovery had begun, Timoleon then was able to
return to his goal of driving out the remaining tyrannies. War was always
an expensive business and although some money had been raised by the sale
of the houses more was needed. The Syracusans voted to condemn their
former tyrants and tear down their public statues. The statues were then
sold at auction. Only the statue of Gelon, the hero of the victory against the
Carthaginians at Himera in 480, was spared.

Once some money had been raised, Timoleon was able to begin his
campaign of liberation. His first target was the city of Messene which
had allied itself with the Carthaginians. The city was quickly captured and

Timoleon then turned against Hicetas. He launched an assault on Leontini but Hicetas' army was still numerous and successfully defended the walls. Unable to accomplish anything, Timoleon broke off the siege and went looking for easier targets. Plutarch has a slightly different version of events: he claims that Hicetas was forced to renounce his alliance with the Carthaginians, dismantle his fortifications and abdicate his tyranny. As Hicetas remained in control of the city and attacked Syracuse soon after, these claims appear to be spurious.[1]

Timoleon met with more success at the city of Engyum, which was controlled by the tyrant Leptines, possibly a relation of Dionysius. He assaulted the city but was forced to call off his attack when Hicetas took advantage of his absence to march on Syracuse. Once again Timoleon defeated him in battle and forced him to retire to Leontini. Leptines was now frightened into surrendering Engyum and several other cities under his control. Timoleon shipped him off to Corinth, 'considering it a fine thing to have the tyrants of Sicily in the mother city where the Greeks could observe them living the lowly life of exiles.'[2] Timoleon returned to these cities their freedom and autonomy. The mercy shown to Dionysius and Leptines would not be repeated and Timoleon would later take a much harder line with the surviving tyrants.

By failing to take Leontini and accepting the surrender of Leptines, Timoleon had not been able to plunder any cities and thereby replenish his war chest. Short of money with which to pay his mercenaries, Timoleon sent a thousand of them on a plundering expedition into Carthaginian controlled territory. He retired to Syracuse to meet with lawgivers who had arrived from Corinth to assist in preparing a new constitution for Syracuse. The expedition went well, winning a large enough amount of booty to pay the mercenaries for a long period. Several cities were captured, while others revolted from the Carthaginians, attracted by Timoleon's policy of restoring autonomy to the cities. Although it is not directly stated, in the usual Greek manner these cities would have been expected to ally themselves with Syracuse. A number of cities of the Sicels and the Sicanians – non-Greek inhabitants of Sicily who were generally allies of the Carthaginians due to their dislike of their Greek overlords – also approached Timoleon and offered to join this alliance.

Such a direct attack on their property and reputation did not go unnoticed by the Carthaginians, who 'recognized that their generals in Sicily were conducting the war in a spiritless manner and decided to send out new ones, together with heavy reinforcements.' The seriousness of their purpose was shown by them raising 'their noblest citizens' alongside the more usual levies of their Libyan subjects and mercenary Spanish, Gauls and Ligurians. A new fleet was also constructed.[3] The commanders, Hasdrubal and Hamilcar were explicitly ordered 'not to carry on the war by piece-meal any more, but at one time to drive the invading Greeks out of all Sicily.'[4] The expedition was dispatched to Sicily and landed at Lilybaeum (Marsala) in either late 340 or early 339. It was certainly of sufficient size to match its intent. The force numbered 70,000 infantry, cavalry and war-chariots whose horses, including spare mounts, totalled 10,000, and 200 warships.

The Carthaginians, the Greeks of North Africa and the Gauls were unusual in that they still used the chariot in warfare; most other nations having replaced them with cavalry. The main reason for their replacement was most likely cost, as chariots were extremely expensive items and only the wealthiest states or individuals could afford them. Their main advantage in battle appears to have been their weight and the fear they caused, especially against troops who were unused to them. Livy describes the impact they had against the Romans when they faced Gaulish Chariots at the battle of Sentinum fought in 295:

> Armed men mounted on chariots and baggage wagons came on with a thunderous noise of horses and wheels, and the horses of the Roman cavalry, unaccustomed to that kind of uproar, became uncontrollable through fright; the cavalry after their victorious charges, were now scattered in frantic terror; horses and men alike were overthrown in their blind flight. Even the standards of the legionaries were thrown into confusion, and many of the front rank men were crushed by the weight of the horses and vehicles dashing through the lines.[5]

What evidence we have shows that the Carthaginian chariots were strongly built and heavier than those of the Gauls, drawn by four horses and were crewed by either two or three soldiers armed with spears. This, along with several descriptions we have of their use in battle, would imply that they were primarily designed as shock weapons rather than missile platforms. This does not mean that the chariots would charge directly into enemy formations as horses will not willingly contact any large object. The fear of the approaching chariots might, however, cause an enemy body to break up, allowing avenues for the chariots to drive through further disrupting, or breaking, the enemy formation. The Carthaginians had earlier brought chariots to Sicily but the coming engagement is the first description of their use in battle.

Timoleon was still at war with Hicetas when he learned of the Carthaginian expedition. The two now came to terms and Hicetas agreed to loan Timoleon a significant number of troops, perhaps as many as 4,000. Why Hicetas made this agreement and what concessions, if any, Timoleon made are not recorded. Perhaps Hicetas feared that now his alliance with the Carthaginians had collapsed their massive force was a greater threat than Timoleon. Plutarch records that Timoleon commanded 4,000 mercenaries, only 3,000 citizen hoplites as most were too scared to obey the call-up and 1,000 cavalry. Diodorus gives a larger figure for the army of 12,000 men.

Perhaps Plutarch's numbers do not include the troops supplied by Hicetas. Even with 12,000 men Timoleon was heavily outnumbered, but such odds had never daunted him previously.

In the summer of 339 Timoleon marched west, determined to wage the campaign on Carthaginian territory 'so as to keep intact the land of his allies while wasting that which was subject to the barbarians.' As he approached the enemy army a revolt broke out among his mercenaries. The rebellion was led by Thrasius, one of those disgraced by serving Phocia and plundering Delphi, but unlike many he had 'eluded divine vengeance.' Comparing the size of the opposing armies, he claimed quite plausibly that 'Timoleon was out of his mind and was leading his men to certain destruction'.[6] He pointed out that once again the mercenaries had not been paid but were foolishly gambling on Timoleon being able to pay them with booty. Thrasius urged them to abandon the campaign, return to Syracuse and demand their money. Timoleon was able to partially quell the mutiny by promising the mercenaries a greater share of the booty. Nonetheless 1,000 deserted with Thrasius.

All the sources agree that the subsequent battle was fought in hilly terrain at the River Crimisus. Unfortunately it is impossible to identify this river with certainty. The Greeks were marching through the territory of Akragas when the mutiny of Thrasius had broken out. This is the best route by which to seek out the Carthaginians who had landed at Lilybaeum and were marching east, probably towards their stronghold of Entella. The most likely site for the battle is therefore along the northern section of the Belice River, somewhere near Entella, modern Rocca d'Entella.[7]

Plutarch records that Timoleon had been on the march for eight days when the mutiny occurred. If this is true then the pace of the march had been in excess of 30km a day; not impossible but a punishing pace to keep up during a Sicilian summer. The date of the battle is given as being early in June. Marching rapidly to surprise the enemy does appear, however, to have been a popular strategy of Timoleon and once again he managed to catch his opponent unawares. The Greeks were able to make their camp in a strong position along the foothills overlooking the river. The Carthaginians were encamped on the other side of the river.

From this position Timoleon was able to observe the Carthaginian army drawn up, 'in a bleak position, directly exposed to the wind and the enemy.' Hoping to take advantage of their situation Timoleon called a council of his officers and claimed that now was the moment of victory: 'For there exists an oracle, which foretells defeat for an army, which occupies the exact position which the Carthaginians have taken. And the time is now at hand, when the oracle will be fulfilled.'[8] This claim would have encouraged the superstitious Greeks. Timoleon further inspired them by recalling the victory of Gelon at Himera and claiming that the Carthaginians were always cowards.

Superstition can, nevertheless, be a double-edged sword. Just as Timoleon had roused his troops' spirits with talk of favourable oracles, a chance incident occurred that threatened to demoralize them. As the army marched out for battle they happened upon a mule loaded with parsley. The Sicilian portion of his army was terrified by the omen: 'for it was customary with them, to cover tombs with parsley.' Timoleon was a master at handling his men. He quickly re-interpreted the omen favourably, and declared that: 'The gods have granted us the victory; for the Corinthians give a crown of parsley as a reward for victory in the Isthmian games.' After saying this, he put a sprig of parsley upon his head as a token of victory and the rest of the army did the same. The army was further encouraged when the seers observed two eagles, one of which carried a snake in its talons, and declared that this too was an omen of victory. The Greeks then 'advanced to battle, in full confidence of victory.'[9]

Timoleon's early arrival at the site had probably allowed him to reconnoitre the location, to discover that although it was summer, the river was flowing strongly and would hamper any Carthaginian attempt to cross and engage. It was now midday, so Timoleon halted his troops and allowed them to lay down their shields and rest before the coming fight. The heat of the day had caused mist to rise above the river and shield the Greeks' movements, but as the sun burnt off the haze the Greeks appeared to the Carthaginians. Timoleon had formed his forces up on a hill directly opposite the Carthaginian camp. He probably hoped that the sight of such a small force would encourage the enemy to attack across the river and he would then be able to defeat them in detail as their column was broken up by the current.

The Carthaginian commanders ordered their army forward, hoping to overwhelm their outnumbered enemy. They advanced with the chariots and 10,000 infantry in the vanguard. These troops the Greeks 'conjectured to be Carthaginians, from the splendour of their armour and the slowness and good order of their march.' The rest of the army was not so well disciplined, as 'the other nations streamed on and were making the crossing in tumultuous confusion.'[10] Diodorus and Plutarch both number the Carthaginian army as being 70,000 strong whereas Polyaenus states that it numbered 50,000. In such cases it is always tempting to accept the lowest of the ancient historians' figures. Either way the Carthaginians heavily outnumbered the 11,000 Greeks.

Timoleon did not, however, plan to fight the entire Carthaginian host. He had skilfully chosen his position to make use of the terrain in order to engage the Carthaginian army a section at a time. As soon as the Carthaginian vanguard had crossed the river he ordered the attack. The cavalry were ordered to charge first 'and fall upon the Carthaginians and throw their ranks into confusion before their array was yet formed.'[11] He had formed up the infantry with the Syracusans in the centre and the allies on the wings, with each contingent bolstered by a detachment of mercenaries. Timoleon took command of the centre, which consisted of the Syracusans and the best of the mercenaries.

At first the Greek infantry was not able to engage the enemy due to the confused combat of the horsemen in front of them. The Greek cavalry had not been able to come to grips with the Carthaginian foot due to the covering screen of the chariots. Timoleon cannot have expected the cavalry to defeat the strong force of chariots that the Carthaginians had brought to Sicily. It is more likely the attack was a hit-and-run raid designed to delay the Carthaginian deployment and draw off the enemy chariots. The cavalry were soon ordered to break off and reform on the flanks of the infantry. From the descriptions of the later fighting, they were probably successful in their attempt to have the Carthaginian chariots pursue them. Our sources are, however, only interested in the coming trial of strength between the Greek hoplites, led by Timoleon, and the Carthaginian infantry, other aspects of the battle are ignored.

Timoleon then 'took up his shield and shouted to his infantrymen to follow and be of good courage' and they responded by 'begging him to lead them on without delay.' The Greek infantry then charged into the Carthaginian vanguard. Although the fight was at equal numbers, as the stream had delayed the crossing of the rest of the Carthaginian army, all the advantages were with the Greeks. Their phalanx was properly formed, with 'their shields in close array,'[12] and they were charging into a disorganized enemy.

For a time the Carthaginian foot resisted stoutly 'owing to the iron breastplates and bronze helmets with which their persons were protected, and the great shields which they held in front of them, repelled the spear thrusts.'[13] Most of the Greek hoplites would have been more lightly armoured, some wearing linen corselets and some with no protection at all other than their shields. From this moment on the accounts of Diodorus and Plutarch differ in their timing of events, particularly over the moment that a thunderstorm struck the battlefield. This account will follow the chronology of Diodorus.

Despite their disadvantage in armour, the Greek phalanx quickly prevailed. Diodorus describes how the Carthaginian vanguard was: 'shattered at the first outset ... there was a sharp fight, but as the Greeks were superior both in bravery and in skill, there was great slaughter of the barbarians;' Plutarch adds the detail that the entire Carthaginian 'first rank of four hundred men' fell. The rapid attack of the Greeks had forced the Carthaginians to fight on a very narrow front, at the unusual depth of twenty-five ranks.[14] Clearly Timoleon's tactics had worked and he had managed to strike the enemy before they could properly form up and bring their weight of numbers to bear. The Carthaginian vanguard had been shattered and was fleeing from the fight.

There is one problem with the description of the battle up to this point. The Greek infantry line, if drawn up in its usual eight man depth would have been three times longer that of the Carthaginians. Even if formed deeper, it still would have been longer than the 400 man frontage of the enemy. The most likely explanation is that the Greek flanks were fully engaged with the surviving Carthaginian chariots. It also is possible that they attacked the flanks of the Carthaginians infantry, ensuring the initial Greek success. If the latter is true, it may have been deliberately omitted by the historians who were more interested in describing the superiority of the Greek fighting man over his Phoenician opponent.

It had been a good beginning but the battle was not yet over as 'the main body of the Carthaginians crossed the river in the meantime and restored the situation.'[15] The Carthaginian numbers began to tell against the tiring Greeks, when once again the Gods appear to have come to the aid of their chosen instrument:

> Suddenly, from the heavens sheets of rain broke and a storm of great hailstones, while lightning flashed and thunder roared and the wind blew in fierce gusts. All of this tempest buffeted the backs of the Greeks but struck the faces of the barbarians, so that, though Timoleon's soldiers were not much inconvenienced by the affair, the Phoenicians could not stand the force of circumstances, and as the Greeks continued to attack them, they broke into flight.[16]

The last of the Carthaginians to resist were 'the Sacred Battalion, 2,500 in number and drawn from the ranks of those citizens who were distinguished for valour and reputation as well as for wealth, were all cut down after a gallant struggle.'[17]

With their demise the entire Carthaginian army broke and fled towards the river with

> horse and foot intermingled, while the chariots added to the confusion – some perished helplessly trodden under foot or pierced by the swords or lances of their comrades, while others were herded by Timoleon's cavalry into the bed of the river and were struck down from behind. Many died without an enemy's stroke as the bodies piled up in the panic. There was crowding and it was difficult to keep one's feet in the stream. Worst of all, as the rain came down heavily, the river swept downstream as a raging torrent and carried the men with it, drowning them as they struggled to swim in their heavy armour.[18]

As usual in battles between the two hated enemies, the Greeks pursued ruthlessly. Many of the Carthaginians were cut to pieces alongside the river. Some managed to escape to the surrounding hills but were caught by the

Greek light-infantry. Carthaginian casualties are recorded as 10,000 dead – among which were 3,000 Carthaginian citizens – and 15,000 captured. As they had after their victory over the Athenians seven decades earlier, the victorious troops stole away many of the captives for their own profit. Only 5,000 were handed in to the authorities to be sold as slaves by the state. The survivors of the Carthaginian army fled back to their stronghold of Lilybaeum.

The Greeks captured huge amounts of booty in the Carthaginian baggage train which

> yielded a great store of wealth also, because the Carthaginians had with them an abundance of silver and gold drinking vessels; these, as well as the rest of the personal property which was very numerous because of the wealth of the Carthaginians, Timoleon allowed the soldiers to keep as rewards for their gallantry.[19]

Much of the booty given to the soldiers was no doubt in order to pay off the promised gifts to those mercenaries who had remained loyal. So much plunder was won that it is recorded that the customary victory trophy was not set up until three days after the battle, as the Greeks were too busy stripping the bodies of the dead.

In addition to the other plunder the Greeks gathered 200 chariots, 1,000 breastplates and 10,000 shields. Timoleon sent the most impressive of these trophies home to Corinth to be dedicated in the Temple of Poseidon. The rest were divided up among the Sicilians and dedicated in their temples.

Although the praise heaped upon Timoleon by the ancient writers is often excessive, on this occasion it appears to be wholly justified. The Battle of Crimisus was a remarkable victory by any standards and Timoleon's leadership was exceptional. His rapid march into Carthaginian territory had forced the Carthaginians to confront him or allow their territory to be ravaged. He had then skilfully selected a site for the battle that would negate the Carthaginian advantage in numbers.

Despite his preparations, even the greatest of commanders needs a slice of luck and Timoleon received his in the form of the storm. Both of our sources claim that the hail blowing into the face of the Carthaginians was decisive to outcome of the battle. Given Timoleon's otherwise careful preparations it is tempting to speculate on whether it was completely a matter of good fortune. The Greeks would have had local knowledge of the weather patterns and may have predicted the possibility of a storm. They might also have known the likely direction of the gale. Polyaenus emphasizes the importance of Timoleon's observation that prior to the battle the Carthaginians were directly exposed to the wind. The timing of the storm could not have been predicted exactly, and it certainly arrived at a fortuitous moment for the Greeks, but, as with so many other factors,

Timoleon appears to have done everything possible to ensure that if it arrived it would favour the Greeks.

Timoleon's victory was so complete that the Carthaginian survivors were reportedly too terrified to embark on their ships and return to Africa for fear 'that they would be swallowed up by the Libyan Sea because their gods had forsaken them.'[20] A more rational concern might have been that they would now be expected to defend the Epicraty from a likely Greek invasion. Their commanders might also have been scared that if they returned they would receive the usual Carthaginian punishment for defeat, crucifixion.

News of the result of the battle caused the same demoralization in Carthage that the defeat at Himera had a century and a half earlier. The Carthaginians feared that the Greeks would follow up their victory with an immediate invasion of Africa. They dispatched an embassy to Sicily with instructions to make peace on whatever terms possible.[21] Such a response was largely the result of panic; Timoleon had neither the resources nor the will to invade Africa. He followed up his victory by leaving his mercenaries to plunder Carthaginian territory while he returned to Syracuse to begin his political reforms and deal with the remaining tyrants.

The battle of Crimisus River was one of the most devastating victories that the Greeks of Sicily ever won over the Carthaginians. Perhaps it was equalled only by those of Gelon in 480 and Dionysius' destruction of Motya in 397. Dionysius' victory had largely been an empty one as the Carthaginians were able to mobilize their immense wealth and quickly recover. Gelon's victory had, by contrast, won seventy years of respite from Carthaginian attack for the Greeks. The results of Timoleon's victory were somewhere in between. The Carthaginians would recover their courage and send a new force to Sicily, soon losing heart and agreeing to a new peace treaty with the Greeks. This treaty would ensure a period of about fifteen years' respite from foreign attacks. As with Gelon's victory, it would allow a long period of uninterrupted economic growth.

Chapter 9

Timoleon's Settlement of Syracuse

In this manner, then, did Timoleon extirpate the tyrannies and put a stop to their wars.

Plutarch, *Timoleon* 35

Timoleon's first item of business after returning to Syracuse was to deal with the 1,000 mercenaries who had deserted with Thrasius. They were paid off and ordered to immediately depart Sicily. Next he welcomed a new group of 5,000 settlers sent from Corinth. The dismissed mercenaries crossed over to Italy and sacked one of the towns of the Bruttians. The Bruttians responded by raising an army and annihilating them. Their violent end was a source of great satisfaction for the ancient writers, who observed that: 'those who had abandoned Timoleon were rewarded by such misfortune for their own wickedness.'[1]

In Carthage, the repercussions of the defeat at Crimisus River were still having an influence on policy. The loss of so many citizens, especially those who made up the Sacred Battalion, also called for a change in strategy. 'For no others were superior to these in birth or wealth or reputation, nor is it recorded that so many native Carthaginians ever perished in a single battle before.'[2] The Carthaginians voted to never again risk the lives of so many citizens in future overseas campaigns but instead 'to enlist foreign mercenaries, especially Greeks who, they thought, would answer the call in large numbers because of the high rate of pay and the wealth of Carthage.'[3] The Carthaginians were keen to recruit Greeks after their defeat 'because they had come to admire them as the best and most irresistible fighters in the world.'[4]

The initial panic seems to have abated fairly quickly. The Carthaginians responded to a new approach from Hicetas and Mamercus, who

> through envy of the successes won by Timoleon, or because they feared him as one who distrusted tyrants and would make no peace with them, formed an alliance with the Carthaginians and urged them

to send a general with an army if they did not wish to be cast out of Sicily altogether.[5]

Once more the Carthaginians opened their coffers and sent a fleet of seventy ships and a force of Greek mercenaries to Sicily under the command of Gisco.

These are the facts as recorded by Plutarch but again they clash with those chronicled by Diodorus. Diodorus records that an embassy had already been sent to Syracuse with orders to make peace on any terms and the treaty was concluded before the campaigns against the remaining tyrants. It is possible, however, that following the approaches of Hicetus and Mamercus the Carthaginians may have repented their initial hasty reaction and decided to recall their embassy, or back it up with a show of force. It is also possible that they, in keeping with their reputation for treachery, simply broke their word. It is, however, unlikely that such a betrayal would have occurred without it being condemned by the Greek historians. Diodorus does at times confuse his chronology by overly abridging his narrative, as may be the case here. On this occasion the more detailed account of Plutarch will be followed, since although he does at times distort his chronology, he is not generally accused of manufacturing evidence.

Timoleon's first target was his old enemy Hicetas. If we accept Plutarch's account, the justification for breaking his treaty with Hicetas would have been the new alliance with Carthage. Hostilities most likely broke out in early 338. The allies united their forces in the territory of Messene, and ambushed a force of Timoleon's mercenaries, killing 400 of them. Mamercus, who fancied himself a poet, celebrated this victory by dedicating the mercenaries' richly decorated shields to a temple and taunting Timoleon in verse: 'These bucklers, purple-painted, decked with ivory, gold, and amber, We captured with our simple little shields.'[6]

The allies won another victory near Panormus (Palermo), wiping out those mercenaries who had been left to ravage Carthaginian territory after Crimisus. Plutarch manages to turn this defeat into a positive for Timoleon, as the mercenaries included some of those who were cursed for their sack of Delphi and had therefore received justice. 'So, then, the good will of the gods towards Timoleon was no less to be admired in his reverses than in his successes.'[7] From the locations of the two battles the campaign was either wide ranging or, more likely, the Carthaginians of Mago had not yet joined forces with their Greek allies. It is possible that Carthaginians were reluctant to rejoin Hicetas as they still hoped to negotiation a peace treaty with Syracuse.

Next Hicetas successfully raided Syracusan territory while Timoleon was campaigning elsewhere. Timoleon pursued Hicetas with a mobile force of cavalry and light-infantry and managed to catch the enemy who were laden with plunder. Hicetas turned to face his pursuers at the Damurias River, confident the steep banks of the river would protect him from his pursuer. In the usual manner of competition between Greek aristocrats, the Syracusan cavalry commanders bickered with one another as to who should have the honour of leading the attack. Timoleon decided to choose one by lot. The victor's men, determined to prove themselves worthy of their position, 'dashed through the river as fast as they could and closed with the enemy. These could not withstand the violence of their onset, but fled, all alike losing their arms, and a thousand being left dead on the field.'[8] Timoleon followed up his victory by invading the territory of Leontini.

Here Hicetas and his family were captured alive, handed over by the tyrant's own troops. The easy defeat of Hicetas' troops and their subsequent handing over of their commander would indicate the morale of his troops was poor. Perhaps their pay was in arrears, which may explain Hicetas' raid into Syracusan territory. Losing their arms and booty on the retreat would not have improved their temper.

Timoleon now abandoned his previous policy of shipping defeated tyrants off to Corinth. He believed that the propaganda advantage of sending them to Greece was no longer necessary. Instead it was more important to demonstrate to the Sicilians that tyrants would be punished by death. Hicetas and his son were summarily executed as tyrants and traitors, his wife and daughters were sent to Syracuse as prisoners where they were put on trial, condemned and executed. For once Plutarch is critical of Timoleon, claiming that he could have prevented the executions but 'he neglected them and abandoned them to the wrath of the citizens.' The Syracusans were determined to punish the entire family of Hicetas as revenge for his murder of Dion's family.[9]

The next tyrant to feel the wrath of Timoleon was Mamercus of Catane. Timoleon defeated him in a pitched battle, killing 2,000 of his soldiers, some of whom were Greek mercenaries supplied by Gisco. With their two major allies now defeated by the Syracusans, the Carthaginians sent an embassy to make peace. The terms are recorded as: 'all the Greek cities should be free, that the river Lycus [Halycus] should be the boundary of their respective territories, and that the Carthaginians might not give aid to the tyrants who were at war with Syracuse.'[10] Despite the peace, Carthaginian power on the island had not been broken. They kept possession of the western end of the island and their undefeated navy ensured they controlled the seas. These assets, along with their wealth, would give them the opportunity to take the offensive at a later time. This is looking forward, however, and at that time the peace must have seemed an enormous blessing to the Greeks.

Mamercus, deserted by his allies, escaped by sea intending to land in Italy and recruit new forces from among the Lucanians. He was, however, betrayed by his comrades who surrendered Catane to the Syracusans. Plutarch has a different version of events, claiming that Mamercus sought refuge with Hippo, the tyrant of Messene. When Timoleon marched on the city, both tyrants tried to flee but were captured by the people of Messene. Hippo was publicly executed and the Messenians 'brought their children thither from their schools to behold, as a glorious spectacle, the tyrant's punishment, and put him to torment and death.'[11]

Mamercus surrendered himself to Timoleon on the condition that he was tried in Syracuse. Perhaps he hoped that the Syracusans would remember his earlier aid to Timoleon in the overthrow of Dionysius and be merciful. If so, he was to be fatally disappointed. He endeavoured to give a defence speech in the Syracusan assembly but was shouted down. Seeing that all was lost he attempted to commit suicide by running head first into the wall of the theatre but failed. The Syracusans dragged him away and crucified him like a common criminal. So, at least, is the tale told by Plutarch.

Polyaenus records a version of Mamercus' surrender that is less flattering to Timoleon's reputation. In this Mamercus only surrendered on one condition:

> Timoleon would promise not to stand forward as his prosecutor. This condition was complied with, and Timoleon conducted Mamercus to Syracuse. As soon as he had introduced him into the assembly, he said: 'I will not prosecute this man, for I have promised him not to. But I order him to be executed immediately. For there is no law more just, than that he, who has deceived many to their death, should for once be overcome by trickery.'[12]

In situations like this is difficult not to prefer those authors who are less obsequious to Timoleon than Plutarch. Plutarch's account has another difficulty, the appearance of the tyrant Hippo. Messene had been liberated by Timoleon four years earlier, shortly after his overthrow of Dionysius. No other source mentions Messene or Hippo in their – admittedly brief – accounts of Mamercus' capture. It is possible that the details of Hippo's death belong to the earlier capture of Messene but have been included here by Plutarch for dramatic effect.

Timoleon followed up his victory by mopping up the remaining tyrannies and expelling the Campanian mercenaries from Aetna. This campaign was the first fought by a young Agathocles, the next tyrant of Syracuse, who distinguished himself and thereby 'gave the Syracusans great proofs of what he could do.'[13] Diodorus concludes his account by stating that: 'all of the tyrants throughout the island were uprooted and the cities were set free and taken into his alliance.' The last phrase would imply that Timoleon was rebuilding the alliance of Sicilian cities with Syracuse as the hegemonic leader. Many cities would have willingly joined such an alliance, out of gratitude for their freedom or from their fear of the Carthaginians, whilst others were probably given no choice. That Timoleon was securing the leading position of his adopted city is borne out by another of his actions: 'Timoleon transferred the people of Leontini to Syracuse.'[14] Leontini had long been a thorn in Syracuse's side and earlier Syracusan governments of all persuasions had been determined to annex the city and its rich farmlands.

With the tyrannies removed and the Carthaginian threat neutralized for the moment, Timoleon was able to concentrate on political reform and the recovery of the prosperity of the Greek cities. Further offers of free land were made to the Greeks and ultimately 40,000 would choose to settle in Syracuse and at least 20,000 in other cities. One of the cities to most benefit from the arrival of the new settlers was Diodorus' home of Agyrium.

Along with the migration to Sicily, the period of peace that followed Timoleon's victories allowed the Greek cities to recover economically in a manner similar to the overthrow of the tyrannies a century earlier:

> For many years, because of domestic troubles and border wars, and still more because of the numbers of tyrants who kept constantly appearing, the cities had become destitute of inhabitants and the open country had become a wilderness for lack of cultivation, producing no useful crops. But now new settlers streamed into the land in great numbers, and as a long period of peace set in, the fields were reclaimed for cultivation and bore abundant crops of all sorts. These the Siceliot Greeks sold to merchants at good prices and rapidly increased their wealth.[15]

Both Diodorus and Plutarch tell us that the increase in population and prosperity enabled a new period of public construction throughout the Greek cities. For once their praise is perhaps understated. The archaeological evidence for this period confirms that the recovery from the previous desolation to prosperity was rapid, significant and long lasting.[16]

Peace also meant that Timoleon now had time to concentrate on his reform of the Syracusan constitution. What form of government immediately replaced the tyranny cannot be determined exactly, but was most likely similar to that after the first overthrow of Dionysius: a type of democracy with the assembly having legislative authority but with the *strategos autocrator*, Timoleon, having extraordinary powers over and beyond the *demos*. During the years of military emergency this duality of power could be tolerated but now that peace had arrived it needed to be resolved. The two solutions were for Timoleon to continue to hold power and become tyrant or to hand political power back to the people. Much to his credit, and the gratitude of the Syracusans, Timoleon eventually abdicated his position.

As with Dion, however, Timoleon had called in constitutional advisors from oligarchic Corinth. This measure had been greatly resented by the democrats when Dion had done so and it must have caused disquiet among the democratic faction once again. Although both Diodorus and Plutarch claim that Timoleon introduced a democracy into Syracuse, the term democracy could take many different forms in the ancient Greek world. At its barest minimum it meant that the city had an assembly that had some legislative authority. In its most extreme form the assembly consisted of all adult male citizens and had total control over initiating and passing laws, as well as control of the law courts. In its more conservative forms, the authority of the assembly could be curtailed by the power of elected officials, with the ability to initiate laws limited to a more exclusive ruling council and a property qualification for admission to these posts. The exact nature of Timoleon's settlement is not described in detail and is much debated by later historians.

Diodorus account is short, merely relating that:

At this time, also, Timoleon revised the existing laws of Syracuse, which Diocles had composed. Those concerning private contracts and inheritance he allowed to remain unaltered, but he amended those concerned with public affairs in whatever way seemed advantageous to his own concept. Chairman and director of this legislative program was Cephalus the Corinthian, a man distinguished for education and intelligence.[17]

This brief account implies that Timoleon imposed his political vision on the Syracusans. Diodorus had earlier named Diocles as the legislator that had introduced the radical democratic reforms in Syracuse after their defeat of the Athenians in 413. If Diodorus is correct then Diocles' constitution was amended by Timoleon.

Plutarch has Timoleon playing a less authoritarian role in the reforms. He states that the Syracusans, in their gratitude, were not content unless their decisions were approved by Timoleon as 'no arrangement of civil polity seemed satisfactory, unless he gave the finishing touches to it.'[18] Plutarch does admit, however, that Timoleon soon fell out with some of the democratic leaders as 'even Timoleon was attacked by two of the popular leaders at Syracuse,' although he calls each 'a false accuser.'[19]

The only office that is recorded as existing under the new constitution was that of the chief magistrate, the Amphipolia of Olympian Zeus. This position was annual, limited to a few noble families and elected by lot. It is not certain whether this was a new position or the elevation of an old office. It is sometimes argued that Timoleon gave executive powers to this magistrate that overrode the power of the assembly. It is not certain, however, whether the Amphipolia had any real political powers or was merely a figurehead. The continued existence of the office after the Roman conquest would imply that it had no real power. Although we cannot be definite about what type of government Timoleon set up in Syracuse, circumstantial evidence would indicate that the earlier radical democracy of Diocles was replaced by a more limited form.

Although Timoleon's measures did significantly increase the prosperity of the Sicilians, later events would indicate that the vast difference in wealth between the different sections of society remained. The nature of the constitutional changes introduced by Timoleon did nothing to permanently solve the enduring problem of political struggle within the city between the rich and the poor. This *stasis* would be the major cause of the collapse of Timoleon's settlement and a return to the rule of the tyrants. Solving such problems was, perhaps, a task beyond the talents of any one man.

What is certain is that after Timoleon had completed his reforms, unlike so many before him, he did not seize the tyranny but resigned his office and retired to the countryside. As a reward for his services the Syracusans gave him a lavish country estate. In recognition of his leadership they also voted that in any future foreign wars they would always call on Corinth to provide them with a commander-in-chief. After his retirement Timoleon did not return to Corinth but brought his wife and family to his adopted city and lived out the rest of his life in comfort and respect. In his house he built an altar to the goddess Fortune who he claimed was responsible for all his victories, which were all supposedly won on his birthday. During his retirement he lost his eye-sight but remained active in the politics of the city, travelling to the assembly in a mule-cart supplied at public expense.

In 336 Timoleon died, eight years after he had arrived in Sicily, and his ashes were buried in the *agora* of the city. Later the Syracusans built a gymnasium near the site, naming it the Timoleonteum, and voted that his life be celebrated with annual games.

At the beginning of the narrative of Timoleon's campaigns it was noted that it was necessary to view the accounts of his life with some scepticism due to the overwhelmingly positive accounts in the main sources who all wrote long after his death. Oddly enough his achievements were largely ignored by his near contemporaries other than the historian Timaeus. His fame was largely eclipsed by events in Greece, with the rise of Macedon and the careers of Philip and Alexander the Great. Polybius is quite scathing in his assessment, claiming that his deeds were done on a tiny scale, unlike the later achievements of Alexander and the Romans:

> Timoleon who not only never seems to have achieved anything great, but never even to have attempted to do so, and in his whole life accomplished but one move and that by no means important considering the greatness of the world, the move from his country to Syracuse. The fact, in my opinion, is that Timaeus was sure that if Timoleon, who had sought fame in a mere tea-cup, as it were, Sicily, could be shown to be worthy of comparison with the most illustrious heroes.[20]

Despite this harsh assessment it cannot be denied that his career in Sicily was a remarkable success. He had landed with a small force of 700 mercenaries and yet had managed to overthrow the tyrannies of eastern Sicily, including that of Syracuse, formerly the most powerful city in the Greek world. His victory at Crimisus had led to a lasting peace with Carthage. These victories had restored peace to the island and this, plus the influx of immigrants, had led to a major economic revival. It is perhaps best to conclude with the opinion of the Syracusans themselves. After his death the assembly passed a decree to be read by a herald at his funeral:

By the people of Syracuse, Timoleon, son of Timodemus, from Corinth, is here buried at a public cost of two hundred minas, and is honoured for all time with annual contests, musical, equestrian, and gymnastic, because he overthrew the tyrants, subdued the Barbarians, re-peopled the largest of the devastated cities, and then restored their laws to the Greeks of Sicily.[21]

Chapter 10

The Rise of Agathocles

More than anywhere else this tendency toward the rule of one man prevailed in Sicily before the Romans became rulers of that island; for the cities, deceived by demagogic wiles, went so far in making the weak strong that these became despots over those whom they had deceived. The most extraordinary instance of all is that of Agathocles who became tyrant of the Syracusans.

Diodorus 19.5

As far as the history of Syracuse is concerned, the twenty year period that followed Timoleon's death is largely unrecorded. Our main source, Diodorus, appeared to lose interest in events on his native island in order to concentrate on the exploits of Alexander the Great. The entire interlude is later summarized in a short account which concentrates on introducing the next dominant character in Syracusan history, Agathocles.

There are three main surviving sources for Agathocles' career: Diodorus, Justin and Polyaenus. Of these Diodorus' account is the most detailed and important. From Diodorus' own testimony we know that he used four earlier sources that were written by Agathocles' contemporaries. Three were Sicilians, Antander, Callias and Timaeus, and the fourth was Duris of Samos. Of these, three were considered to be biased in favour of Agathocles. Antander was Agathocles' brother. Callias was accused by Diodorus of being a paid pen of the tyrant, for: 'ever since he was taken up by Agathocles and for a great price in gifts sold into bondage Madam History, the mouthpiece of truth, he has never ceased singing dishonest praises of his paymaster.'[1] It is generally assumed that Duris' account was favourable to Agathocles as he too was a tyrant. Duris' histories were often attacked by other ancient writers for being superficial. Plutarch in particular disliked him, claiming that: 'it is not the wont of Duris, even in cases where he has no private and personal interest, to hold his narrative down to the fundamental truth.'[2]

The fourth of these sources, Timaeus, is quite different from the other three in that he was notorious in antiquity not only for his open admiration of Timoleon but also his violent hatred of Agathocles. Polybius describes how: 'Timaeus, blinded by his own malice, has chronicled with hostility and exaggeration the defects of Agathocles and has entirely omitted to mention his shining qualities, being unaware that it is just as mendacious for a writer to conceal what did occur as to report what did not occur.'[3]

Diodorus echoes Polybius' criticisms. He notes that because Timaeus was banished by Agathocles from Sicily he was determined to blacken his name, claiming that:

> The greater part of his history of Agathocles consists of lying propaganda against the ruler because of personal enmity. For since he was banished from Sicily by Agathocles and could not strike back while the monarch lived, after his death he defamed him in his history for all time. For, in general, to the bad qualities that this king did in fact possess the historian adds others of his own invention. He strips him of his successes, leaving him his failures – not only those for which the king was himself responsible, but even those due to ill luck, which he transfers to the score of one who was not at all at fault.[4]

Despite holding these reservations, it is generally believed that Diodorus used Timaeus as the major source for his account of Agathocles' rule. Justin's history of Agathocles' career is consistently hostile but the sources are unknown.

As with the careers of many famous men in the ancient world, tales of Agathocles' childhood are replete with numerous stories of omens which need not be believed. His father, Carcinus, was an exile from the Italian city of Rhegium and settled in Thermae, also known as Himera, in northern Sicily. The city had been founded by the Carthaginians in 407 after their destruction of the original Himera, 10km to the east. Most of its inhabitants were Greek survivors of that city, forced to abandon their ancestral home by the Carthaginians. Thermae lay on the border of Carthaginian and Greek territory and as a result had changed alliances many times depending on which power was dominant. At the time of Agathocles' birth it was under Carthaginian control.

Carcinus, who already had at least one son and may therefore have been a widower, formed a union with a native woman. Some writers assume she was a Carthaginian but she might just as likely have been descended from one of the indigenous peoples of Sicily. From this relationship another son, Agathocles, was born in 361. Prior to the birth Carcinus suffered from bad dreams and instructed a delegation of Carthaginians heading to the oracle at Delphi to ask the Gods about his son. The reply came back that the child would be a cause of great misfortune to the Carthaginians and all of Sicily. Carcinus decided to kill his son by exposing him to the elements and posting guards to ensure that no-one took the child away. This was a common form of both infanticide and adoption in Greek cities. Parents left unwanted children out in a public area and anyone who wished to adopt could come and take them away. Those not chosen simply died or were eaten by scavenging animals.

The guards grew lax and the mother came secretly at night and took her child away, leaving him in the care of her brother. The boy grew up strong for his age and handsome and was later admired by his father while performing at a festival when seven-years-old. The mother confessed to her act and Carcinus reclaimed his son. Supposedly the family was poor and Carcinus taught him the trade of a potter. Later, fearing that Carthaginians might remember the oracle, he moved his household to Syracuse, taking advantage of Timoleon's offers of citizenship. The family probably moved to Syracuse in 343 when Agathocles was in his eighteenth year.

Carcinus died soon after the family arrived in Syracuse. Agathocles' mother then set up a carved stone image of her son upon an altar. This effigy was settled on by a swarm of bees and the omen interpreted that the boy would obtain great fame. Agathocles was renowned for his beauty and as a youth soon caught the attention of one of the leading nobles of the city, Damas, who fell in love with him. Although homosexual relationships between adult men were open to ridicule, a relationship between an older man and a youth was considered normal, at least among the upper classes. The older partner was expected to be responsible in assisting the education of the younger and to help in his career development. When the youth entered adulthood the relationship would cease to be sexual but the two would remain friends. This of course is the idealized view and such relationships would vary greatly in their nature.

Damas certainly played his anticipated role in the relationship. He assisted Agathocles by supplying him with lavish gifts and assisting in his promotion in the army. After Damas died, Agathocles married his widow and thereby became one of the richest men in Syracuse. Agathocles' relationship with Damas, and his marriage, have been twisted by his disparagers in order to assassinate his character. Justin accuses him of being a prostitute: 'for, being remarkable for beauty and gracefulness of person, he supported himself a considerable time by submitting to the infamous lust of others. When he had passed the years of puberty, he transferred his services from men to women.'[5] This is pure slander coming from the pen of Timaeus and was seen as such by other writers.[6] Although Agathocles was the beneficiary of particularly good fortune in his choice of lover, none of this would have been seen as unusual by the citizens of ancient Syracuse.

The stories of the poverty of Agathocles' upbringing should also be discounted. It is clear that his family mixed in the highest circles whilst in both Thermae and Syracuse. Agathocles was the favourite of one of the noblest men in the city and his brother was later elected to the important post of general. All this demonstrates that the family was rich and well respected. If Agathocles was a potter as claimed, then it would have been as the owner of a pottery factory where slaves and labourers did the physical work. The myth may have been a part of the Hellenistic tradition of creating humble backgrounds for famous men, thereby exaggerating their achievement of making it to the top. An alternative interpretation would be that his enemies wished to discredit him by falsely claiming a low born family. As this story again comes from Timaeus the latter motive is the more likely.

Despite these problems, an outline of Agathocles' early life can be sketched. His father was an exile from Rhegium and later took advantage of Timoleon's offer to take up Syracusan citizenship. The family moved within with the circle of the aristocratic governing class of the city, Agathocles formed a relationship with one of the leading nobles, Damas, and married his widow. All this ensured that he became a wealthy and prominent member of the Syracusan elite.

There was, however, another important reason for Agathocles' high-standing: he had already earned an impressive military record and reputation for bravery and great physical strength. 'Even before his military service Agathocles had been much respected on account of the great size of his armour, for in military reviews he was in the habit of wearing equipment so heavy that no one of the others was able to use it handily because of the weight of the armour.'[7] These were important assets in the highly competitive world of the Greek elite whose ideal was to emulate the behaviour of the heroes of Homer's *Iliad*. Even Justin acknowledges his courage:

> Enlisting in the army as a common soldier, he showed himself ready for every kind of audacity, his life being then not less distinguished by restlessness than it had previously been by infamy. He was noted for activity in the field, and for eloquence in making harangues. In a short time, accordingly, he became a centurion, and soon after a tribune. In his first campaign against the people of Aetna, he gave the Syracusans great proofs of what he could do: in the next, against the Campanians, he excited such hopes of himself throughout the army, that he was chosen to fill the place of the deceased general.[8]

Although Justin's version is slightly garbled it does emphasize the importance of Agathocles' military reputation. The actions against Aetna and the Campanians were a part of Timoleon's last campaign. Agathocles would have been in his early twenties, the usual age at which Greek youth were expected to begin serving in expeditions outside of their own city's territory. Depending on the extent of the wealth of his family he would have served either as a hoplite among the heavy infantry or in the cavalry.

Later, Agathocles took part in an expedition against Akragas which was commanded by his former lover Damas. The only mention of this war is that of Diodorus, and it is impossible to determine when or why it was fought; the period immediately after Timoleon's campaigns was renowned as one of relative peace. The results of this campaign are not recorded but, even allowing for the favouritism of his patron, Agathocles again performed well and was promoted to the rank of *chiliarch*, commander of a thousand men.

The next campaign in which Agathocles took part can be dated to about 325. He was now a married man in his mid-thirties. The expedition was sent to Italy to relieve the city of Croton, which was ruled by an oligarchy, and was under attack from the Bruttians. The Syracusan commanders were two of the leading oligarchs of Syracuse, Heracleides and Sostratus, 'men who had spent the greater part of their lives in plots, murders, and great impieties.'[9] These two were the leaders of an oligarchic clique known as the 'Six Hundred' who came from the noblest Syracusan families and were determined to overthrow the democratic aspects of Timoleon's constitution.

Agathocles held a command on this expedition and his brother took part as one of the elected generals. Agathocles is again reported as fighting with distinction but 'was deprived of the award for his deeds of valour by Sostratus and his friends because of jealousy.'[10] Deeply offended by this injustice, Agathocles became a personal enemy of Sostratus. As so often was the case in the ancient Greek world, personal enmity soon became political rivalry.

Up until his quarrel with Sostratus, Agathocles was possibly either a supporter of the Six Hundred or a member of their circle. His falling out with Sostratus appears to have led to a change of political allegiance and he decided to throw in his lot with the democrats. Whether this change in political alliance was from genuine conviction or merely from political expediency and personal hatred is impossible to determine. It is always easy to be cynical in such cases and to assume that the motive was thwarted ambition rather than ideology. In antiquity there are, however, surprising examples of such leaders who, once they had made their choice, remained steadfastly loyal to their followers and committed remarkable acts of self-sacrifice.[11]

On his return to Syracuse from Croton, Agathocles denounced Sostratus and his supporters in the assembly for plotting to overthrow the democracy. The oligarchs were, however, in the ascendant and Agathocles lost his case. With such a powerful enemy at home, Agathocles wisely determined to return to Italy. Sostratus now went on the attack. He persuaded the Syracusan assembly to banish Agathocles' associates, along with their families. These people were murdered by Sostratus' followers as they left the city. Sostratus sentenced to death *in absentia* the few who had escaped, and confiscated the property of the exiles and the dead. With this money he hired mercenaries and released criminals from the prisons, enrolling them as his own bodyguards. With a private army within the walls of the city, the Six Hundred were able to use them to overthrow the democracy. They introduced an oligarchic form of government ruled by a narrow, aristocratic council.

Agathocles, in exile in Italy, joined a failed revolt by the democrats of Croton and was forced to flee to Tarentum. There he enrolled as a mercenary but again became involved in local politics and was expelled from the city. Agathocles then joined a group of political exiles who had gathered together to aid the democratic government of Rhegium, which was under attack from an expedition led by his nemesis, Sostratus. Justin asserts that by involving himself in such actions, Agathocles was not fighting to reclaim his rights but merely 'engaged in piracy against his own country.'[12] Soon after, perhaps in 322, there was a democratic revolution in Syracuse. Sostratus and many other members of the Six Hundred were driven into exile and the moderate democracy restored. Agathocles, with his new reputation as a defender of democracy, was now able to return to Syracuse.

Agathocles came back to a city on the verge of civil war. The exiled oligarchs had allied themselves with the Carthaginians. This was the first time the Carthaginians had intervened in Greek Sicily since their treaty with Timoleon. Once again they had decided to take advantage of the factional strife within Syracuse. There is no coherent account of the war but Diodorus describes the nature of the fighting and Agathocles' role in it: 'there were constant engagements and pitched battles between strong forces, in which Agathocles, sometimes as a private soldier, sometimes appointed to a command, was credited with being energetic and ingenious, for in each emergency he contrived some helpful device.'[13] The fighting spread beyond Syracuse and drew in the surrounding cities. They too were probably split by political conflict, democrats against oligarchs and rich against poor.

In one attack on the city of Gela, Agathocles is supposed to have saved his fleeing soldiers by organizing a rearguard action in the narrow gap in the fortifications. He then ordered his trumpeters to mount the walls and sound the attack. The Geloans, believing that another assault had commenced, abandoned their pursuit. Despite being wounded seven times and weak from blood loss, Agathocles was thus able to spare the 700 survivors of his command.

After his return from Italy, Agathocles appeared to have attached himself to the most extreme faction of the radical democrats. He may even have joined such a group while in Tarentum, as Diodorus describes him as having been 'suspected of revolutionary designs.'[14] The extreme democrats of Syracuse now proposed the two most revolutionary of demands in the ancient Greek world: the redistribution of land and the cancellation of debts. Such attacks on private property were an anathema to the rich, regardless of whether they were oligarchs or democrats. The political struggle in Syracuse now appears to have been one of rich against poor rather than one of conflicting political ideologies. The extremists seem to have despaired of making reforms through the assembly and began to plot the overthrow of the democracy. They planned to set up a dictatorship in order to enforce their policies. Many of them probably believed that such a regime would be short-lived but, like many revolutionaries throughout history, they would end up creating an entrenched tyranny.

As the war involved fighting against the Carthaginians, the Syracusans had, in accordance with the law passed during the time of Timoleon, brought in a general from Corinth, Acestorides, to assume the role of supreme commander. Akin to most of his countrymen, he was probably politically inclined towards oligarchy or a very limited form of democracy. Acestorides was given information of a plot by the revolutionaries to seize power. Unwilling to move directly against Agathocles, who by then appears to have been the leader of the extreme democrats, he arrested a number of his supporters. Agathocles survived only because of the loyalty of his friends, who 'when apprehended and put to the torture, denied his guilt.'[15] Whatever his faults may have been, Agathocles certainly appears to have been a charismatic leader, capable of inspiring great devotion from his supporters.

Unable to produce direct evidence against Agathocles, Acestorides exiled him for a second time but plotted to have him murdered after he had left the city. Diodorus records a tale of Agathocles' flight designed to highlight his reputation for cunning. Agathocles dressed one of his slaves in his own clothes. The slave was duly murdered but Agathocles managed to escape dressed in rags. These events can best be dated to 319.

After the exile of Agathocles and the arrests of his supporters, democrats of all persuasions were in disarray. Acestorides took advantage of the situation by making peace with the Carthaginians and forcing a reconciliation between the moderate democrats and the exiled oligarchs. His work done, Acestorides vanishes from the record. It is probable that he returned to Corinth.

Agathocles retreated inland to the city of Morgantina and gathered together an army of his own supporters. They were joined by many of the smaller cities of the interior. Most of these cities would have been populated by Sicels, a people who occupied eastern Sicily before the arrival of the Greeks. They had a long history of being oppressed and exploited by the Syracusans. They probably joined Agathocles on the basis that my enemy's enemy is my friend. Although Diodorus does note that: 'they were unceasingly hostile to the Six Hundred, who had been magistrates of the oligarchy in Syracuse, and hated the populace in general because they were forced to carry out its orders.'[16]

Agathocles was made commander of their combined forces and launched a war against his own city. The rebels captured Leontini, marched on Syracuse and laid siege to it. The Syracusans, probably at the suggestion of the returned oligarchs, called on the Carthaginians to assist them. One of the results of the constant civil strife within the Greek cities was that many now saw their former mortal enemies as less of a threat than their own political opponents. Justin reflects on the irony of these events:

> Hamilcar, general of the Carthaginians, being entreated to aid it, laid aside his hatred as an enemy, and sent a body of troops thither. Thus, at one and the same time, Syracuse was both defended by an enemy with the love of a citizen, and attacked by a citizen with the hatred of an enemy.[17]

The arrival of Hamilcar and the Carthaginian troops tipped the campaign in favour of the Syracusans and Agathocles was forced to seek terms. In 317 he was allowed to return to Syracuse but only after he had sworn at the shrine of Demeter that he would 'undertake nothing against the democracy.' Agathocles had come back to a city that was still split along class and political lines, 'for it happened that the political clubs of those who were holding meetings were divided into many factions and that important differences of opinion existed among them.' He joined forces with the moderate democrats and 'by pretending to be a supporter of democracy and by winning the favour of the people in artful ways that he secured his own election as general.'[18]

With the return of Agathocles to the city and to a position of power, it was now the turn of the hard-core oligarchs to attempt to overthrow the democracy by force. They gathered together an army at the city of Herbita. Agathocles was appointed to command an expedition against the rebels and allowed to recruit a force as he saw fit. The Syracusan section of Agathocles' army was deliberately recruited from 'those of the citizens who because of poverty and envy were hostile to the pretensions of the powerful.'[19]

Once again Agathocles was joined by 3,000 troops from the cities of the interior. These cities appear to have remained loyal to Agathocles not only because of their hatred of the oligarchs but also as they had 'received many benefits from him during the campaigns.'[20] Most likely, these cities feared that a restored oligarchy in Syracuse would once again attempt to impose direct rule and garrisons upon them. Agathocles may have promised to give them their freedom and autonomy. Such guarantees would soon become politically expedient and fashionable. A year later the Successor king Antigonus the One-Eyed promised that all the Greek cities were to be 'free, not subject to foreign garrisons and autonomous.'[21] The popularity of this promise was such that all the other Successor kings were forced to adopt a similar policy. None, except possibly Antigonus, was prepared to adhere to it.

The political situation within Syracuse had deteriorated to such an extent that both extremes of the political divide were ready to take up arms.

Before Agathocles could strike, he first needed to remove the threat of the Carthaginians. Polyaenus relates that he achieved this by concluding 'a peace with Hamilcar; who drew off his forces, and returned to Africa.'[22] Justin claims that Agathocles 'swore to Hamilcar that he would be faithful to the Carthaginians' and 'received from Hamilcar five thousand African troops.'[23] Justin's account of the deal with the Carthaginians is not repeated elsewhere and can confidently be dismissed as libel.

With the Carthaginians now absent, things began to move rapidly. Three or four days after Hamilcar withdrew, Agathocles was advised that the Six Hundred were preparing to attack him. He decided to strike first. He ordered the Syracusan part of his expedition to gather at the Temple of Timoleon the next day. Meanwhile, he lulled his enemies into a false sense of security by telling them that they would take command of the force and march out to relieve an allied city. 'They received his commands with rapture; hoping to have forces put into their hands, which they intended to employ against him.'[24] The next morning they arrived at the meeting accompanied by 200 of their supporters determined to arrest him. Agathocles denounced the plot of the gathered oligarchs to the assembled troops. His supporters, perhaps in a stage-managed scene, now demanded that he strike and 'inflict the just penalty on the wrongdoers out of hand.'[25] Agathocles willingly acceded to their demands and ordered the deaths of the plotters. Eager to settle scores with the hated oligarchs his troops killed the 200 gathered along with 600 onlookers who attempted to assist the victims.

Agathocles then unleashed his troops against his political opponents throughout the city, giving them orders 'to plunder the property of the Six Hundred and their supporters.' The troops were joined in their hunt by gangs of the poor who not only killed and looted, but inflicted 'something worse than death' on the wives and daughters of the wealthy. Many of the rich rushed unarmed into the streets to learn the source of the tumult, thereby hastening their own demise. Agathocles' soldiers 'made savage both by greed and by anger, kept killing these men who, in their ignorance of the situation, were presenting their bodies bare of any arms that would protect them.'[26]

Once unleashed, class hatred in a Greek city could be murderous. The killing got out of hand:

> The armed mob having seized power did not distinguish between friend and foe, but the man from whom it had concluded most profit was to be gained, him it regarded as an enemy. Therefore one could see the whole city filled with outrage, slaughter, and all manner of lawlessness. For some men because of long-existing hatred abstained from no form of insult against the objects of their enmity now that they had the opportunity to accomplish whatever seemed to gratify their rage;

others, thinking by the slaughter of the wealthy to redress their own poverty, left no means untried for their destruction. Some broke down the doors of houses, others mounted to the housetops on ladders, still others struggled against men who were defending themselves from the roofs; not even to those who fled into the temples did their prayers to the gods bring safety, but reverence due the gods was overthrown by men. In time of peace and in their own city Greeks dared commit these crimes against Greeks, relatives against kinsfolk, respecting neither common humanity nor solemn compacts nor gods.[27]

Despite the excesses of the mob, the coup was obviously well planned. Agathocles' troops had barred the gates to the city and arrested those that tried to flee. Many tried to escape over the walls, some were killed but others succeeded and sought refuge in the neighbouring cities. The killing and looting continued for two days before Agathocles, 'since he was now sated with the slaughter of his fellow citizens,' called an end to the murders and ordered the survivors to be taken prisoner. The most hostile oligarchs were separated and executed, the remainder exiled. Altogether, over the two days of the coup, it is reported that 4,000 were killed and 6,000 sent into exile.[28]

Once his power had been secured Agathocles' adopted a more conciliatory approach to his enemies. One of his first acts was to declare an amnesty for his political opponents. Diodorus ends his description in a tone quite different from his earlier description of the violence of the coup. He describes Agathocles' later behaviour:

With a complete change of humour he showed himself affable to the common people and won no slight popularity by aiding many, by encouraging no small number with promises, and by currying favour from all by philanthropic words. Although he possessed such power, he neither assumed a diadem, nor employed a bodyguard, nor affected a haughty demeanour, as is the custom of almost all tyrants.[29]

The obvious conclusion is that Diodorus has now switched to one of the more favourable sources for Agathocles' rule. The general sentiment was, however, repeated by Polybius who claims that Agathocles after 'showing himself exceedingly cruel in his first enterprises and in the establishment of his power, afterwards, when once he thought that he had securely attached the Sicilians to his rule, he became to all appearance the gentlest and mildest of men.'[30] This is perhaps an overstatement as Agathocles would carry out several more political purges during his reign. It may refer instead to the period of peace in Sicily after 304.

Here is perhaps the appropriate place to insert a word of caution regarding the bloody purges that both of our main sources accuse Agathocles of carrying out against his opponents. The most likely source for such incidents in Agathocles' rule is Timaeus, a historian who hated Agathocles and had good reason to exaggerate their extent. Although in no way should such massacres be excused, they should be viewed within the context of the era. The execution and exiling of political opponents usually accompanied changes of regime within Greek cities. Agathocles was probably no worse than many of his contemporaries. It should also be remembered that it was less than a year since Sostratus had carried out his own massacre of Agathocles' followers.

Once the dust had settled, Agathocles called an assembly in order to justify his actions. He announced that the Six Hundred had been plotting to restore the oligarchy and that he had 'cleansed the state of those men who were trying to become her masters; and he proclaimed that he was restoring liberty undefiled to the people.' Next he laid down his military insignia and claimed he wished to be relieved of the burden of command and retire to private life. In yet another stage-managed scene Agathocles was acting the democrat and artfully bringing to mind the deeds of Timoleon. Such actions can, nonetheless, be a dangerous stratagem if the offer is accepted. On this occasion, however, Agathocles had again primed his adherents and they led the assembly in 'begging him not to leave them but to accept the general administration of the state.' In this they had little trouble, for as Diodorus so adroitly points out, 'the majority of the members of the Assembly had had a share in his unholy acts and for this reason would not be willing to vote the generalship to anyone else.'[31]

Agathocles clearly understood his audience and increased the drama of the scene by at first remaining silent, forcing the mob to clamour for him to accept. Finally he acceded but only on the condition that he was elected general with sole command, *strategos autocrator*. The assembly voted to give Agathocles sole power. Any opposition was silenced by the enthusiasm of the many.

As soon as he was in power, Agathocles kept his word to his followers and 'promised in the Assembly both to abolish debts and to distribute land to the poor.'[32] There is no record of Agathocles actually carrying out these policies. Nonetheless, his reported popularity among the people of Syracuse, being able to walk about the city without an official bodyguard, would indicate that they must have been at least partially carried out. The occasional political purge of his wealthy opponents, so castigated by the ancient writers, themselves wealthy aristocrats, were probably popular among the poor of Syracuse. As well as dealing with the hated oligarchs, the executions would have made available the land necessary for redistribution.

There is no surviving description of how Agathocles ruled Syracuse, although we do know that the assembly continued to meet. Probably he governed in a similar manner to Dionysius the Elder: the assembly continued to manage the day to day administration of the city but Agathocles was in control of foreign policy and the military. Agathocles certainly attended the assembly where he ridiculed his opponents:

> But by nature also a buffoon and a mimic, not even in the meetings of the assembly did he abstain from jeering at those who were present and from portraying certain of them, so that the common people would often break out into laughter as if they were watching one of the impersonators or conjurors. With a crowd serving as his bodyguard he used to enter the assembly unattended, unlike Dionysius the tyrant.[33]

As well as never affecting a haughty demeanour, Agathocles supposedly preferred to drink from earthenware rather than from gold or silver goblets. There are no reports of his court being populated by artists or philosophers. Plutarch recounts how he supposedly 'used to place earthen and golden vessels together, and show them to young men, telling them, those I made first, but now I make these by my valour and industry.'[34] These tales, along with his buffoonery, would imply that Agathocles appears to have consciously projected an image of a man of the common people. The stories of him being a simple potter who rose to be a king may have been encouraged by Agathocles himself, as an ancient example of political spin.

This genial façade disguised the political reality. Agathocles was always able to intimidate the assembly into obeying his wishes, through the assassination of his enemies and his command of large numbers of mercenaries within the city walls. From his seizure of power in 317 until his death in 289, Agathocles would rule Syracuse first as a tyrant and later as a self-appointed king.

The biggest difference between Agathocles' rise to power and that of Dionysius the Elder forty years previously, was the importance that the internal struggles within the city had played. Although a demagogue who had played to the poor, Dionysius had largely come to power on the promise of providing effective military leadership against the hated Carthaginians. Agathocles won power primarily on the promise to redress the economic condition of the poor at the expense of the rich. This political division along the lines of wealth had always existed, but since the return of Dion and the overthrow of Dionysius the Younger it had played an increasingly important role in the city's politics.

Whatever the real nature of Agathocles' rule it is clear, that the Syracusan democracy – always a fragile institution – had once again been destroyed. Syracuse, with the exception of a few brief but vain attempts to restore the democracy, would largely be ruled by a succession of tyrants, some masking their power with the guise of kingship, but tyrants nonetheless.

Chapter 11

Agathocles' Defeat at the Battle of Himera

Agathocles, the tyrant of Sicily, broke the oath he pledged to his enemies, and slew his prisoners. He told his friends with a laugh, 'After supper we will throw up our oaths.

Polyaenus 5.3.1

Once Agathocles felt secure in his position as tyrant, he demonstrated that his regime would be just as imperialistic as the Syracusan governments that had preceded it. Early in 315, he commenced a campaign of conquest against the other Greek cities of Sicily. The first city to be targeted was Messene. The conflict arose over a Messenian fort that had somehow come into the possession of the Syracusans during the preceding wars. The Messenians wanted their fort back and they approached Agathocles. He offered to sell it back to them for thirty talents of silver. The Messenians handed over the money but Agathocles showed that his reputation for treachery was well deserved. He took the money but refused to hand back the fort. As with Dionysius the Elder before him, Agathocles had a casual attitude towards the breaking of oaths.

Agathocles then followed up this affront by attacking Messene. Apart from the strategic position of Messene on the Straits, another motive for this might have been the large population of Syracusan exiles who had taken refuge in the city. Learning that a section of the city's walls was in ruins, he ordered his cavalry to attack the breach while he sailed on the city with a fleet of *hermiolas*. These were warships lighter than triremes, literally a one and a half, and were popular vessels for pirates. They were possibly a pirate fleet hired by the Agathocles, as the Syracusan navy appears to have been neglected during the years of chaos after the downfall of Dionysius. They could have been old allies of Agathocles from his days as a freebooter in Italy. Justin might be literally correct in his description of Agathocles having been being a pirate during that part of his career.

The Messenians were warned of the attack and managed to repel it. Many of the Syracusan cavalry would have had friends amongst the exiles and one had probably betrayed the assault. Not daunted by his failure, Agathocles turned his attentions to the smaller city of Mylae (Milazzo) which occupied a headland on the northern coast about 20km west of Messene. The city surrendered and Agathocles was able to use it as a base for further attacks on Messene. Later that same year, after the harvest had been brought in, Agathocles renewed his attack. He camped near to the city and made repeated attacks on its walls but to no good effect. Resistance in the city was bolstered by the desperation of the exiles, who 'fought furiously both for the sake of their own safety and because of their hatred for the tyrant.'[1]

The Carthaginians, no doubt alarmed at this revival of Syracusan imperialism and fearful of Syracuse controlling the Straits, sent an embassy to Agathocles. They demanded that he withdraw, claiming that he had violated their treaty. This can only mean the agreement made between Agathocles and Hamilcar the previous year, which must have included the usual provisions of earlier treaties and guaranteed the autonomy of the Greek cities not already controlled by the two signatories. The Carthaginians also successfully demanded that he return the fort to the Messenians as he had promised. Agathocles, not yet ready to confront the power of the Carthaginians, surrendered to their stipulations. Humiliated, Agathocles retired southwest to the allied city of Abacaene. Here, perhaps still in a bad humour, he executed forty of his political opponents.

Another group of Syracusan exiles had found refuge in the city of Akragas. Frightened by Agathocles' aggressive campaigning, they urged their hosts to fight Agathocles before he became too powerful. Convinced by this argument, and always ready to challenge their traditional rival, Syracuse, the Akragantian assembly voted for war and formed an alliance with the cities of Gela and Messene. The allies sent a delegation to Sparta to request that they send a general to Sicily to take command of the war. Diodorus states that this offer was made by the Akragantians, as they suspected their own leaders of plotting to impose a tyranny and did not trust them with the command. The Sicilians, optimistically 'remembering the generalship of Timoleon the Corinthian, assumed that leaders from abroad would honestly devote themselves to the common cause.'[2] Unfortunately for the cause of the allies, the ambassadors decided to recruit a Spartan general rather than a Corinthian.

The embassy to Sparta found a willing leader in the person of Acrotatus, the son of King Cleomenes. He was widely hated in Sparta for being alone in opposing a decree that would have returned full citizenship to those Spartan citizens who had survived the defeat at the battle of Megalopolis in 331. The usual punishment for Spartans who fled from the battlefield was a loss of their political rights. Acrotatus was so detested by these men and their families, that he was the subject of beatings and constant plots against his life. Glad to escape Sparta, he accepted the offer of the Sicilians without bothering to get the consent of the Spartan government.

Arriving in Tarentum, a colony of Sparta, Acrotatus convinced the people to join the alliance against Agathocles and provide twenty ships. Without waiting for the Tarentines to prepare their fleet he sailed immediately for Akragas. Once he had assumed the command, Acrotatus indulged in the sort of behaviour that gave Spartan commanders overseas such a notorious reputation:

> He accomplished nothing worthy either of his fatherland or of the distinction of his family, but on the contrary, being bloodthirsty and more cruel than the tyrants, he continually gave offence to the common people. Moreover, he abandoned his native manner of living and devoted himself so unrestrainedly to pleasure that he seemed to be a Persian and not a Spartan.[3]

Acrotatus squandered most of the funds for the war on his own amusement rather than on fighting Agathocles. As the mood in Akragas turned against him, he committed one final outrage. He invited Sostratus to dinner and murdered him merely because he believed him to be a rival for his command. The assembly removed Acrotatus from his command and, once he had lost the protection of his office, his enemies attempted to stone him to death. Acrotatus fled back to Sparta. As result of his removal, the Tarentines left the alliance and recalled their fleet. The remaining cities of the alliance, with their military position now compromised by having lost much of their funds and the support of Tarentum, decided to make peace with Agathocles. Hamilcar, the Carthaginian commander in Sicily, brokered the agreement. The main terms of the treaty were: 'the Greek towns in Sicily, Heraclea, Selinus, and Himera were to be subject to the Carthaginians as they had been before, and all the others were to be autonomous under the hegemony of Syracuse.'[4] These terms were very favourable to Agathocles, as Syracuse was officially recognized as the leader of all the Greek cities east of the traditional border with Carthage, the Halycus River.

Justin uses his account of these events to continue his accusations of Agathocles' double dealing with Hamilcar. According to him, Agathocles had launched an unprovoked attack on the cities. The favourable treaty was a result of the secret deal Agathocles is supposed to have made with Hamilcar before his seizure of power. Hamilcar is then accused by his Sicilian allies of being a traitor to Carthage, 'by whom the possessions of their allies, under a settled compact, were betrayed to the bitterest of enemies,'[5] the city of Syracuse. As a result of these accusations, the Carthaginian government recalled Hamilcar from Sicily while secretly condemning him to death. He died before the sentence could be carried out. Although Diodorus does record that Hamilcar was censured for the terms of the peace, once again Justin's accusations can be treated with scepticism.

Agathocles, living up to reputation for breaking oaths, soon breached the terms of the treaty and began yet another campaign of conquest against the Greek cities. With the Carthaginian leadership in disarray, he was able to quickly capture a number of cities and overawe the rest. These campaigns probably occurred over the years 314–3. As a result 'he built up for himself a host of allies, ample revenues, and a considerable army.'[6] Agathocles' conquests had succeeded in returning Syracuse to its former position of power and domination over an extensive alliance of cities. He predicted that the Carthaginians would not long tolerate this renewal of the Syracusan threat to their Sicilian possessions, especially now the pliable Hamilcar was dead. Agathocles prepared for the coming conflict by recruiting a force of mercenaries, totalling 10,000 infantry and 3,500 cavalry.

By 312 only Messene among the Greeks cities remained openly hostile to Agathocles, therefore the remaining Syracusan exiles had concentrated there. Agathocles was eager both to capture Messene and destroy the gathering of his most determined enemies. He sent a detachment of troops, under his general Pasiphilus, with orders to intimidate the Messenians into surrendering by ravaging their territory. Pasiphilus' attack carried the element of surprise and he was able to plunder the countryside at will. The campaign achieved its desired result as the Messenians soon requested terms. They were offered peace on condition that they ally themselves with Syracuse and expel the exiles.

Agathocles now advanced on Messene with his entire army, falsely professing friendship as he approached. Polyaenus records an anecdote set during the surrender of Messene designed to show the more merciful side of Agathocles' character. According to this version the resistance to Agathocles was led by Megacles of Messene. One of Agathocles' conditions for the surrender of the city was that they hand over this general. Megacles, who despised death, proposed to his fellow citizens, that he should be appointed to be their ambassador; in which case, he would voluntarily surrender himself into the hands of the tyrant. Brought before Agathocles he did plead for his life but declared:

'I come in the name of my city, as an ambassador from the Messenians; and the object of my embassy is to die. But first convene your friends, and give me a hearing.' Agathocles therefore summoned his friends, and Megacles was brought before them. After pleading for the rights of his country, he said: 'If the Messenians had engaged in an expedition against Syracuse, with the intention of completely destroying it, would you not have done the same things against the Messenians, which I have done against the Syracusans?' Agathocles smiled at the question; and his friends, who were present, interceded on behalf of Megacles.

Accordingly, Agathocles sent him back unhurt, concluded the war, and entered into an alliance with the Messenians.[7]

Agathocles' good-will did not stretch far beyond Megacles. During the negotiations he intimidated the Messenians into accepting the return of their own exiles. These men, owing their homecoming to Agathocles, would become his partisans within the city. Once this had been achieved, Agathocles ensured the future loyalty of Messene by eliminating all opposition to his rule. He arrested 600 of those politicians who had been his opponents from both Messene and Tauromenium and executed them. It may have been as a result of this purge that the historian Timaeus was forced into exile. He fled to Athens, where he wrote his histories and never forgave Agathocles.

Diodorus explains these purges by stating that Agathocles' 'intention was to wage war on the Carthaginians, and he was getting rid of all opposition throughout Sicily.' He adds that the Messenians soon 'regretted what they had done; but they were forced to submit, since they were completely cowed by the superior power of those who had become their masters.'[8] For the first time since the reign of Dionysius the Elder, Syracuse was ruled by a government both determined to expel the Carthaginians from the island and possessing the military power with which to make it possible.

Now that the alliance of Messene had been secured, Agathocles marched against Akragas, hoping to install a regime more favourable to his purposes. The events of the last few years had, however, finally convinced the Carthaginians that force was necessary to stop Agathocles' progress. They sent a fleet of sixty ships to Akragas which saved the city. Now that open conflict with the Carthaginians had begun, Agathocles invaded Carthaginian territory, plundering the countryside and capturing a number of strongholds.

Meanwhile, one of the Syracusan outcasts, Deinocrates, gathered together an army of exiles in central Sicily totalling 3,000 foot and 2,000 cavalry. The cavalry component of the force was much higher than what was usual for a Greek army, certainly due to the high percentage of aristocrats who made up the opposition to Agathocles' rule. Deinocrates had been one of the leading oligarchs arrested when Agathocles had seized power in Syracuse but had been spared death on account of their long standing friendship. Deinocrates attempted to seize the city of Centuripae in central Sicily. The city was held by a Syracusan garrison but the opponents of Agathocles had offered to open their gates to Deinocrates. With their connivance, a detachment of the exiles' army managed to force its way into the city but the garrison was alert and drove them out. This success was insufficient to satisfy Agathocles; he marched on the city and executed all those whom he considered to be his opponents.

While Agathocles was busy in the interior of the island, the Carthaginians decided to retaliate against his incursions by sending a fleet of fifty ships to raid Syracuse. The attack achieved nothing except the capture of two

Athenian merchant ships. Diodorus, as a good Sicilian, was never one to ignore a Carthaginian atrocity and condemns the raiders for cutting off the hands of the captured crews.[9] With satisfaction he records the divine justice handed out to them for mutilating

> men who had done them no harm at all, and the gods quickly gave them a sign of this; for immediately, when some of the ships were separated from the fleet in the vicinity of Bruttia, they were captured by the generals of Agathocles, and those of the Phoenicians who were taken alive suffered a fate similar to that with they had inflicted upon their captives.[10]

The war had only just begun and both sides were already displaying the viciousness and tit for tat atrocities so prevalent in their earlier conflicts.

After failing to capture Centuripae, Deinocrates' army was invited by opponents of Agathocles to occupy the city of Galeria. The population of the city had expelled the supporters of the tyrant from the town. Agathocles sent an army of 5,000 men under Pasiphalus to attack the exiles. A battle was fought during which the fighting was inconclusive until the commander of the exiles' left wing was killed and his troops fled, exposing the flank of the right wing of the army. Deinocrates, commanding the right, was forced to withdraw. The Syracusans pursued with an enthusiasm unusual for a battle fought between two Greek armies and killed many of those fleeing. The hatred shown towards the oligarchs in the civil strife within the city appears to have spilled over onto the battlefield. The Syracusans captured Galeria and 'punished those guilty of the uprising.'[11]

Meanwhile, Agathocles learned that the Carthaginians had invaded the territory of Gela and occupied a fortified position on a hill called Ecnomus. The mount is best identified as Monte Cufino, part of the modern town of Licata. It lies about 30km to the west of Gela and its occupation would have been a permanent threat to Gela and its surrounding farmlands. The hill had been a stronghold of Phalaris, the notoriously cruel sixth-century tyrant of Akragas. It gained its name, which means 'lawless,' from the tortures and executions that had been carried out there by the tyrant. Agathocles advanced upon Ecnomus determined to bring the Carthaginians to battle and thus bring the war to a speedy conclusion. The Carthaginians refused to come down and fight and eventually Agathocles, with winter approaching, gave up the attempt and retired to Syracuse. There he celebrated the earlier victory over the exiles by decorating the temples of Syracuse with the spoils of battle.

Agathocles' growing power had alarmed the Carthaginians and they decided that it was necessary to send reinforcements to the island. They raised a force of 130 triremes, 2,000 Carthaginians, 10,000 Libyans, 2,000 mercenaries, 1,000 slingers from the Balearic Islands and 200 cavalry from

Campania. The force was commanded by Hamilcar, son of Gisco (not the deceased Hamilcar who had made the peace deal with Agathocles).

In the spring of 311 the fleet sailed for Sicily but was struck by a storm on the way and sixty triremes, along with many transport ships, were sunk. Diodorus uses this episode to inform his readers of the mourning customs of the Carthaginians. 'Not a few of the Carthaginian nobles were lost, for whom the city instituted public mourning; for it is their custom whenever any major disaster has befallen the city, to cover the walls with black sackcloth.'[13] Upon landing in Sicily, Hamilcar recruited mercenaries to replace his losses and enlisted troops from those Greek cities that still favoured Carthage. When mustered, his army totalled 40,000 infantry and 5,000 cavalry.

Hamilcar now marched into the territory of Gela. Presumably Akragas had remained loyal to Carthage, having been saved from Agathocles by a Carthaginian fleet only a year earlier. Diodorus sums up the strategic problems that faced Agathocles, stating that as the 'forces of the Carthaginians were superior to his own, he surmised that not a few of the strongholds would go over to the Phoenicians, and also those of the cities that were offended with him.'[14] The situation was made worse when the Carthaginians won a naval victory off Messene, capturing twenty Syracusan ships. The invasion of Geloan territory was his most pressing problem as the loss of such a large city would seriously deplete his resources. The next passage of Diodorus is interesting in that it supports the proposition that, in building his alliance, Agathocles had promised to respect the autonomy of at least some of his allies and not impose a garrison upon them.

Deciding nevertheless to make the city of Gela secure with a garrison, he did not venture to lead an army in openly lest the result be that the Geloans, who were looking for an excuse, forestall him and he lose the city, which provided him with great resources. He therefore sent in his soldiers a few at a time as if for particular needs until his troops far surpassed those of the city in number.[15]

Agathocles could have claimed to be sending allied troops to assist in the defence of the city rather than an as occupying garrison. At first such troops would have been welcomed as the Carthaginians were so near. Once he had sufficient forces within the walls, Agathocles entered the city and launched his coup. He accused his opponents within the city of treason, executed many and confiscated their property. Agathocles extorted further money out of the remainder of the population. Now that the Geloans had been terrorized into obedience, Agathocles secured the city with a garrison. Although strategic considerations and avarice were the most likely motives for Agathocles' violation of his ally's freedom and autonomy, politics may also have played a role. Diodorus claims that it was possible that Agathocles embarked on this course of action against the Geloans 'either because they were actually planning to do something of this sort, or because he was persuaded by false charges made by exiles.'[16] One of the sad realities of Greek politics was the swarm of exiles from both sides of the political divide ready to hurl accusations against, and to betray, their fellow countrymen

Once he had secured Gela, Agathocles marched out to confront the Carthaginians. Meanwhile, Hamilcar's army had taken up position on the steep hill of Ecnomus. Agathocles built his camp on another hill which was also a former stronghold of Phalaris, called the Phalarium. This position was probably Monte Gallodoro, which is about 8km from Monte Cufino and has a gentler slope. The two camps were separated by the Himera River. There was supposed to exist an ancient prophesy predicting that many men would die at this place, but did not record who they would be. The men of both sides were 'filled with superstitious fear and shrank from battle.'[17]

What is more likely is that Agathocles was cautious in engaging an army that was considerably larger than his own. The size of Agathocles' force is not recorded other than that the number of mercenaries was 13,500. The usual range in size for the field armies of the earlier tyrant, Dionysius the Elder, was 30–40,000. It is probable that Agathocles' army was at the lower end of this range, giving the Carthaginians an advantage in numbers. As Agathocles was unwilling to engage a superior enemy, the Carthaginians resorted to the usual strategy employed to force an enemy to fight; they commenced raiding the Geloan countryside.

Agathocles countered by sending forces to attack the Carthaginian foragers and their supplies. After a successful raid on the Carthaginian camp, one of the Syracusan detachments was pursued by the enemy. Agathocles, observing events from his hill, predicted that the Carthaginians would press the attack too far and cross the river. Although the mouth of the river silts up and forms a brackish pool in summer, it can easily be forded several kilometres inland. The ambush succeeded and the Carthaginians were driven back to their own camp with heavy losses. Agathocles believed that an opportunity had arisen to inflict a decisive defeat on the enemy while they were panicked by the refugees attempting to enter their camp. He led the entire Syracusan army out to assault the enemy stronghold, 'thinking that the time had come to fight to a finish.'[18] With the Carthaginians at a disadvantage, Agathocles had changed strategies and was now seeking a decisive battle, the traditional method of the Greeks for settling wars. The best place to attack the Carthaginian position was not the steepest face near the mouth of the river, but the gentler slope on the northern side.

Diodorus describes the beginning of Agathocles' assault on the camp:

Falling on them unexpectedly and quickly filling up a part of the moat, he overthrew the palisade and forced an entrance into the camp. The Carthaginians, who had been thrown into a panic by the unexpected attack and could find no opportunity for forming their lines, faced the enemy and fought against them at random. Both sides fought fiercely for the moat, and the whole place round about was quickly covered with dead; for the most notable of the Carthaginians rushed up to give aid when they saw the camp being taken, and the forces of Agathocles, encouraged by the advantage gained and believing that they would end the whole war by a single battle, pressed hard upon the barbarians.[19]

Hamilcar, seeing the success of the Greek attack, brought up his slingers to attempt to slow the enemy advance. The close-packed Greeks made an easy target and suffered badly from the barrage. At close range the Balearic slingers were able to fire large stones, each about 400g in weight. Such heavy missiles, even if they did not penetrate the armour of the Greeks, could cause broken bones and concussions. Wherever the slingers were stationed the attack faltered but they were too few in number to defend the entire perimeter. Reinforcing success, Agathocles continued the assault at those points where his troops were still advancing. The Greeks were close to victory when disaster struck. A relief force, which had arrived by sea from Africa, marched to the battlefield. Most likely the fleet had landed initially at Lilybaeum and been ordered to rendezvous with Hamilcar. Sailing from the west it would have been visible to Hamilcar's position but screened from Agathocles' position by Monte Cufino. It is possible that Hamilcar, knowing of the imminent arrival of the fleet, had deliberately drawn Agathocles into the attack by staging the earlier flight of the Carthaginian attackers.

Whether by good planning or blind luck, Hamilcar now had the Greeks caught in a trap. The Carthaginians in the camp rallied, while the relief force attacked the Greek's rear. Assaulted from all sides, the Greeks broke and fled. Their escape route back to their camp was over 7km of flat plain and gentle slopes. The cavalry of the Carthaginians pursued and inflected heavy losses on the fugitives. Normally the Greek cavalry would be expected to cover the retreat of their infantry but on this occasion they appear to have shirked their duty. Diodorus later records that in this defeat 'the greater part of the foot-soldiers had been killed, but almost all the horsemen had survived uninjured.'[20] Perhaps the aristocratic cavalry were not un-happy to see Agathocles decisively defeated, as similar disasters had caused revolts against earlier tyrants. A further calamity struck the Greeks when they reached the river. Desperately thirsty from fighting in the hot sun, they drank the brackish waters and as a result many died from dehydration.

The battle was a decisive defeat for the Greeks who lost 7,000 killed compared to the Carthaginians' 500. Agathocles, after gathering the survivors, was forced to burn his camp and retreat to Gela. Here he decided to with-stand a Carthaginian siege rather than retreat to the greater safety of the walls of Syracuse. Agathocles' reasoning was to keep the Carthaginians engaged before Gela, while leaving the Syracusans free to gather in their harvest unmolested. Hamilcar marched on Gela and began preparations for a siege. He soon abandoned the attempt when he learned that Agathocles was there in force and well supplied. Instead he decided to break Agathocles' power by winning over the other Greek cities with offers of friendship. Most likely he proposed the usual Carthaginian terms of respecting their autonomy in return for them accepting Carthaginian leadership and the payment of a modest tribute.[21] The cities 'vied with each other in deserting to Hamilcar.'[22] In fact they were recognizing the reality of the situation; the Carthaginians were on the ascendant and, for now, the Syracusans in decline.

Once the harvest was secure, Agathocles retreated to Syracuse and strengthened the walls, preparing for the coming Carthaginian siege. Hamilcar, now that he had successfully isolated Syracuse, advanced on the city and began to besiege it. Justin speaks of a second defeat of Agathocles by Hamilcar before the siege began. As it is not recorded elsewhere it would be easy to dismiss this episode except that Polyaenus records an incident that does seem appropriate:

> Hamilcar noticed that a Greek tactician, whom he kept as an advisor, was disclosing all his plans to Agathocles. Therefore, he announced that he intended to send his fleet to capture the Olympium, near Syracuse. The tactician secretly passed on this information to Agathocles; but Hamilcar ordered his sailors, after sailing for part of the night, to turn round and return as quickly as possible. Agathocles was fooled into sending a force to Syracuse, to defend the Olympium. He led the rest of his army by night against Hamilcar, who he expected to be left with only a small force. But Hamilcar, after disembarking a large number of troops from the ships, with a loud yell attacked the enemy, and killed seven thousand of Agathocles' soldiers.[23]

The Olympium is the Temple of Zeus to south of the city, and would be a suitable location for such a final attempt by Agathocles to prevent a siege. The casualty figure appears suspicious, however, as it is the same as that for the earlier battle at Ecnomus.

The Carthaginians were superior in both troops and ships and were able to completely cut off the city. Such a situation was a politically dangerous time for tyrants. Dionysius the Elder twice faced revolts against his rule after defeats by the Carthaginians and the threat of a siege. Agathocles could see that his forces were no match in the field for the Carthaginians and there was no hope of any relief from an outside force. Although Syracuse had successfully stood siege many times before, to retreat totally within the walls would surrender all the initiative to the attacker. Agathocles, always an energetic commander, decided to risk everything on a brilliant, albeit dangerous strategy. He would leave an adequate garrison in Syracuse under the command of his brother, Antander, but take the best of his forces to Africa and attack Carthage directly. Diodorus explains Agathocles' logic:

> For he hoped that, if he did this, those in Carthage, who had been living luxuriously in long-continued peace and were therefore without experience in the dangers of battle, would easily be defeated by men who had been trained in the school of danger; that the Libyan allies of the Carthaginians, who had for a long time resented their exactions, would grasp an opportunity for revolt; most important of all, that by appearing unexpectedly, he would plunder a land which had not been ravaged and which, because of the prosperity of the Carthaginians, abounded in wealth of every kind; and in general, that he would divert the barbarians from his native city and from all Sicily and transfer the whole war to Libya.[24]

The rulers of Carthage, who had lived in relative peace and security for over a century while they campaigned in other peoples' lands, were about to experience war at first hand.

Chapter 12

The Invasion of Africa and the Battle of Tunis

The victorious Carthaginians, in consequence, having invested Syracuse with a close siege, Agathocles, perceiving that he was neither a match for them in the field, nor provided for enduring a blockade, and being deserted, moreover, by his allies, who were disgusted at his cruelties, resolved to transfer the war into Africa; a resolution formed with wonderful audacity.

Justin 22.4

Agathocles made his plans to invade Africa with the utmost secrecy, telling nobody of the target of his design. Most assumed he was planning a plundering raid on Italy, the Epicraty or Sardinia. Agathocles gave orders for the infantry and the cavalry to prepare their equipment, except for the cavalry's mounts. The cavalry would hopefully be supplied with captured horses after landing. The number of hoplites available was low due to their losses at Himera River.

In selecting those troops to accompany him, Agathocles kept a watchful eye on his political security. Families were deliberately split, with some members remaining in the city and others going to Africa. The number of Syracusans taken by Agathocles is not certain although a contingent in Africa is recorded as numbering 3,500. Whatever the true total, they were outnumbered by the 7,000 mercenaries who accompanied the expedition. The Syracusans were, in effect, hostages for their relatives' good behaviour. Agathocles also took both of his adult sons, Archagathus and Heracleides, with him.

The loss of his empire meant that Agathocles was short of funds for his expedition. In the usual manner of tyrants, he contrived a number of methods by which to extort money from his subjects. He took control of the estates of orphans from their guardians, extracted loans from the merchants, stripped some of the dedications from the temples and confiscated the jewels of the women. This was still not enough and Agathocles adopted an even more ruthless method. He offered to allow those not prepared to endure a siege to depart the city. Both Diodorus and Polyaenus state that Agathocles then killed everyone who took up the offer as they were the 'wealthiest and most bitter against the tyrant' and expropriated their property. With this 'single unholy act, he gained an abundance of wealth and had cleared the city of those who were opposed to him.'[1]

Oddly enough, Justin does not repeat this accusation, stating that 1,600 left the city. He then goes to claim that after collecting the money Agathocles left most of it with Antander for the defence of Syracuse and took 'away with him only fifty talents for present use, and intending to get further supplies rather from his enemies than his friends.'[2] This amount of money would have been only about two weeks pay for his expedition, so clearly Agathocles was pinning all his hopes on successfully pillaging Carthaginian territory.

The shortage of manpower in the city must have been acute as Agathocles recruited: 'all the slaves that were of age for war, after receiving their freedom, to take the military oath, and put them and the greater part of the soldiers, on ship-board, supposing that, as the condition of both was made equal, there would be a mutual emulation in bravery between them.'[3] Usually freed slaves would serve as rowers in the fleet but after the heavy losses in infantry at Himera they may have made up some, or all, of the unidentified infantry who are recorded as fighting in Africa. Such troops were equipped by the state, usually with the bare minimum of a hoplite's equipment, a spear and shield.[4]

Once all the preparations had been made, Agathocles gathered a fleet of sixty ships to transport the force to Africa. Agathocles' first problem was to evade the Carthaginian fleet that was blockading Syracuse and which heavily outnumbered the Syracusans. An opportunity came when a grain fleet approached Syracuse. Agathocles' tight security had succeeded and the Carthaginians were not expecting any enemy activity. They attacked the approaching ships with their entire fleet. With the blockade temporarily lifted, Agathocles sailed out with his flotilla. The Carthaginians, observing Agathocles' ships assumed they had come out to rescue the grain ships and formed a battle line to face this threat. Much to their surprise, Agathocles sailed straight past. The more experienced Carthaginian fleet rapidly gained on the Greek ships who were saved only when night fell and darkness allowed their escape. Meanwhile, the Carthaginian pursuit had left the harbour unguarded, allowing the cargo ships to enter port bringing needed supplies into the city.

The next day Agathocles had to overcome another crisis when a solar eclipse occurred, as 'utter darkness set in and the stars were seen everywhere.' Eclipses were generally considered to be bad omens and Agathocles' men believed 'that the prodigy portended misfortune for them, fell into even greater anxiety about the future.'[5] Re-interpreting such omens was an essential skill for all good ancient commanders and Agathocles soon put a positive spin on the eclipse. Justin states that he reassured his men by telling them that 'if it had happened before they set out, he should have thought it a portent unfavourable to their departure, but since it had occurred after they had set sail, its signification was directed against those to whom they were going.'[6] Frontinus records a different version, in which the well educated Agathocles 'explained the reason why this happened, and showed them that, whatever it was, it had to do with nature, and not with their own purposes.'[7] Given the superstitious nature of the ancient Greeks, Justin's version of events is the more believable.

The recording of the eclipse does, however, provide us with two interesting pieces of information: the date and route of Agathocles voyage. The eclipse occurred on August 15, 310 and was strongest along the northern coast of Sicily. Agathocles must have taken the longer but less perilous voyage along the northern coast of Sicily. This is a much safer route weather-wise but would have risked interception by any Carthaginian ships stationed at Panormus or Lilybaeum. The choice of the northern route may have helped to mislead the Carthaginians into believing the rumours that Agathocles was planning to raid Italy, Sardinia or the Epicraty.

Six days later, as Agathocles' fleet approached the African coast, the Carthaginian fleet again threatened to intercept them. A race followed during which the experienced Carthaginians rapidly closed on the Greeks. This time they were saved when they made land moments before the Carthaginians could catch them. So close were the fleets that the leading Carthaginian vessels had already come within bowshot. Once the Greeks had landed, they were able to deploy their troops and the Carthaginian fleet drew off beyond missile range.

Agathocles' fleet landed at a place known as the Quarries which is located on the eastern end of Cape Bon, near the modern Tunisian fishing town of El-Houraria. The Quarries are now, somewhat inaccurately, known as the Roman Caves. They were the source of much of the marble used to construct Carthage. This spectacularly located archaeological site is now unfortunately closed to visitors due to safety concerns. Agathocles could not, however, have landed at this exact location as the coast consists of rocky cliffs that stretch well to the south. Fortunately for Agathocles' fleet there is a long stretch of beach located about 2km to the north of the Quarries and this must have been where the Greek fleet made landfall.

Once the Greeks were securely ashore, Agathocles called an assembly of the army and announced to them that during the pursuit he had promised the patron goddesses of Sicily, Demeter and Core, that if they allowed the Greeks to land safely he would burn all their ships as an offering. He added that the goddesses had promised him that they would grant victory in the war to the Greeks. It was now time to honour his vow:

While he was saying this, one of his attendants brought forward a lighted torch. When he had taken this and had given orders to distribute torches likewise to all the ship captains, he invoked the goddesses and himself first set out to the trireme of the commander. Standing by the stern, he bade the others also to follow his example. Then as all the captains threw in the fire and the flames quickly blazed high, the trumpeters sounded the signal for battle and the army raised the war-cry, while all together prayed for a safe return home.[8]

It was a stirring piece of theatre but Diodorus then goes on to relate the real motives for Agathocles' theatrical gesture: 'this Agathocles did primarily to compel his soldiers in the midst of dangers to have no thought at all of flight; for it was clear that, if the retreat to the ships was cut off, in victory alone would they have hope of safety.'[9] It would also relieve Agathocles of the need to split his small force in order to provide security for the ships.

Justin gives a more detailed version of the address in which Agathocles justifies his decision to take the war to the Carthaginians. Agathocles promises the men great plunder and concludes by appealing to the Greek's lust for eternal fame:

By these means the Carthaginians might not only be conquered, but Sicily might be delivered from them; for they would not continue to besiege Syracuse, when they were suffering from a siege of their own city. Nowhere else, therefore, could war be found more easy, or plunder more abundant, for, if Carthage were taken, all Africa and Sicily would be the prize of the victors. The glory, too, of so honourable an enterprise, would be so celebrated through all ages, that it could never be buried in oblivion; for it would be said that they were the only men in the world who had carried abroad against their enemies a war which they could not withstand at home; who, when defeated, had pursued their conquerors, and besieged the besiegers of their own city. They ought all accordingly, to prosecute, with equal courage and cheerfulness, an enterprise, than which none could offer them a more noble reward if they were victorious, or greater honour to their memory if they were conquered.[10]

Once the theatre of the assembly was over, however, the troops began to reflect with fear on the situation they now found themselves in, 'as they considered the vastness of the sea that separated them from home, they abandoned hope of safety.'[11] In order to restore their morale Agathocles determined to make good his promise of plunder. He decided to sack the nearest Carthaginian town. Diodorus describes the wealth of the rich farm-land territory through which they marched:

There were also country houses one after another, constructed in luxurious fashion and covered with stucco, which gave evidence of the wealth of the people who possessed them. The farm buildings were filled with everything that was needful for enjoyment, seeing that the inhabitants in a long period of peace had stored up an abundant variety of products.[12]

The pillaging of such countryside quickly buoyed the Greeks' spirits as they went about 'devastating the country wherever they went, and laying farmhouses and fortresses in ashes.'[13] The exact route that Agathocles took when marching on Carthage is unknown. He is recorded as quickly taking and sacking the large city of Megalepolis, whose location is not certain. One proposition is that Agathocles used the shortest route to Carthage, along the northern coast of Cape Bon. If this route was taken, on a clear day the city itself might have been in view of the invaders, across the Gulf of Tunis. Megalepolis would probably have been the modern town of Soliman.

A more attractive option is that Megalepolis was instead the city that occupies the archaeological site at Kerkouane, on the southern coast of Cape Bon. This site is only a day's march from Agathocles' landing site and it would certainly have satisfied his need for a quick victory. He had promised his troops 'that the cities and fortresses of Africa were not secured with walls, or situated on eminences, but lay in level plains without any fortifications.'[14] Excavations at Kerkouane, whose ancient name is unknown, show that this claim is largely accurate. Despite occupying a flat, coastal site with no natural defences, the walls of the city were too low to form an effective defence. Archaeological evidence shows that the city was sacked and largely destroyed by Agathocles.

Another 20km south of Kerkouane lays the fort of Aspis, so named because it occupies a dome shaped hill that resembles the concave shield of a Greek hoplite. From its top, the entire eastern tip of Cape Bon is visible. It has been occupied by many armies throughout history. The hill is now dominated by a medieval Arab fortress. Inside its walls are the remains of earlier fortresses built by the Carthaginians, Agathocles and the Byzantines. At some time the fort was stormed by Agathocles.

Strabo (17.3.16) records that Agathocles built a town here after he captured the fort. Below the fort is a small harbour where evidence of shipbuilding from about the time of Agathocles has been found. Sometime after landing in Africa, Agathocles is recorded as building two light ships in order to establish communications with Syracuse and they may have been built here. The fort is now a part of the Tunisian fishing and resort town of Kelibia. Both Aspis and Kerkouane are impressive sites and well worth a visit by anyone travelling in Tunisia. If Kerkouane was Megalepolis, then Agathocles must have first travelled along the southern coast of Cape Bon before turning north past Aspis. This is an easier but longer route than that along the northern coast.

The next city to fall was Tunis, near the site of the centre of modern Tunis, about 20km from Carthage.[15] The victorious Syracusans wished to occupy the captured cities and secure their booty within, but Agathocles would not allow it. Instead he destroyed both towns, claiming that real security could only be found by defeating the Carthaginians in battle. As Tunis was later used as a base by the Syracusans, the destruction cannot have been complete. Agathocles now advanced directly against Carthage in an attempt to force them to come out and fight. He would have hoped that a successful battle before the city would force the Carthaginians to seek terms.

When news of Agathocles' arrival reached Carthage, the ruling council was at first unnerved, believing that their forces in Sicily had been destroyed. What else could explain the presence of a Greek army in Africa? The Carthaginian council met to discuss the danger. The situation appeared grim as there were no significant forces at hand and the citizens had little experience in warfare. Some urged that envoys be sent to seek peace terms from Agathocles, although with the usual Punic cunning they should also act as spies while in the Greek camp. Before a decision was made messengers from the fleet arrived and explained the real state of affairs.

Now aware of the true nature of the situation the Carthaginians regained their composure. They appointed two generals, Hanno and Bomilcar, to lead their forces. This was an unfortunate choice as the two men were political rivals and loathed each other. Many within the city feared that Bomilcar had ambitions to set himself up as a tyrant. The split command may have been the result of internal divisions within the council, with neither side willing to give sole command to the other.

Diodorus states that the two generals did not wait for reinforcements from their allied cities or the garrisons of the interior but instead merely called up all the available citizen soldiers in the city: 40,000 infantry, including the reformed Sacred Band, 1,000 cavalry and 2,000 chariots. Justin directly contradicts Diodorus by claiming that the army was 30,000 strong, drawn from troops from the countryside (*paganorum*) and commanded by Hanno alone. On this occasion it is necessary to prefer aspects of Justin's account over that of Diodorus. Based on the area of the city, the population of urban Carthage cannot have been more than 100,000 people.[16] Even allowing that the Carthaginians conscripted every able-bodied man, regardless of social class and age, they could not have raised over 40,000 troops from the city alone.

A more likely scenario is that Bomilcar remained in Carthage recruiting the citizen levies while Hanno quickly toured the neighbouring cities, raising what forces he could. When the two joined forces the combined army totalled between 30,000 and 45,000 troops. Whatever the real number, such a large force, quickly raised, must have included many untrained and poorly-armed men. Despite the shortcomings of the army, the Carthaginian generals would have been under pressure to do battle with Greeks as soon as possible in order to prevent further pillaging of the countryside

The coming encounter would have taken place on the plain that lies between Tunis and Carthage and is usually known as the Battle of Tunis. The Carthaginians are recorded as making camp on a low hill. Unfortunately, even when looking down from the hill of Carthage, the urban sprawl of modern Tunis makes it impossible to confidently locate this rise and thereby the actual site of the battlefield. From the terrain maps of the area the most likely site would be a rise midway between Carthage and Tunis on the northern side of the Lake of Tunis.

The Carthaginian commanders divided their army into two wings. Hanno commanded the right flank, with the Sacred Band holding the position of honour on the extreme right. Bomilcar, commanding the left, was forced to form up his phalanx extremely deep 'since the terrain prevented him from extending it on a broader front.' The most likely explanation of this was that Bomilcar's flank rested on the marshy shore of the Lake of Tunis. The Carthaginian chariots and cavalry were stationed in front of the infantry in order to launch an immediate attack 'and test the temper of the Greeks.'[17] A better tactic would have been for the Carthaginian mounted troops to attempt to attack the exposed flank of the Greek phalanx while it was engaged with the infantry. However the Carthaginian nobles who made up such troops were probably eager to win glory for themselves in battle.

After viewing the formation of the Carthaginians, Agathocles drew up his army to match their deployment. Instead of taking position on the traditional right wing or centre, Agathocles placed himself and his bodyguard of 1,000 of the best hoplites opposite the Sacred Band. He hoped to quickly defeat the enemy's best troops and spread dismay among the rest of the army. From right to left the Syracusans then drew up as: 3,000 Samnite, Etruscan and Celtic mercenaries, 3,000 Greek mercenaries 3,500 Syracusans, 2,500 unidentified infantry and finally Agathocles' bodyguard. The unidentified infantry might have consisted of allied Greeks from Sicily, although according to the sources all the Sicilian allies had deserted Agathocles. Instead it possibly consisted of pro-Agathocles exiles from the Sicilian cities, freed slaves and/or some sailors equipped with spare arms. The right flank was commanded by Agathocles' son Archagathus. Five hundred light infantry, archers and slingers, were spread along the front of the army. There is no record of the Syracusan cavalry so presumably they had not yet found enough mounts. The cavalrymen would have fought as infantry hoplites, probably as part of the Syracusan detachment.

The 13,500 strong Greek army would clearly have appeared smaller than the Carthaginian host. In order to match the frontage of the enemy line Agathocles would have been forced to draw up his line as shallow as possible, perhaps as few as four deep. In order to prevent the Carthaginians from gaining heart from his lack of numbers, Agathocles decided to create the illusion of more troops and a greater depth to his battle line. He equipped the largely unarmed sailors with shield covers stretched over sticks and placed them behind the heavy infantry. Once positioned, 'these men, of no use at all for real service but when seen from a distance capable of creating the impression of arms in the minds of men who did not know the truth.'[18]

Believing that his own troops would be intimidated by the greater numbers of the enemy, Agathocles had artfully prepared his own favourable omen. He released captured owls, sacred to the goddess Athena, to fly among the army. The appearance of an owl was supposed to have foretold an earlier Greek victory over another barbarian people, the Persians, at Salamis.

The battle began with a charge of the Carthaginian chariots. This was met by the Greeks with the usual tactics used against these vehicles. The light infantry shot at them for as long as possible before falling back behind the protection of the phalanx. Their fire wounded many of the drivers and horses, causing their vehicles to go out of control. Some of these turned away from the missiles and raced back towards their own ranks. The Greek infantry then opened up lanes in their ranks and allowed those chariots that survived the fire to pass through to the rear. Here they would have been finished off by the light infantry and perhaps the sailors.

The cavalry were next to charge. Although Diodorus claims that they were dealt with in the same manner as the chariots, it is more likely that the Greek phalanx would have adopted its normal tactics when facing cavalry.[19] Agathocles' hoplites would have formed up in their closest order, with the light infantry supporting them by firing over their heads. It was impossible for the cavalry of the Carthaginians to defeat such a formation, provided the infantry held their nerve, and they too were driven off.

With their first two attacks having failed, the Carthaginians launched a third attack with their infantry. Although it is not certain how all of the Carthaginian infantry were equipped, what evidence there is suggests that their best armed were the equivalent of the hoplites of the Greeks – armed with spear and shield and fighting in the close-packed phalanx formation. The clash of the two infantry lines would therefore have been typical of the clash of any two lines of hoplites.

The routing chariots and cavalry would have disorganized the inexperienced Carthaginian infantry, giving the Syracusans the advantage at the moment of impact. When the two lines clashed, the only Carthaginians to have any effect on the Greek line were Hanno and the elite Sacred Band. Hanno, hoping to obtain the decisive breakthrough, pushed forward too eagerly. The Greeks were able to the isolate the enemy commander and bring him down. Hanno's death panicked the untried troops under his command and the Carthaginian right wing collapsed.

The disunity among the Carthaginian command now played a decisive role in deciding the outcome of the battle. Bomilcar's left wing had been slower to engage the enemy. Possibly this was a result of it being hemmed in by the shores of the sea. The fleeing chariots and cavalry would have had no way by which to avoid the deeply packed ranks of the infantry and crashed through them, disrupting their battle line. On the open right wing of the army many of the fleeing Carthaginian cavalry may have been able to avoid such a collision. Given what happened next, however, it is also possible that Bomilcar was deliberately slow in bringing his troops forward, hoping that disaster might strike his unsupported rival.

With the Carthaginian right wing in flight, the Greeks went onto the offensive and pushed forward eagerly. When Bomilcar heard of the death of his competitor he decided that:

> The gods had given him the opportunity for gaining a position from which to make a bid for the tyranny, he reasoned thus with himself: If the army of Agathocles should be destroyed, he himself would not be able to make his attempt at supremacy since the citizens would be strong; but if the former should win the victory and quench the pride of the Carthaginians, the already defeated people would be easy for him to manage, and he could defeat Agathocles readily whenever he wished.[20]

Bomilcar now abandoned the fleeing Carthaginians of the right to their fate and attempted to withdraw his own command intact. He ordered them to retreat back to the high ground of their original position, beginning with the troops of the front ranks. Such a manoeuvre in the face of the enemy was difficult for even the most disciplined troops and the inexperienced Carthaginians were unable to carry it out. The rearmost troops, believing that the retiring front ranks had been defeated, turned and fled. The entire Carthaginian army was now in rout. The victorious Greeks pursued the enemy, giving them no opportunity to rally.

The Carthaginians did not cease their flight until they had reached the safety of the city. Only the Sacred Band did not flee, instead they closed their ranks and withdrew from the battle in a solid body. Such an organized retreat often saved those involved, as the victorious enemy would look for easier targets rather than risk their own lives. At some point Agathocles called a halt to the pursuit and turned his troops back to plunder the enemy camp. Numbers of casualties for both sides vary in the sources. The Carthaginian dead are recorded variously as 1,000, 2,000, 3,000 or more than 6,000, with the Greeks losing 2, 200 or 2,000.[21] The lack of Greek cavalry to pursue the beaten enemy would have spared many of the fleeing Carthaginians.

Diodorus uses an incident during the sacking of the Carthaginian camp to indulge his penchant for including moral lessons. The Syracusans are reported to have found 20,000 pairs of fetters with which to lead the defeated Greeks away to the slave markets. The Greeks believed that such hubris was frequently punished by the gods. The author takes the opportunity to give us his thoughts on the matter: 'but, I think, the divinity of set purpose in the case of men who are arrogant in their calculations, changes the outcome of their confident expectations into its contrary.' Herodotus records how the Spartans in a campaign against Tegea had also carried fetters for the same purpose, and been punished in the same way.[22]

Despite their defeat, the Carthaginians did not seek terms but resolutely decided to continue to resist. Their defeat did, however, cause them to believe that their gods must be angry with them. At such times the Carthaginians often resorted to an archaic ritual despised by Greeks and Persians alike. Three hundred children from the noblest families were sacrificed. Diodorus gives us a description of the ritual: 'There was in their city a bronze image of Cronus, extending its hands, palms up and sloping toward the ground, so that each of the children when placed thereon rolled down and fell into a sort of gaping pit filled with fire.'[23] It is generally believed that the children were either killed or drugged prior to them being thrown into the flames.

The remains of the temple and the furnace can be visited just south of the acropolis of Carthage. The site is staffed by a charming Tunisian pensioner who, for a small consideration, will guide visitors around the ruins. To my surprise he was somewhat reticent in discussing the murderous ceremonies that occurred at the site and was more interested in describing the construction of the later Roman plumbing.

Agathocles was now unopposed in the field at the gates of Carthage. His victory had created the incongruous situation where both sides' capitals were threatened by an enemy force. Carthage was a different proposition to the cities that Agathocles had already captured, though; it was a large city, with the citadel strongly situated atop a hill. Excavations have shown that the city was protected on the landward side by two walls, the tallest being up to 18m high. Well sheltered within the walls were two harbours, an outer commercial port and an inner naval facility. Agathocles' army was too small to have any real chance of successfully storming Carthage. His ongoing strategy would to isolate the city while he attempted to break its power by winning over its subject Phoenician cities and African allies.

Chapter 13

Agathocles' Campaigns in Africa and the War in Sicily

This wonder was gradually changed into a contempt for the Carthaginians; and not long after, not only the populace of Africa, but the most eminent cities, out of fondness for change, revolted to Agathocles.

Justin 22.6.

Following his victory at Tunis, Agathocles built a fortified camp about 8km distant from the city. From there the Syracusans plundered the surrounding countryside at will. The Carthaginians penned-up within the city were forced to watch the devastation of their property without any chance of reply. Although Agathocles was able to blockade Carthage from the land, without a fleet he could not hope to starve it into submission. In the coming months the Carthaginians would experience some shortages of food but as long as they controlled the seas they were never in any danger of being forced into submission through starvation. Their fleet ensured that supplies of food could be brought in from Sardinia and Sicily.

Carthage's defeat at Tunis was seen as a sign of weakness by many of her allied cities and much of the native population. Many of them took the opportunity to rebel. Some of the cities allied themselves with Agathocles and supplied him with food and money. Justin describes the attitude of the Carthaginian allies: 'not only their tributary towns, but even princes that were in alliance with them, began to fall off, estimating the obligations of confederacy not by the standard of honour but by that of fortune.'[1] In a manner similar to the Greek cities of Sicily, the smaller Phoenician cities of Africa were simply recognizing the new strategic reality and throwing in their lot with the side that appeared to be the strongest. Others, more ambitious, would have seen it as an opportunity to throw off the Carthaginian yoke and regain their independence.

The Carthaginians, with no effective forces in the field, sent messengers into Sicily ordering Hamilcar to send aid as soon as possible. They also told the envoys to spread the word that Agathocles' force had been defeated and destroyed. The bronze rams of Agathocles' burnt ships were to be displayed as trophies to give credence to their lie. Hamilcar sent the envoys into Syracuse to announce the supposed victory and demand the surrender of the city. The rams were presented as proof.

The stratagem worked to an extent, as many among the people of Syracuse, believing that their family members were dead, filled the city with mourning and uproar against the officers of the tyrant. Agathocles' magistrates were not so easily convinced, however, and expelled the delegation from the city. Perhaps they were privy to Agathocles' plan to burn his ships or simply thought to secure their own positions. They rounded up 8,000 of their opponents and banished them from the city. Fortunately for the outcasts, Hamilcar took pity on them and took them in. The usual fate for people expelled from besieged cities was to be barred by the besiegers, slowly starving to death in the no man's land separating the opposing armies.

With the Syracusans now in disarray, Hamilcar prepared to assault the city but first made one more attempt to win it without fighting. He sent another delegation into the city to offer safety to Antander and his associates if he surrendered the city. Despite the fact that Antander had once been a general of Syracuse, Diodorus (20.16) describes him as 'unmanly by nature' and he was ready to yield. This description of Antander is a deliberate play on words by the author as his name in Greek is 'Antandros' and the word for unmanly is '*anandros*'. Agathocles, perceiving that such a situation might arise, had given joint command of the city to his mercenary commander, Erymnon. He was made of sterner stuff and convinced the council to hold out until it was certain that Agathocles was defeated. Hamilcar, somewhat tardily, now began building the rams and towers necessary for the assault.

After his victory, Agathocles had built two thirty-oared ships, *triaconters*, and dispatched them to Syracuse to bring the good news. The ships had good weather and made the crossing in five days. As they approached the city the Carthaginian pickets caught sight of them and tried to intercept. Once again the Greeks won the race and the ships entered the harbour in safety. The crews had decked themselves out in victory garlands and were singing hymns as they docked. During the chase the people of Syracuse had gathered around the harbour to receive the news from Africa. The sight of the crews in their finery told them the truth without words being necessary.

Hamilcar, observing the commotion in the city, decided that the distraction offered a chance of catching the Syracusans unprepared. He ordered an immediate assault against those portions of the wall furthest from the port. The Carthaginians found a section of the defences had been deserted and scaled them unopposed. Before the attackers could secure a foothold, a Syracusan patrol discovered them and raised the alarm. The Syracusans rushed to attack the bridgehead and were able to drive back the invaders.

The success of their counter-attack and the news from Africa revived the failing morale of the Syracusans. Hamilcar despaired of taking the city and withdrew. Answering the call from Carthage he sent 5,000 troops to reinforce the city.

Back in Africa, Agathocles' decided to exploit his victory before the winter rains set in. He left garrisons in the fort near Carthage and in Tunis, while the rest of the army marched south to attack other Phoenician cities. Many of the cities surrendered, either from fear of the Greeks or hatred of Carthage. Others resisted and needed to be captured by force. Neapolis (Nabeul) was taken by storm. Agathocles treated the survivors with unusual mercy, perhaps hoping that their humane treatment would induce other cities to surrender. Agathocles' success also convinced one of the Libyan chieftains, Aelymas, to ally himself with the Syracusans. The Libyans were an agricultural people who had been conquered and forced into servitude by the Carthaginians. Some worked on Carthaginian estates but many lived in their own communities, paying tribute to Carthage. Like many such peoples they resented their position and were predisposed to rebellion.

Next Agathocles marched on Hadrumetum (Sousse) and laid siege to the city. Agathocles' main force was now about 120km from Carthage. The Carthaginians decided that his absence was an opportunity to break the blockade of their city. They marched out and quickly overran Agathocles' forward camp. Next they advanced on Tunis and after bringing up siege engines they made constant assaults on the walls. Agathocles, learning of the attack on Tunis, left most of his army to continue the siege but took a detachment to relieve Tunis. Diodorus now relates a strange tale of one of Agathocles' supposed stratagems. He claims that Agathocles' force occupied a mountain in view of both Tunis and Hadrumetum and lit many fires so both Carthaginian forces could see his camp. 'Both of them, deceived by the deceptive stratagem, suffered an unexpected defeat: those who were besieging Tunis fled to Carthage abandoning their siege engines, and the people of Hadrumetum surrendered their home-land because of their fright.'[2]

Tillyard claims that the story is clearly fictitious as 'the distance between Hadrumetum and Tunis was too great for the fires to have been seen from both places at once.' He further adds that even if it were possible: 'At all events there would have been nothing more than a faint glow in the sky, which could hardly have frightened the Carthaginians into such headlong flight, that they forgot to move or even to burn their siege-engines.'[3] Here Tillyard is too sceptical, all that would be needed is a hill somewhat greater in height than 200m. There are a number of these, some over 1,000m, between Tunis and Hadrumetum and widespread campfires on their slopes could be recognized as such. Agathocles' ploy was therefore possible.

After Hadrumetum fell, Agathocles advanced further south along the coast and took Thapsus by storm. By now he won over or captured more than 200 towns and controlled the coast of Tunisia south of Carthage. If they had not been captured immediately after Agathocles' landing, it is now that the cities at Kerkouane and Aspis must have fallen. Although Diodorus' narrative continues without a break, it is perhaps at this point that Agathocles went into winter quarters as the rains of the Tunisian winter begin in October. The first few months of Agathocles' African campaign had ended with him in a dominant position. Carthage was isolated and many of its subject cities had changed sides.

In the spring of 309, once the winter rains had ended, Agathocles decided on a campaign into inland portions of the Carthaginian domains. The most likely motive would have been to win over more of the Libyans and Numidian tribes of the interior. The Numidians were nomadic peoples living further inland. They would ally with the Carthaginians whenever they were forced to or thought it profitable. At other times they would raid Carthaginian territory. Many Numidians served as mercenaries in Carthage's armies.

Agathocles absence, plus the arrival of the reinforcements sent from Sicily emboldened the Carthaginians'. They waited until Agathocles was several days march away and launched their offensive. The Carthaginians re-captured a number of their outposts and laid siege to Tunis. The successes of the Carthaginians convinced the Libyan chieftain, Aelymas, to once again change sides.

When messengers brought word of the attack to Agathocles, he immediately turned around and marched back towards Tunis. Agathocles made camp some distance from the city and, in order to maintain secrecy, forbade his troops from lighting campfires. Making a night march, Agathocles took the Carthaginians by surprise, killing 2,000 and taking many captives. The Carthaginians once again lost heart and they retreated back to the city. With the threat to Tunis at an end, Agathocles now decided to punish the renegade Libyans. He defeated them in battle and killed Aelymas. With these two victories Agathocles had once more confirmed his dominance over the countryside and the Carthaginians were again confined within the walls of their city.

Meanwhile, in Sicily, Hamilcar had used the winter to regain his composure and rebuild his forces. In 309 he again marched on Syracuse. In preparation for the coming siege, he captured the outlying forts, blockaded the city by sea and ravaged the countryside. He again occupied the Temple of Zeus and had his priests take the sacrificial omens. After the seer declared that 'that on the next day he would certainly dine in Syracuse,'[4] Hamilcar is supposed to have changed his plans and decided to launch an all-out assault on the city the next day. Hamilcar's army included a number of Greek allies, including the Syracusan exile Deinocrates. Some of these deserted during the night, bringing the Syracusans word of the Carthaginians' plans and their proposed line of march.

Antander, or more likely Eurymnon, decided to lay an ambush for the attackers. Early in the evening they sent out 3,000 infantry and 400 cavalry to occupy the pass of Euryalus that led up to the heights of the Epipolae, which lie to the north and west of the city. Hamilcar had decided to march his army into position during the night in order to achieve surprise for his attack the next morning. The cavalry took the lead, followed by infantry, which was separated into Carthaginian and Greek contingents. The army was accompanied by: 'a mixed crowd of rabble also followed along for the sake of booty, men who are of no use whatever to an army, but are the source of tumult and irrational confusion, from which the most extreme dangers often arise'[5] At the rear of the army marched its baggage train. Hamilcar's army is recorded as containing 120,000 infantry and 5,000 cavalry. The figure is too large to be confidently accepted. If accurate, it probably represents all the Carthaginian forces in Sicily or alternately includes those serving on the fleet as well as the various servants and hangers on.

The road up to the pass was rough and narrow and the column soon fell into disarray. This situation was not helped by the mix of nationalities and accompanying freebooters, the various contingents started jostling for position and the ethnic rivalries led to fights breaking out. The Syracusans occupying the pass observed the confusion of the enemy and decided to attack. The light infantry occupied the heights above the road and unleashed a torrent of missiles into the column while the rest of the force charged downhill into the disorganised enemy. The leading units of the Carthaginians panicked and fled. This increased the confusion among their ranks and the Carthaginian troops began fighting their Greek allies believing them to be the enemy. Hamilcar and his bodyguard held their ground against the Syracusan attack but, with the troops around them in flight, they were quickly isolated and overwhelmed.

The Carthaginians, now leaderless, fled, scattering across the countryside. The victorious Syracusans captured Hamilcar and the baggage train. The next day Hamilcar was taken as a prisoner into the city, completing the prophecy. The Syracusans paraded him through the streets and handed him over to the families of those killed in battle against the Carthaginians. They took their revenge by torturing him to death. His head was cut off and sent to Agathocles along with the news of the victory. Tillyard rejects the account of Hamilcar's brutal execution, claiming that: 'this story does not sound like sober history. It is not likely that Hamilcar, an unusually generous foe, would have been made away with in so outrageous a way.'[6] This opinion seems to be a product of its time and reflects the general pro-Greek bias of the Edwardian gentleman and scholar. The Syracusans had many times demonstrated that they were capable of such vicious actions towards defeated enemies.

Another account of the prophecy and Hamilcar's defeat has survived from antiquity. Cicero records that:

We read in a history by Agathocles that Hamilcar, the Carthaginian, during his siege of Syracuse heard a voice in his sleep telling him that he would dine the next day in Syracuse. At daybreak the following day a serious conflict broke out in his camp between the troops of the Carthaginians and their allies, the Siculi. When the Syracusans saw this they made a sudden assault on the camp and carried Hamilcar off alive. Thus the event verified the dream.[7]

Tillyard uses these sources to dismiss Diodorus' account of the battle on the basis that such an experienced general as Hamilcar would never have risked his entire army on a night march through the narrow Euryalus pass. He claims that the fight must have occurred further south in the Anapus valley as Hamilcar was approaching the city.[8] Tillyard was, however, writing in a period when Diodorus was held in much lower regard as an historian than he is now. On balance, however, neither a passing reference in a work on divination nor the objections of a modern historian would appear to be adequate reasons to reject Diodorus' detailed account of the battle.

Following their defeat, the survivors of the Carthaginian army were in complete disarray as there was no obvious successor to assume Hamilcar's position. The Greek component of the army deserted; Deinocrates had also left and gathered another army together comprising of oligarchic exiles. The people of Akragas, the traditional rival of Syracuse for the leadership of the Sicilians, saw an opportunity to renew their ambitions; they observed that the defeat of Hamilcar had created a power vacuum in Sicily. With the Carthaginians in confusion and the Syracusans friendless and weakened from the repeated ravaging of their countryside, they believed now was the time to strike.

Akragas, which appears to have been a democracy at this time, elected Xenodicus as general. They began a campaign to liberate the Sicilian cities from the domination of Carthaginians, oligarchs and Syracusans alike, believing that: 'if they took the field to secure the independence of the cities, all would gladly answer the summons both through hatred for the barbarians and through the desire for self-government that is implanted in all men.' Xenodicus first marched on Gela and 'the people of Gela, having been thus freed, joined in his campaign very eagerly and unanimously, and set about freeing the cities. As news of the undertaking of Xenodicus spread throughout the whole island, an impulse toward liberty made itself manifest in the cities.'[9] Next the city of Enna came over voluntarily and Herbessus was captured from its Carthaginian garrison.

Wherever they were successful the Akragantians restored democracy to the cities. The Syracusans responded by plundering the territories of Leontini and Camarina but were driven off by the advance of Xenodicus. Despite their victory over Hamilcar, the Syracusans were limited in their capacity to make war as they were still under blockade from the Carthaginian fleet and

The theatre of Syracuse, either built or expanded by Dionysius the Younger, could hold 16,000 spectators. As the population of the city expanded, meetings of the assembly and important trials, such as that of the tyrant Mamercus, were held here. (*Author's photograph*)

The 'Ear of Dionysius'. Part of the quarries in Neapolis, the cave was used as a prison cell for political prisoners as the acoustics are so good any whisper can be heard at the entrance. This phenomenon can still be experienced by visitors today. (*Author's photograph*)

The massive walls of the fort guarding the pass of Euryalus. Designed by Archimedes, the fort was supposedly impregnable. It was surrendered to the Romans without a fight. (*Author's photograph*)

The Fountain of Arethusa, one of the many fresh water springs within the walls that allowed Syracuse to survive prolonged sieges. The papyrus plants were originally a gift from Ptolemy II to Hieron II. It was here that the Romans landed on Ortygia. (*Author's photograph*)

The theatre of Tauromenium (Taormina). The city was the birthplace of the historian Timaeus, the nemesis of Agathocles. It was here that both Timoleon and Pyrrhus landed in Sicily and began their campaigns of liberation. The bay of Naxos, the site of the first landing of the Greeks in Sicily can be seen in the background. (*Author's photograph*)

The walls of the city of Akragas. The city was captured and sacked by the Romans after a long siege. It was supposedly this success which led the Roman Senate to hope that 'that it would be possible to drive the Carthaginians entirely out of the island.' Polybius. (*Author's photograph*)

Fourth century vase painting of hoplite being bid farewell by his family as he leaves for war. A common image over centuries of vase painting; Hoplites, either citizen or mercenary, were the main strength of the Greek armies in Sicily. Now in the Whitaker Museum, Mozia. (*Author's photograph*)

A plate from Bactria showing an Indian war-elephant with tower and crew. Pyrrhus' elephants would have been similar in appearance. Their presence made such an impact on the Carthaginians that they soon raised their own force of smaller African elephants. Taken from a reproduction on display in the War Museum, Athens. (*Author's photograph*)

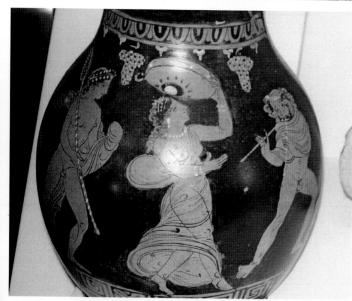

The good life enjoyed by the citizens of the Greek cities of Sicily and Italy, so despised by Plato, 'The kind of life which was there called the life of happiness, stuffed full as it was with the banquets of the Italian Greeks and Syracusans, who ate to repletion twice every day, and were never without a partner for the night.' Now in the Museo Archaeologico Nazionale, Taranto. (*Author's photograph*)

(*Left*) Bust believed to be Dionysius the Younger. This is probably an idealized image or produced in the early years of his reign as later he 'fell into indolence, and contracted, from excessive indulgence at table, great corpulence of body.' Justin. Now in the Museo Archaeologico Nazionale, Naples. (*Author's photograph*)

(*Right*) King Pyrrhus of Epirus, descendant of the hero Achilles and king of the Sicilians from 278?–276, arrived in Sicily with great expectations that he would expel the Carthaginians only to be driven out by his own subjects. As Pyrrhus sailed away from Sicily he is quoted as saying, 'my friends, what a wrestling ground for Carthaginians and Romans we are leaving behind us!' Plutarch, *Pyrrhus*. Now in the Museo Archaeologico Nazionale, Naples. (*Author's photograph*)

A coin depicting King Hieron II. Polybius claimed that, 'although he lived constantly in the midst of affluence, luxury, and most lavish expenditure, he survived till over ninety, and retained all his faculties, as well as keeping every part of his body sound.' (*Courtesy of Wildwinds, Freeman & Sear and Harlan J. Berk*)

The remains of an altar to the Phoenician God of the Sea. Located in the centre of the boatshed in the Carthaginian Naval Harbour. (*Author's photograph*)

The remains of the *tophet* of Carthage. It was here that the Carthaginians carried out their sacrifice of children to their God Molech. This practice horrified the Greeks, Persians and Romans. (*Author's photograph*)

All that remains of the once great city of Carthage after its destruction by the Romans. (*Author's photograph*)

The Arab fort atop the hill of Aspis, so named because it resembles the concave shield of a hoplite, inside its walls are the remains of earlier Phoenician, Greek and Byzantine fortifications. The hill and the Phoenician fort were captured by Agathocles. (*Author's photograph*)

One of the towers built to strengthen the fortifications of the Phoenician city at Kerkouane. After the city was sacked by Agathocles, attempts were made to improve its defences. These failed as Regulus later sacked the city and it was then abandoned. (*Author's photograph*)

The *Quarries (Roman Caves)* at Cape Bon where most of the marble used in the construction of Carthage was obtained. Agathocles was supposed to have landed here but the coast is too rough. A more likely site is the beach about 2km to the north. (*Author's photograph*)

suffering from the effects of famine. The people of Sicily had become engaged in a four way struggle for power, with the Akragantians, Carthaginians, Syracusans and oligarchic exiles of Deinocrates all vying for control.

Agathocles received the head of Hamilcar and news of the victory in Sicily soon after his own victories over the Carthaginians and Libyans. He displayed the head outside of the nearest Carthaginian position and gave them the news of their defeat. Naturally, Agathocles was elated by events and 'borne aloft by soaring hopes.' Such hubris could not go unpunished by the Gods and: 'Fortune notwithstanding did not permit success to remain long on the same side but brought the greatest danger to the prince from his own soldiers.'[10] The political tensions within the Syracusan army were about to boil over.

During a party, one of Agathocles' officers, Lyciscus, became drunk and insulted him. Agathocles laughed it off but his son Archagathus became angry and threatened Lyciscus. As all were leaving Lyciscus could not resist one last insult; he returned and accused Archagathus of having committed adultery with his stepmother. Archagathus became enraged and, seizing a spear from one of the guards, murdered Lyciscus. The next day Lyciscus' friends gathered and demanded Agathocles either give up his son for punishment or surrender and pay the penalty himself. More soldiers joined the demonstration and demanded their arrears of pay. Agathocles' plundering of Africa must have given him sufficient funds to pay his troops but, like many Hellenistic rulers, he may well have kept his troops' wages deliberately in arrears to ensure their loyalty. It could, however, be a dangerous game. The resentment of the soldiers over their arrears and the murder meant that the demonstration quickly became a full scale mutiny. The mutineers elected their own generals and seized the walls of Tunis. Agathocles was isolated within the city, a prisoner of his own troops.

The Carthaginians, learning of the revolt, offered to pay the mercenaries in full if they changed sides. Most of Agathocles' army was composed of mercenaries and many agreed to accept the Carthaginians offer. Agathocles' political instincts had not deserted him and he sensed the danger of the situation. In a scene reminiscent of his seizure of the tyranny, he put aside his purple garments, the signs of his office, and donned humble clothing. Agathocles walked into the middle of the army and appealed to them as a common citizen:

> After recalling his earlier achievements, he said that he was ready to die if that should seem best for his fellow soldiers; for never had he, constrained by cowardice, consented to endure any indignity through love of life. And declaring that they themselves were witnesses of this, he bared his sword as if to slay himself. When he was on the point of striking the blow, the army shouted bidding him to stop, and from every side came voices clearing him from the charges. And when the

crowd kept pressing him to resume his royal garb, he put on the dress of his rank, weeping and thanking the people, the crowd meanwhile acclaiming his restoration with a clash of arms.[11]

Agathocles, ever the opportunist, was not content with a single success. Knowing that the Carthaginians were waiting for the mutineers to desert to them, he led the army out against them. Believing that the approaching Greeks were about to join them, the Carthaginians were taken completely by surprise when the Greeks attacked. Diodorus admiringly comments on the energy and abilities of Agathocles: 'after having fallen into the most extreme danger on account of his son, through his own excellence not only found a way out of his difficulties, but even defeated the enemy.'[12] Despite the apparent reconciliation, 200 of the leaders of mutineers were fearful enough of Agathocles' revenge to desert to the enemy.

With the war in Africa now stalemated around Carthage, both sides looked to win the alliance of the Numidian tribes of the interior. The Carthaginians sent out an army to attempt to win back those tribes who had allied themselves to Agathocles. Agathocles left his son Archagathus in command of the garrison in Tunis and pursued the enemy with an army of 8,000 infantry and 800 cavalry. Accompanying the army were fifty chariots supplied by his Libyan allies. The Carthaginian expedition had already achieved some success when Agathocles caught up with it. The Carthaginians camped on an easily defended hill, surrounded by deep streams, and sent out their Numidian allies to harass the Syracusans.

The Numidians were renowned for the quality of their light cavalry. Their armies also included light infantry; both troop types were predominately armed with javelins. Their usual tactics were to surround and harass the enemy with missile fire while avoiding close combat. When they began to harass the Greek column, Agathocles sent out his skirmishers, bowmen and slingers to drive off the Numidians. The range of their weapons was greater than that of the javelins of the enemy and allowed them to engage at a greater distance.

Once the Numidians were neutralized, Agathocles marched his heavier troops against the camp of the Carthaginians. The Carthaginians drew up their army outside the camp and attacked the Greeks as they were fording one of the streams. The difficult nature of the stream broke up the Greek formation and gave the Carthaginians the advantage in the fight. Agathocles nonetheless pressed the attack, confident in the superiority of his troops. While the fighting continued, the African allies of both sides withdrew from the fighting and decided to join the winning side in sacking the camp of the loser.

The battle ended when Agathocles' bodyguard broke through the Carthaginian line. With a gap now opened in their formation, the rest of the army fled. A contingent of Greek mercenary cavalry, most likely political exiles, fought desperately to cover the Carthaginian retreat but they were caught between the camp, the streams and the advancing Syracusan phalanx. With no room to manoeuvre they were destroyed by the heavy infantry.

The sacrifice of the cavalry had allowed the survivors of the Carthaginian army to reach the safety of their camp. Agathocles pressed the attack but the difficult nature of the terrain hindered his assault. The African allies, who had stood aloof until this point, now realized that with the fighting all about the Carthaginian camp, it was impossible to loot. Instead they decided that the Greek camp, some distance from the fighting, was an easier target. They overwhelmed the few defenders and sacked the camp. Agathocles, learning of the assault, rushed his army back. He managed to overrun some of the Numidians, now loaded down with booty, but most escaped into the night. Agathocles compensated his men by sharing out what booty he had collected. He also set up a trophy for the initial victory over the Carthaginian army. It was, however, a hollow success as the bulk of the Carthaginian army had escaped and his Libyan allies had deserted.

The prisoners taken by the Greeks in the battle included 1,000 Greek mercenaries, including 500 Syracusan exiles. Agathocles imprisoned them in one of his captured fortresses. He probably intended to raise money by ransoming the non-Syracusans and keeping the Syracusans as hostages to ensure their families' loyalty. The prisoners were, on the other hand, terrified that Agathocles intended to crucify them as an example to other Greeks, as Dionysius the Elder had once done. If the captives included the 200 deserters from the mutiny they may have had good cause to fear punishment. The prisoners rebelled and managed to capture a section of their prison. Agathocles convinced them to surrender by offering terms. Once they had quit the safety of their position he broke his oath and executed them.

With the war once again stalemated and the news from Sicily no longer so favourable, Agathocles decided he needed a new source of reinforcements. He sent an embassy to Ophellas the governor of Cyrene. Ophellas was a former companion of Alexander the Great. He governed Cyrene in the name of the Macedonian king of Egypt, Ptolemy. Like all the Macedonian commanders after the death of Alexander, Ophellas had ambitions of carving out his own kingdom. Agathocles offered to cede to Ophellas the rule of all the Carthaginian territory in Africa if he would assist him in defeating them. Agathocles claimed that once the threat of Carthage was removed he would be content to rule over Sicily and the Greek cities of Italy. 'For Libya, separated by a wide and dangerous sea, did not suit him at all, into which land he had even now come through no desire but because of necessity.'[13]

Ophellas, with the bait of Carthage dangling before his eyes, agreed to the alliance. He had strong ties with Athens, his wife being an Athenian aristocrat, and hired a number of mercenaries from that city. The wars of the Successors had caused great disruption throughout the Greek world and many landless and stateless men joined Ophellas hoping to secure for themselves fertile land and plunder. In the spring of 308 the expedition set out from Cyrene. Many of the mercenaries brought their families with them and, as it set out, Ophellas' force was said to have resembled a colonizing expedition rather than an army. The fighting troops of the army numbered 10,000 infantry, 600 cavalry and 300 chariots.

The army soon ran into trouble as it marched through the waterless desert between Libya and Tunisia. Food and water quickly ran out and many died from snake bites. After a march of two months the army finally arrived in Tunisia and was met by Agathocles. The two armies camped separately but Agathocles was all friendship, supplying the newcomers with food and dining with Ophellas. Agathocles used these visits to spy on the camp of Ophellas. He waited until a large part of his army had scattered to forage and then called an assembly of his own army. Agathocles accused Ophellas of plotting against him. The Syracusan army attacked Ophellas' camp and easily overwhelmed the scattered forces. Ophellas died in the fighting. Agathocles won over the captured soldiers with the promise of generous rewards, although they would have had little alternative. Their families were despatched to Syracuse as hostages to ensure their continued loyalty. With a single assassination Agathocles had doubled his forces. Diodorus ends his account with the wry observation: 'thus Ophellas, who had cherished great hopes and had rashly entrusted himself to another, met an end so inglorious.'[14]

If Polyaenus (5.3.4) is to be believed, Agathocles had sent his son Heracleides, who like his father, was famed for his beauty, to Ophellas as a hostage. Ophellas was well known for his predilection for young men and Agathocles ordered his son to lead him on for a few days before submitting to his lust. Agathocles then claimed that Ophellas had mistreated his son in order to stir outrage in his troops against their new ally. This story follows, however, the tradition of Agathocles prostituting himself as a youth and can be easily dismissed.

Diodorus' account of Ophellas' murder is believed to derive from the pen of Duris of Samis, a fellow tyrant. Although it emphasizes Agathocles' treachery, it may be designed to highlight his cleverness rather than to condemn him. There are numerous instances in the wars of the Successors of allies plotting to murder one another and Ophellas is unlikely to have been as innocent, or as naïve, as portrayed. Agathocles' accusations may well have had a basis in reality or, if false, there were certainly enough precedents to make them believable.

News of the arrival of Ophellas' army caused a fresh outbreak of desperation to descend upon the people of Carthage. Justin claims that after recruiting Ophellas' army Agathocles defeated the Carthaginians in another major battle before the city. This battle is not recorded in any other source but it does provide a credible basis for the events about to take place in Carthage. The uncertainty caused by defeat was the perfect opportunity for a self-appointed saviour to arise with promises of a united and effective resistance to the invader. Bomilcar decided that now was his moment and launched a coup to seize control of the city. He had raised a private army of 500 supporters and 1,000 mercenaries and declared himself tyrant. Bomilcar, as joint commander of the army, would already have been one of the two chief magistrates, *suffetes*, of the city. He must have disavowed his colleague and appointed himself the Carthaginian equivalent of 'general with full powers.'

Bomilcar divided his force into five death squads and gave them orders to eliminate all his opponents. One detachment entered the market and proceeded to murder indiscriminately the unarmed citizens gathered there. The presence of armed troops, many of them foreign mercenaries, rampaging through the city, convinced the Carthaginians that Agathocles had entered the city. They rushed to arms and after learning the truth, turned instead on the rebels. The outnumbered insurgents were soon surrounded. The revolt ended when the Carthaginian council promised an amnesty to all the rebels. After their surrender, the council broke their oath to Bomilcar and crucified him in same market where his troops had carried out their massacre. While on the cross Bomilcar 'bore the cruelty of his countrymen with such fortitude, that from his cross, as if he had been on a judgment-seat, he inveighed against the injustice of the Carthaginians.'[15] Given the reasons for his execution, few of the listeners could have had any sympathy.

In 307 Agathocles decided to complete his conquest of the coastal cities of Tunisia. His next target was the large city of Utica, situated on the coast about 40km to the north of Carthage.[16] His advance must have caught the city by surprise as Agathocles was able to capture a number of prisoners outside the walls. When he arrived at Utica he offered generous terms if the city surrendered but the citizens remained loyal to Carthage and refused. The Greek engineers then advanced a siege tower against the walls of the city. Agathocles had tied a number of the unfortunate prisoners to the tower to act as a human shield. At first the defenders hesitated to fire on their kinsmen but as the tower neared the walls they decided that 'the liberty of all of more account than the safety of these' and in defending the city they had 'to slaughter mercilessly a large number of unfortunate fellow citizens.'[17] Despite the best efforts of the defenders the walls were soon breached, with the city sacked and occupied by a Syracusan garrison. Next to fall was the city of Hippacritae (Bizerte). After taking the city, Agathocles made Hippacritae his new naval base, 'with walls, citadel, harbour, and dockyards handsomely built by Agathocles.'[18]

With the completion of his northern campaign, Agathocles had 'became master both of most of the places along the sea and of the peoples dwelling in the interior except the Nomads, of whom some arrived at terms of friendship with him and some awaited the final issue.'[19] With his position in Africa apparently so strong, Agathocles decided that his presence was more urgently required in Sicily where the situation had continued to deteriorate. After a fleet was constructed at Hippacritae, Agathocles left his son Archagathus in command of Africa and, along with 2,000 troops, returned to his native city.

Chapter 14

The End of the War in Africa

Agathocles, meanwhile, having overcome all opposition in Africa, left the command of his army to his son Archagathus, and went back to Sicily, thinking that all he had done in Africa was as nothing, if Syracuse was still to be besieged.

Justin 22.8

While Agathocles had been continuing his campaigns of conquest in Africa, the situation in Sicily had continued to deteriorate. Xenodocus, general of the Akragantians, had continued his campaign by marching on Syracuse with an army of 10,000 infantry and 1,000 cavalry. The Syracusan generals had marched out to meet him with an army of 8,200 foot and 1,200 horsemen.[1] In the ensuing battle the Syracusans defeated Xenodocus and killed 1,500 of his army. The defeat convinced the people of Akragas to end their war with Syracuse and sue for peace. The news of this victory had not reached Agathocles before his departure.

Agathocles arrived in Sicily at Selinus. The city had been a subject of Carthage and, along with the nearby city of Heraclea, must have declared its independence as a result of Xenodocus' earlier campaigns. Agathocles intimidated both cities into submitting to him. He then marched north and won over the city of Thermae after giving the Carthaginian garrison safe conduct. Next he took Cephaloedium (Cefalu) and installed a Syracusan garrison. Leaving the north coast, Agathocles headed inland. He was repulsed at Centuripae when a plot to admit him into the city was discovered. A similar plot failed at Apollonia but Agathocles stormed the city and sacked it.

The Greek opposition to Agathocles had not ended, however, as Deinocrates and his army of oligarchic exiles were still in the field. Deinocrates decided that a change of image was necessary and 'proclaiming himself champion of the common liberty, caused many to flock to him from all sides; for some eagerly gave ear to his appeals because of the desire for independence inborn in all men, and others because of their fear of Agathocles.'[2] He quickly gathered together an army of 20,000 infantry and 1,500 cavalry, and marched against Agathocles. Despite his successes since returning to Sicily, Agathocles army was inferior in numbers and he retreated to Syracuse with Deinocrates in close pursuit.

In spite of Agathocles absence, the war in Africa continued to go well for the Syracusans. Archagathus sent an expedition into the interior under the command of Eumachus. He succeeded in capturing a number of cities, took much booty and won over a number of the Numidian tribes. The success of the campaign encouraged Archagathus to send Eumachus out on another expedition further into the interior. This time Eumachus met with mixed success, capturing some towns but failing at others, eventually being forced to withdraw when the tribes of the region formed an alliance against him. He began to retire back towards the coast, again accompanied by large amounts of plunder. There are a number of exotic tales about this journey, including the existence of three cities where the population shared their homes and food with apes whom they worshipped as gods.

Eventually the Carthaginan council appears to have recovered from the shock of Agathocles' victories and the coup of Bomilcar. They raised a force of 40,000 soldiers and divided it into three separate armies. These were sent out to recover their lost cities and to force the Syracusans to respond by lifting their blockade of the city. One army would operate along the coast, one in the immediate vicinity of Carthage and the third was sent into the interior to hunt down Eumachus. Archagathus was now in a dilemma. It would have been best to keep his smaller army together but this would allow the Carthaginians to dominate the open countryside and win over the Syracusans' allies. In the end Archagathus decided to divide his army in two. He would operate along the coast while another force would head into the interior. A garrison was left in Tunis to continue the blockade of Carthage. A better general might have kept his army united and hunted the Carthaginian armies down one at a time.

The Carthaginians had immediate success. The Syracusan army sent into the interior was ambushed along the way with more than 4,000 soldiers and its commander killed. The survivors fled over 100km to rejoin Archagathus. Another Carthaginian force lured Eumachus' force into an ambush by a part of the army pretending to flee before him. The Greeks were routed and forced to take refuge on a nearby hill which was without water. Once the Greeks were exhausted from thirst the Carthaginians attacked and overwhelmed them. Of the 8,400 Greeks in the army only seventy managed to escape.

The limited resources available to the Syracusans had always made the African campaign vulnerable to heavy losses. With perhaps as much as half his total force lost, Archagathus was forced to call off his campaigns and retreat to Tunis. The defeats caused the cities and tribes of Africa to abandon their alliances with the Syracusans. The three Carthaginian armies now converged on Tunis and set up separate camps to blockade the city. The formerly victorious Greeks were now shut off by both land and sea and began to suffer from hunger. Archagathus managed to get a message out to his father, imploring him to come to their rescue. In two short campaigns the Carthaginians had completed reversed their fortunes. The African territories were once again under their control and the remaining Syracusans under siege.

Despite his difficulties in dealing with Deinocrates, Agathocles decided that he must come to the rescue of his forces in Africa. He made ready a fleet of seventeen warships but was prevented from leaving by a blockading force of thirty Carthaginian vessels. Agathocles' luck again held as a reinforcement of eighteen warships from Italy managed to enter the harbour of Syracuse under the cover of night. The ships were Etruscan, a people who had traditionally been allies of the Carthaginians against the Greeks. The Carthaginians had, however, later aligned themselves with the Romans who were busily conquering the lands of the Eutruscans. At some unrecorded time, Agathocles might have formed an alliance with the Etruscans on the old basis that my enemy's enemy is my friend. It is also possible that the ships were simply hired mercenaries.

Agathocles now used the undiscovered ships to ambush the Carthaginian fleet. He set sail with his seventeen ships luring the Carthaginians into pursuing him. The Etruscan ships then emerged from hiding and Agathocles turned his ships about. Caught been two forces the Carthaginians fled but lost five ships captured by the enemy. The Carthaginian commander, fearing that his ship was about to be taken, committed suicide moments before his ship caught a favourable wind and escaped under sail.

The victory at sea persuaded Agathocles to delay his departure to Africa and renew the offensive in Sicily. It had other benefits in that now the naval blockade of the city was lifted, trade was able to return to the Syracuse. As a result, 'the people of Syracuse, goods being brought to them from all sides, in place of scarcity of provisions soon enjoyed an abundance of everything.'[3] Despite Agathocles' constant wars, Syracuse under his rule showed a remarkable ability to recover its wealth whenever things were going well. The archaeological and literary records show that the prosperity enjoyed by the city following the settlement of Timoleon, continued throughout Agathocles' rule.[4]

Agathocles sent an army commanded by Leptines to attack Akragas. Leptines plundered the countryside in an attempt to provoke the enemy to come out and decide the campaign in battle. The people of Akragas, despairing of the damage being done to their property, lost patience and ordered Xenodocus out to fight, even though his army was inferior in numbers. Diodorus uses this opportunity to again criticize the fighting spirit of the Akragantians, claiming that their force 'in morale was far inferior since the citizen army had been formed amid indulgence and a sheltered way of life and the other had been trained in military service in the field and in constant campaigns.'[5]

The Syracusans easily won the battle, killing 500 of the enemy. As a result the people of Akragas turned on Xenodocus and brought charges against him. Prudently, he departed the city and went into exile in Gela. There is no record of any settlement between the two cities but presumably Akragas was compelled to ally itself with, and accept the leadership of, Syracuse. Justin goes as far as to claim that after Agathocles' return 'all the cities of Sicily, having previously heard of his achievements in Africa, unanimously submitted to him; and being thus enabled to drive the Carthaginians from Sicily, he made himself master of the whole island.'[6] Although an exaggeration, since his return Agathocles had won over the important cities of Selinus, Heraclea, Thermae and Akragas, and lifted the Carthaginian blockade of Syracuse.

Only Deinocrates' exile army stood against him. It is possible that it was because of the continued opposition of Deinocrates, that Agathocles committed one last outrage in order to secure Syracuse before he departed. Agathocles gave a feast to celebrate the two victories before he left for Africa. According to Polyaenus, Agathocles had been informed that 'some of the Syracusan leaders intended to attempt a revolution.' During the celebration Agathocles behaved in his usual entertaining manner, playing the genial host he 'advanced into the midst of them, and sang, and played on the harp, and danced; while mirth and revelry prevailed around.'[7] Most importantly he encouraged everyone to drink up and 'giving men license to speak against him in their cups he used to discover exactly the opinion of each, since through wine the truth is brought to light without concealment.' Once he had learned who his enemies were, Agathocles later invited 500 of those most opposed to him to another banquet 'and surrounding them with suitable men from his mercenaries he slaughtered them all.' In this brutal manner Agathocles 'was taking very careful precautions lest, while he was absent in Libya, they should overthrow the tyranny and recall Deinocrates and the exiles. After he had made his rule secure in this way, he sailed from Syracuse.'[8] Agathocles could now return to Africa confident that the situation in Sicily was manageable for his commanders.

In 307, Agathocles returned to Africa. There he found that his army was demoralized by its defeats and on the verge of mutiny due to lack of pay and shortage of food. Agathocles summoned the army to a general assembly and there he told them frankly that he did not have enough money to pay them. Instead: 'pay was not to be asked of him, but to be taken from the enemy; that they must gain a common victory, and common spoil; and that they must continue to support him for a short time, till what remained of the war was finished, as they were certain that the capture of Carthage would satisfy all their desires.'[9] This device was common enough among cash strapped ancient commanders and is especially attributed to Agathocles.[10] It shows the faith his troops had in his ability that they at once agreed to follow him.

Agathocles gathered his forces and challenged the Carthaginians to battle. His army consisted of 6,000 Greek infantry, 6,000 mercenary infantry made up of Gauls, Samnites and Etruscans, and 1,500 cavalry. In addition he had an allied force of 10,000 Libyan infantry and a large force of Libyan chariots. The Libyans proved once again to be treacherous and withdrew to see which way the battle would go. The Carthaginians, who had occupied a strong position on some hills, were unwilling to risk a battle. All they needed to do was hold their positions while starvation and mutiny won the victory for them.

Agathocles decided that under the circumstances he must attack, whatever the odds, and force the Carthaginians to fight. At first the desperate uphill assault looked like succeeding, but eventually the Carthaginian advantages of numbers and position told. Agathocles' mercenaries lost heart and withdrew. He was forced to order the retreat of the whole army back to their camp, having achieved nothing and losing 3,000 dead in the battle and pursuit.

After the defeat, the situation of the Greeks looked hopeless but once again luck came to Agathocles aid. The Carthaginians celebrated their victory by sacrificing to their gods the most handsome of their prisoners. A sudden gust of wind caused the sacrificial fires to flare up and set fire to a hut. Carthaginian camps were notorious for their lack of organization and poor construction. The fire soon spread among the reed huts, killing many, destroying much equipment and causing panic.

Meanwhile 5,000 of the Greeks' erstwhile Libyan allies had decided to desert to the Carthaginians. As they approached the camp the guards believed they were they Greeks taking advantage of the fire and advancing to attack. The fire had caused a complete breakdown in the Carthaginian command. Learning of the column advancing on their camp some of the Carthaginians fled in panic while others advanced out to confront the Libyans whom they took to be the enemy. A fight took place in which many were killed. Those who had fled ran all the way back to Carthage, where they caused consternation as they spread news of the fire and supposed defeat by the Greeks. Over 5,000 Carthaginians were killed as a result of the fire, the fighting and accidents caused by their flight in the dark. Diodorus piously believed that the Carthaginians had: 'suffered due punishment on the spot for their cruelty to the captives, the impious act itself having brought about a punishment to match it.'[11]

The disaster in the Carthaginian camp may have been an ideal chance for Agathocles to attack, provided his defeated troops could be convinced to fight again. The Greeks were, however, also caught up in the confusion of the night. After their clash with the Carthaginians, the Libyans fled back towards the Greek camp. The nervous Greek sentries believed that they were the Carthaginians advancing to attack. Many of the already demoralized Greeks fled into the night where they too ran into groups of Libyans and fought them as the enemy. Once the morning had revealed the truth both sides set about gathering their scattered forces.

Following his defeat by the Carthaginians and the desertion of the Libyans, Agathocles' position in Africa was no longer tenable. His major problem in evacuating his army was a shortage of shipping and the Carthaginian control of the sea. Nor could he expect the Carthaginians, who held such a dominant position to come to terms. Agathocles therefore determined to escape by sea, taking only a few friends and his son Heracleides.

According to Diodorus Archagathus was to be left behind as Agathocles had begun to suspect his son of plotting against him. Archagathus, suspecting his father's design, betrayed him to the rest of the army who arrested him and placed him in irons. This version of events appears to be at odds with the description of Agathocles' nature and more in keeping with the paranoia attributed to Dionysius the Elder. On this occasion Justin's account, where Archagathus accompanies his father on his escape attempt but gets lost in the darkness would appear to be more plausible. Archagathus' eventual fate would also tend to support Justin's version of events.[12]

Whatever the truth, the troops captured Agathocles and bound him in chains. The sight of their ruler in shackles dismayed many of those still loyal to Agathocles and they demanded his release. Despite this generosity, Agathocles fled during the night and sailed away abandoning his army. Both of his sons were also left behind, most likely they had become separated from him in the dark. The forsaken soldiers vented the anger on Agathocles' sons and executed them. When Archagathus recognized his killer as 'Arcesilaus, a former friend of his father, asked him "what he thought Agathocles would do to the children of him by whom he was rendered childless?"' Arcesilaus replied, that 'he felt no concern, since he knew that his children would certainly survive those of Agathocles.'[13]

Arcesilaus' nonchalance may have been justified. Polybius records how: 'two brothers had been serving for some time under Hannibal, having adopted Carthage as their country, since their grandfather had been exiled because he was thought to have assassinated Agatharchus, one of the sons of Agathocles.'[14] After the executions, the soldiers elected new leaders and made peace with the Carthaginians. In return for handing over the cities they still held they would receive 300 talents, those who wished to do so entered service with the Carthaginians and rest were settled in Soluntum in Sicily. A few of Agathocles' garrisons remained loyal and refused to surrender. They were attacked and captured, their leaders crucified and the remainder sold as slaves.

Agathocles' escape can be dated to November of 307. After four years of campaigning his African expedition, so successful at first had ended in total failure. However it had always been a desperate venture, given the limited resources that Agathocles could commit to it. Continued success, in order to gain plunder and win over allies, was essential for its survival. Any major defeat, such as those suffered by Archagathus, could, and did, spell disaster. The superior wealth and resources of Carthage meant that all it had to do was survive and eventually the Greeks would be worn down. Perhaps the major cause of Agathocles' defeat was the continued domination of the sea by the Carthaginians. This ensured that Carthage could never be starved into surrender. The Syracusan force in Africa could expect little help from home and was always reliant on winning the alliance of the peoples of Africa. Once the Carthaginians gained the upper hand with their victories over Archagathus, this support vanished and the expedient was doomed.

From a different perspective, however, the campaign could be seen as a success. Four years earlier Syracuse had been isolated and under siege. Agathocles' invasion of Africa had forced the Carthaginians to abandon their siege and divert most of their resources to the fighting in Africa. After the initial raising of funds, Agathocles' expedition had been largely self-sufficient and had only involved about 4,000 Syracusan troops. The loss of his mercenary troops would not have unduly bothered Agathocles. By contrast, the devastation of their countryside had cost the Carthaginians greatly. According to Richard Miles this destruction and cost of the war had 'brought Carthage to the brink of financial ruin,'[15] as demonstrated by the dramatic devaluation of its coinage. Although Agathocles was no doubt disappointed that he had not been able to conquer Africa, his tyranny had survived and he would return to a much stronger Syracuse than he had left.

Perhaps the last word on Agathocles' failure should go to Diodorus who saw it as further proof of the existence of divine justice:

Fortune, as if of set purpose, displaying her peculiar power when a situation has become hopeless. After he had come to such a position of superiority and had murdered Ophellas although he was a friend and a guest, the divine power clearly showed that it established through his impious acts against Ophellas a portent of that which later befell him; for in the same month and on the same day on which he murdered Ophellas and took his army, he caused the death of his own sons and lost his own army. And what is most peculiar of all, the god like a good lawgiver exacted a double punishment from him; for when he had unjustly slain one friend, he was deprived of two sons, those who had been with Ophellas laying violent hands upon the young men. Let these things, then, be said as our answer to those who scorn such matters.[16]

Chapter 15

The Last Years of Agathocles' Rule

As he lay dying, he summoned the populace, denounced Archagathus for his impiety, aroused the masses to avenge him, and declared that he restored to the people their self-government.

Diodorus 21.16

Upon landing in Sicily, Agathocles found that the supremacy of Syracuse was still challenged by the army of Deinocrates. The renewal of trade had not yet allowed the economy to recover and the Syracusan war chest was almost empty. Desperate to raise money he resorted to the traditional expedient of sacking a city. After gathering together a force, he advanced on the allied city of Segesta, a city that contained a population of 10,000 inhabitants. The poor were slaughtered and the rich tortured to surrender their wealth. In Diodorus' account, lest we be too dazzled by the civilisation of the Greeks, he gives us a reminder of the violence and brutality that existed under the sophisticated veneer of some ancient societies:

Some of them he broke on the wheel, others he placed bound in the catapults and shot forth, and by applying knucklebones with violence to some, he caused them severe pain. He also invented another torture similar to the bull of Phalaris: that is, he prepared a brazen bed that had the form of a human body and was surrounded on every side by bars; on this he fixed those who were being tortured and roasted them alive, the contrivance being superior to the bull in this respect, that those who were perishing in anguish were visible.[1]

Once he had extracted the money, Agathocles murdered the men and sold the women and children into slavery. Agathocles then settled the city with a group of exiles and renamed it *Dicaeopolis*, 'Just City'. Not surprisingly the name did not endure and despite Agathocles' treatment the city continued to exist under its original name.

It is, however, unlikely that even someone as ruthless as Agathocles would have treated an allied city in such brutal manner. It is more likely that the city was either hostile, neutral or had broken its alliance with Syracuse. If so, then Agathocles response, although extreme, was justified by the standards of the time. Alexander the Great had dealt with Thebes in a similar manner less than thirty years earlier.

On learning of the murder of his sons, Agathocles is supposed to have ordered his brother, Antander, to execute the relatives of all those Syracusans who had accompanied him to Africa. Antander is reported to have murdered not only all their male relatives, including infants, but also their female relatives. The terror this caused in Syracuse was supposed to have been so great that the surviving friends and relatives of the victims, against all propriety, refused to claim the bodies lest they become associated with them. This is the last political massacre of Syracusans by Agathocles that is recorded by the ancient sources.

There may have been motive other than revenge for Agathocles' purge. His defeat in Africa undermined his reputation and thereby weakened his hold over Syracuse and the allied cities. One of Agathocles' commanders, Pasiphilus 'regarded the tyrant with contempt; and, deserting to Deinocrates and establishing friendship with him, he both kept a firm grip on the cities which had been entrusted to him and by alluring the minds of his soldiers with hopes alienated them from the tyrant.'[2] Deinocrates now ruled many of the Greek cities of Sicily and commanded an army of 23,000 men. This threat provoked Agathocles to secure control over his remaining allied cities with garrisons, always an unpopular move.

The loss of Africa, the death of his sons, the desertion of Pasiphilus and the growing strength of Deinocrates is supposed to have caused Agathocles to have an unusual crisis of confidence. He approached Deinocrates offering to surrender the tyranny of Syracuse and restore the democracy on the condition that he was allowed to retire in peace to rule Thermae and Cephaloedium. Diodorus expresses amazement as this turn of events as Agathocles: 'had shown himself resolute in every other situation and had never lost confidence in himself when his prospects were at their lowest, at this time became a coward.'[3]

Deinocrates had no intention of accepting these terms. Although officially he was 'called general of the exiles, he really possessed the authority of a king, his power being absolute.' He desired to replace Agathocles as tyrant, not to re-enter the city as a private citizen under a restored democracy, where 'in the elections he might be defeated by any chance demagogue.'[4] Deinocrates responded to Agathocles' advances by insisting that Agathocles quit Sicily completely and demanding his surviving children as hostages. Deinocrates' intransigent position roused Agathocles out of his melancholy. He sent messages to the exiles claiming that it was Deinocrates' ambition that prevented their return. It is possible that Agathocles was never genuine in his offers to resign, and by negotiating with Deinocrates was attempting to both buy time and expose his opponent's ambitions.

In order to free himself for the coming struggle against Deinocrates, Agathocles made peace with the Carthaginians

> on terms such that the Phoenicians should regain all the cities which had formerly been subject to them, and in return for them he received from the Carthaginians gold to the value of three hundred talents of silver (or, as Timaeus says, one hundred and fifty), and two hundred thousand measures of grain.[5]

Justin adds that 'Agathocles made peace with them on equal terms.'[6] From this statement, and Agathocles later campaigns, it would appear that it was agreed that the Halycus River was once again the border of Carthaginian territory. This peace held until Agathocles death in 289. It was probably this prolonged period of peace that finally allowed Syracuse, and the other Sicilian cities, to fully return to prosperity. The Carthaginians most likely agreed in order to prevent the drain of their resources to Sicily and allow their own economic recovery.

The following year, 305, Agathocles determined to confront Deinocrates, 'believing that it was necessary for him to fight a battle with them and stake everything on the result.' Agathocles' power had dwindled to the point where he could only raise an army of 5,000 infantry and 800 cavalry, most likely all Syracusans. Deinocrates, with an army of 25,000 infantry and 3,000 cavalry, confident in his numbers, advanced to meet Agathocles. The two sides met at Torgium, the location of which is unknown.

During the battle, Agathocles' tactic of undermining Deinocrates' credibility had the decisive effect. Over 2,000 of Deinocrates' troops switched sides, causing others to flee in dismay. The exiles' cavalry succeeded in fleeing the field but many of the infantry sought refuge in a hill fort where they were surrounded by the Syracusans. Agathocles offered them quarter but after they had surrendered he disarmed them and executed 4,000, possibly his most determined opponents. After this massacre Agathocles accepted the surrender of the surviving Syracusan exiles. He also came to terms with Deinocrates who re-entered his service and served him loyally for the rest of his reign.

Polyaenus records an incident where, after defeating the army of Leontini, Agathocles sends Deinocrates to the survivors to offer them terms, saying 'that it was his intention, in the preservation of his prisoners, to rival the glory of Dionysius, who after the battle at the river Eleporus preserved the lives of all the Italian prisoners he had taken.'[7] After their surrender, Agathocles ordered them to meet him un-armed and had his men kill them all. Polyaenus is not the most careful of compilers but it is possible that this tale refers to the above battle. Somewhere near Leontini would be a likely location for the battle. If Deinocrates did his deal with Agathocles prior to the surrender of the survivors, his word may have made the offer seem more credible.

It is very likely that Agathocles had subverted part of the enemy army before the battle, hence his confidence. The changing of sides of part, or sometimes all, of an army on the battlefield was not unknown during this period, when two rulers were engaged in a struggle for personal power. Many of the troops involved would have believed they were risking their lives merely to replace one tyrant with another. As Plutarch observed when commenting on such struggles: 'we see that kings have no reason to find fault with popular bodies for changing sides as suits their interests; for in doing this they are but imitating the kings themselves, who are their teachers in unfaithfulness and treachery, and think him most advantaged who least observes justice.'[8]

In a similar vein, Diodorus ends his account of this whole distasteful episode with the despairing observation that: 'indeed, this tyrant always scorned faith and his oaths; and he maintained his own power, not by the strength of his armed forces but by the weakness of his subjects, fearing his allies more than his enemies.'[9]

Agathocles followed up this victory by reasserting his rule over the Greek cities outside of Carthaginian control. Deinocrates embarked on a two year campaign, during which he finished off Pasiphilus and the remaining exiles and won back many of the cities. It is perhaps form this point on that Diodorus' and Polybius' accounts of the mildness of Agathocles' rule belong, with his internal enemies finally defeated and Syracuse enjoying prolonged prosperity.

In 307, Demetrius, son of the Successor commander Antigonus the One-Eyed, had won a great naval victory over Ptolemy at Salamis, off the island of Cyprus. This victory ensured their pre-eminence over the other Successors. When bringing the news to Antigonus, his courtier began his message with the salutation, 'Hail, King Antigonus' According to Plutarch it was from this moment on 'the multitude for the first time saluted Antigonus and Demetrius as kings.'[10] The scene was almost certainly stage-managed by Antigonus, as he and the other Successors had long adopted both the powers and trappings of monarchy. The title itself, however, had not been used since the murder of Alexander the Great's son four years earlier. Over the next three years all the Successor rulers would also adopt the title of king.

We know from Agathocles' dramatic scene during the mutiny in Tunis that he had already adopted the trappings of royalty by wearing purple. Although Diodorus describes Agathocles assuming the royal title soon after Demetrius, he is not always strict in his chronology when he inserts his digressions. It is perhaps now that he was once again the ruler of all the Sicilian cities outside of Carthaginian territory that Agathocles assumed the title of king, 'since he thought that neither in power nor in territory nor in deeds was he inferior to them, he called himself king.'[11]

The usual symbol of Hellenistic kingship was the wearing of a diadem – an embroidered white silk ribbon which ended in a knot and two fringed strips. For reasons of vanity, Agathocles decided not to adopt the diadem but continued to wear a laurel wreath, the symbol of an earlier priesthood, as it better covered his rapidly thinning hair. Julius Caesar was said to have worn a wreath for the same reason. Whether the mechanics of Agathocles' government of Syracuse changed after his adoption of the kingship is unknown but unlikely.

After he had described Deinocrates' campaigns, Diodorus lost interest in events in Sicily for the next three years, other than describing a raid by Agathocles on the island of Lipari. Unfortunately his later books, describing the final years of Agathocles' rule, have been lost. All that survive are the summaries of later Byzantine librarians. To this can be added Justin's account of his death and a few details of his final campaigns. It is, therefore, possible only to give the briefest outline of the final fifteen years of Agathocles' life. Justin's less dramatic version of events is generally more plausible than what remains of Diodorus' account.

Once Agathocles had regained control over the Greek cities of Sicily, like Dionysius the Elder before him, he attempted to add the Greek cities of Italy to his empire. As with his predecessor, he was aiming to build up his strength and revenues before attempting another war with Carthage. Although the Italian cities were under constant pressure from the tribes of southern Italy – the Bruttians, Lucanians and Apulians – they were still wealthy. As such they were seen as a rich source of revenue by a number of would-be conquerors.

Since the collapse of Syracusan power in Italy, the defence of the Greek cities had largely fallen to the leadership of the largest and wealthiest of them, Tarentum. Tarentum's leadership was, however, hamstrung by long term rivalries with the other cities. Nor was it powerful enough to impose its control effectively over the other cities, or to face the challenge alone. As a result, the Tarentines had developed a strategy of bringing to Italy forces and generals from Greece, using the wealth of the Italian cites to pay their expenses. This system had not provided any lasting results.

In 343 Tarentum appealed to Sparta for assistance in yet another war against the Lucanians. The Spartan king Archidamus answered the call and landed with an army. In 338 he was defeated and killed at the battle of Manduria by the Apulians. Archidamus was followed, in 334, by Alexander of Epirus who, after initial success, fell out with the Tarentines and built a new alliance centred on the city of Thurii. Two years later, he was betrayed, ambushed and killed by his Lucanian allies.

In 303 the Tarentines were threatened by both the Lucanians, and the newly emerging Italian power, the Romans. Initially the Tarentines had supported Rome's expansion, as they were attacking Tarentum's enemies. This benign attitude would when the Romans began to encroach into the Tarentines' sphere of influence.

The Tarentines again approached their founding city Sparta for assistance. They requested that the experienced general Cleonymus be sent to assist them, despite Cleonymus having been passed over as king in Sparta because of his violent nature. Cleonymus' arrival frightened the Lucanians into making peace. His first action was to capture the Greek city of Metapontum. Flushed with his success, Cleonymus' behaviour reverted to its true character He is said to have demanded 200 virgins as hostages and also extorted 600 talents in cash, an enormous sum, from Metapontum. Turning his back on his Spartan upbringing, he violated the maidens and wasted the money raised by his allies on a luxurious lifestyle.

Cleonymus now planned to use the wealth of Italy to build his own empire. He made grandiose plans to invade Sicily and overthrow Agathocles. Sensibly postponing this campaign, he instead captured Corcyra, an island off the west coast of Greece, and dreamed of creating a kingdom within Greece. As a result his Italian allies turned on him. In 302 Cleonymus returned to Italy and captured a number of cities including Thurii.

The Romans, using Cleonymus' behaviour as an excuse to intervene in the Greek area of southern Italy, marched against him. They defeated him in battle, forcing him to abandon his foothold in Italy and retreat back to Corcyra. From there he continued to ravage the eastern coast of Italy. His power was finally shattered when he was later ambushed and defeated by the Gauls, while raiding northern Italy.

Due to the chaos caused by Cleonymus, Tarentum was forced to accept the Roman conquests in Apulia and enter into a treaty with Rome. The full terms are not recorded but one clause is certain: the Romans agreed not to send ships east of the Cape of Lacinum (Capo Noto) or into the Bay of Tarentum. The Tarentines would have assumed that this meant that Rome thereby recognized their hegemony over the region. Such a concession had, however, never been a part of Roman policy, as they would later discover.

This is the situation that prevailed in Italy when Agathocles decided to invade. Neither of the accounts of Agathocles' campaigns in Italy is continuous or complete. Therefore only an outline of events can be attempted. Even the date is uncertain but they must have begun in either 301 or 300. Nor is there any mention of fighting against the nominal hegemon, Tarentum. Perhaps this is because Agathocles' initial campaign was against a common enemy, the Bruttians, who occupied the toe of Italy. In the preceding years they had expanded their power as they

seem to have been the bravest and most powerful people of the country, and to have been extremely ready to attack their neighbours; for they had driven the inhabitants of many of the Greek cities from

Italy, and had conquered in war the Lucanians their founders, and made peace with them on equal terms.[12]

Agathocles defeated the Bruttians and forced them into an alliance. At some stage he also made an alliance with Menedemus, the tyrant of Croton, possibly an old friend from Agathocles' period of exile in Italy. Agathocles' victories and alliances ensured that his hold over south-eastern Italy was secure enough for him to attempt to emulate Dionysius the Elder, and expand his empire into the Adriatic Sea. In 299, Agathocles intervened against the Macedonian king, Cassander, who was attempting to capture Corcyra. The inhabitants of the island had driven out Cleonymus a few years earlier, possibly with the help of Demetrius. Agathocles destroyed the Macedonian fleet but failed to take the opportunity to wipe out Cassander's army. As the island came into his possession, Agathocles must have come to some arrangement with Cassander. From an anecdote recorded by Plutarch, Agathocles' rule of the island appears to have been harsh. When the people of Corcyra complained, he told them that it was their own fault for giving shelter to the legendary hero, Odysseus, who later ravaged Sicily.[13]

On his return to Italy, Agathocles was forced to put down a mutiny of his mercenaries. In doing so he alienated the Bruttians and was defeated by them in battle. This defeat ended Agathocles' first campaign in Italy and he returned to Syracuse, probably in 298.

While in Syracuse, Agathocles continued to involve himself in the ongoing wars of the Successor kings. In 295 he completed an alliance with Pyrrhus, king of Epirus who had recently been restored to his throne with the assistance of King Ptolemy of Egypt. Agathocles married his daughter, Lanassa, to Pyrrhus and gave him Corcyra as a dowry. What Agathocles received in return, or hoped to gain, is unreported but it might have involved a three way deal with Ptolemy. At some stage during this period Agathocles received a new wife, Texena, the step-daughter of Ptolemy. It would appear that with his gains in both Sicily and Italy, and his victory over Cassander, Agathocles clearly saw himself as an equal player in the struggles of the other Hellenistic kings. Diodorus describes how, when fighting the troops of Cassander: 'the Siceliotes wished not only to be regarded as victors over the Carthaginians and the barbarians of Italy, but also to show themselves in the Greek arena as more than a match for the Macedonians, whose spears had subjugated both Asia and Europe.'[14]

Perhaps as a result of his alliance with Pyrrhus, Agathocles now felt strong enough to depose Menedemus and seize Croton. Gathering his naval forces, he reassured Menedemus, claiming that the fleet was escorting Lanassa in state to her wedding. Menedemus was therefore taken completely by surprise when the Syracusans attacked. They were able to land unopposed and besiege the city. Diodorus' description of the attack confirms how the art of siege-craft had continued to improve among the Greeks over the last century, due to the innovations of the tyrants of Syracuse and the Macedonian kings: 'he then invested the city and encircled it with walls from sea to sea, and by means of a stone-thrower and by tunnelling brought down in ruins the largest of the towers.'[15] Part of the population either panicked or betrayed the city to Agathocles by throwing open the gates. The Syracusans sacked the city and slaughtered the male population. Agathocles then made an alliance with the Apulians of south-eastern Italy, leaving them a number of vessels with which to carry out raids against his enemies. Little encouragement was probably needed, as the Apulians were an Illyrian people, notorious for their piracy and slave raiding. Leaving a garrison in Croton, Agathocles returned to Syracuse.

Agathocles continued to dabble in the wars of the other kings and in this he was assisted by the actions of his daughter, Lanassa. Although she had borne Pyrrhus a son named Alexander, she objected to her husband taking other non-Greek wives for diplomatic reasons. In about 293, Lanassa left Pyrrhus and retired to Corcyra. Once there, 'since she desired a royal marriage, she invited Demetrius, understanding that he, of all the kings, was most readily disposed to marry wives. So Demetrius sailed thither, married Lanassa, and left a garrison in the city.'[16]

Agathocles saw this as a chance to break his alliance with Pyrrhus and switch his allegiance to the rising star of Demetrius, who had seized the throne of Macedonia in 294 by murdering the son of Cassander. He sent his son, also named Agathocles, to the court of Demetrius. The treaty was made but Demetrius was just as ambitious and devious as Agathocles. Demetrius despised all 'those who gave the title of King to anyone except his father and himself, and was well pleased to hear his revellers pledge him as King, but Seleucus as Master of the Elephants, Ptolemy as Admiral, Lysimachus as Treasurer, and Agathocles of Sicily as Lord of the Isles.'[17] Agathocles was reported to be amused by this conceit. Demetrius, always ambitious, sent an ambassador, Oxythemis, to Syracuse, 'ostensibly to receive pledges of the alliance, in reality to spy out Sicily.'[18]

With many of the Greek cities of Italy and Sicily now firmly under his control, Agathocles looked once more to his ambition of conquering Africa. Realizing that it was Carthage's naval dominance that had allowed the city to survive his earlier siege, Agathocles determined to build a fleet large enough to challenge them at sea. This ambitious plan did not come to fruition before Agathocles' death, owing to further events in Italy.

The Bruttians had broken their treaty and commenced to attack the Greek cities of Italy. In desperation, Tarentum now turned to Agathocles for assistance. He responded to the call by raising a large army of 30,000 infantry and 3,000 cavalry, and crossing over into Italy. His fleet was sent to raid Bruttian territory but lost most of its ships in a storm. Agathocles took the city of Hipponium by breaching its walls with artillery. The Bruttians sued for terms and surrendered 600 hostages. During the negotiations Agathocles fell seriously ill, 'being affected by the distemper through his whole body, and a pestilential humour spreading through all his nerves and joints, he was tormented, as it were, by an intestine war among all his members.'[19] As a result of this illness he was forced to return to Syracuse, leaving an occupying army in Italy. The Bruttians, apparently as faithless as their enemy, once again broke their treaty, defeated the Syracusans and recovered their hostages. With this victory they 'freed themselves from the domination of Agathocles.'[20]

After returning to Syracuse, Agathocles' condition continued to decline. In such situations contention invariably arose between the potential heirs to a throne. In this case the rivalry was between his son Agathocles and his grandson Archagathus – the son of the Archagathus who had died in Africa. Archagathus the younger had earlier commanded Agathocles' troops in Italy and was now the commander of his forces in Sicily. Diodorus claims that he was very young to hold such a position but 'in manliness and fortitude he far surpassed ordinary expectations.'[21]

Little is known of Agathocles' personal life other than that he married at least three times. His known wives were: the unnamed widow of Damas, Alicia, the step-mother who supposedly had an affair with Archagathus, and Texena. From these unions six children are recorded. Archagathus and Heracleides must have been the children of his first marriage. Texena bore him two sons. The mother of his other son, Agathocles, and Lanassa is not recorded. It could have been either Damas' widow or Alicia.

Agathocles favoured his son, Agathocles, to be his heir and announced this to the Syracusans. He sent him to the camp of Archagathus near Mount Aetna with orders that Archagathus hand over command of the army to Agathocles. Archagathus had no intention of surrendering his power; he gave a feast in honour of the younger Agathocles, got him drunk and murdered him. The body was thrown into the sea but washed ashore and was recognized. Archagathus was then declared to be king by his troops.

When news of the murder was brought to the dying Agathocles he realized that he could not protect his new wife and their two infant sons from the ambition of Archagathus. He ordered them to escape to Egypt, along with all his wealth. His wife, Texena, refused to abandon her husband, saying that: 'By marrying him, she not only engaged to share his good fortune, but all his fortune'[22] Agathocles insisted that they escape. In one of his few passages sympathetic to Agathocles, Justin describes the pathos of their final goodbye:

> The little children, at parting, embraced and clung to their father with doleful lamentations; while the wife, who was to see her husband no

more, could not desist from kissing him. Nor were the tears of the old man less moving; the children wept for their dying father, the father for his banished children. They bewailed the forlorn condition of their parent, a sick old man; he lamented that his offspring, born to the prospect of a throne, should be left in want. At the same time the whole palace resounded with the cries of those who were witnesses to so cruel a separation. The necessity for departure, however, at length put a stop to their weeping, and the death of the prince followed the leave-taking of his children.[23]

Diodorus has a somewhat different account of Agathocles last days. After his sack of Segesta, Agathocles took as a slave into his personal household one of the survivors named Menon. Due to his physical beauty he became one of the king's favourites. Although he outwardly appeared to accept his lot, 'the disaster to his city and the outrage to his person produced a rankling enmity to the king, and he seized an opportunity to take his revenge.'[24] Archagathus persuaded Menon to poison the king on the same night that he would murder the son. Diodorus describes the king's murder:

Now it was the king's habit after dinner always to clean his teeth with a quill. Having finished his wine, therefore, he asked Menon for the quill, and Menon gave him one that he had smeared with a putrefactive drug. The king, unaware of this, applied it rather vigorously and so brought it into contact with the gums all about his teeth. The first effect was a continuous pain, which grew daily more excruciating, and this was followed by an incurable gangrene everywhere near the teeth.[25]

After learning of his son's murder, Agathocles still had enough energy to summon the people, denounce Archagathus and call on them to avenge him. As a final gesture of defiance against his grandson, he announced the end of the kingship and a return to the democracy. This was unwelcome news to anyone who had designs on ruling Syracuse. The envoy of King Demetrius, Oxythemis, supposedly murdered the king by placing the still living, but paralyzed, Agathocles on his pyre and setting it ablaze. Due to his condition Agathocles was unable to call for help and was burned alive.

Diodorus delights in the divine justice of the manner of Agathocles' death. 'Agathocles had committed numerous and most varied acts of slaughter during his reign, and since to his cruelty towards his own people he added impiety towards the gods, the manner of his death was appropriate to his lawless life.'[26] It is generally considered that on this occasion Justin's account is the more believable and that Agathocles died of his disease, most likely cancer of the mouth.

Agathocles died at the age of seventy-two, having ruled Syracuse for twenty-eight years. Diodorus, in his summing up of Agathocles' life, acknowledges the difficulty in assessing his career due to the biased nature of the earlier writers. He admits that Timaeus is not to be trusted as 'the greater part of his history of Agathocles consists of lying propaganda against the ruler because of personal enmity.'[27] Other historians, particularly Callias, are criticized for being too generous. This makes any overall appraisal of his rule a difficult enterprise. Opinions are divided among both ancient and modern writers. Depending on the point of view of the author he has been described at one extreme as the worst tyrant possible or, at the other, as a heroic character, the saviour of Hellenistic Sicily and brutal only in the pursuit of his ideals.

As a general Agathocles was courageous and energetic but not always successful in the field. It is perhaps his ability to capture cities where he stands out. Diodorus describes him as using all the techniques, particularly artillery, in breaching the walls of strong positions such as Croton and Utica. Lack of numbers prevented him from ever seriously being able to assault Carthage. As a commander he is best remembered for his inspired strategic decision to save Syracuse by invading Africa. Although ultimately unsuccessful, this campaign probably saved Syracuse from being captured by the Carthaginians. By weakening Carthaginian power it also laid the foundation for Agathocles' later reconquest of eastern Sicily.

In summing up his career it is perhaps best to compare the position of Syracuse when he came to power to that it held when he died. In 317 Syracuse was racked by civil war between political factions, one of which had allied itself with the old enemy, the Carthaginians. It had lost its leadership of the Greek cities and had a Carthaginian army on its doorstep. By the end of his reign Syracuse was once again the undisputed leader of the Sicilian Greeks, the Carthaginians had been forced back behind the Halycus River and Syracuse controlled a number of Italian cities.

The last seventeen years of peace with Carthage had also led to era of prosperity for the Sicilians, and is often described as another golden age. Agathocles had used this period to embark on a round of building in the city, particularly in the much needed repair and strengthening of the city's fortifications. On Ortygia he built a public banqueting hall known as the 'Hall of the Sixty Couches' which was then largest and grandest building in the city. Even his arch enemy Timaeus admitted that Syracuse was 'the greatest of the Grecian towns. It was indeed a most beautiful city; and its admirable citadel, its canals distributed through all its districts, its broad streets, its porticoes, its temples, and its walls, gave Syracuse the appearance of a most flourishing state.'[28]

Agathocles' monuments to himself were all supposed to have been destroyed after his death but at least one survived. Two centuries later Cicero saw a picture in the Temple of Athena on Ortygia in which: 'there was a cavalry battle of their king Agathocles, exquisitely painted in a series of pictures, and with these pictures the inside walls of the temple were covered. Nothing could be more noble than those paintings; there was nothing at Syracuse that was thought more worthy going to see.'[29]

All this would lead to the conclusion that, for the majority of Syracusans, Agathocles' reign was a success. Unfortunately for them his good work was undone by the struggle for succession that broke out during his final few weeks of his life. After his death civil war would once again break out in the city, Syracuse's leadership would collapse and the Greek cities would fall under the control of a number of petty tyrants. The Carthaginians would take advantage of the weakness of the Greeks to again impose their control over much of eastern Sicily. The Sicilians would be forced to once more look to Greece for a potential saviour to free them from Carthaginian domination.

Chapter 16

The Invitiation to King Pyrrhus

But in future, if they were wise, they would not admit any one of the kings into their city nor open their gates to him.

Plutarch, *Pyrrhus* 12

After the death of Agathocles, Syracuse and the Greek cities of Sicily once again descended into a series of costly wars between petty tyrants. The main source that survives for this period is a brief summary of Diodorus. As a result, only a bare outline of events can be reconstructed.

Menon, the supposed assassin of Agathocles, had fled the city to join his co-conspirator, Archagathus. However, Menon held his own ambitions to rule Syracuse. He murdered his erstwhile ally and won over Archagathus' army. Presumably it was comprised mostly of mercenaries whose loyalty was easily bought, as it is difficult to believe that an Elymian ex-slave could win over an army consisting of mostly Syracusan citizens.

The new democracy in Syracuse had celebrated its freedom by confiscating the property of Agathocles and tearing down his statues. Although Agathocles was a demagogue who appears to have ruled largely in favour of the poor, he shared the fate of most dead or deposed tyrants. Regardless of how he had acted during his life, he would be hated by all but his most fervent supporters after his death. The Syracusans appointed another Hicetas as general and ordered him to destroy the army of Menon. Menon's army must have been smaller than that of Hicetas, as he refused to settle the issue in battle but instead conducted a skilful guerrilla campaign.

The Carthaginians, learning of the death of Agathocles and the chaos it had caused, decided it was a favourable time to re-impose their control over the eastern part of the island. Seventeen years of peace had no doubt allowed them to recover economically. Justin states that they, 'thinking that an opportunity was afforded them of securing the whole island, crossed over to it with a great force, and reduced several cities.'[1] The Carthaginians marched against Syracuse and due to their 'vastly superior forces ... the Syracusans were compelled to give four hundred hostages to the Phoenicians, to make an end of hostilities, and to restore the exiles.'[2] As a result of the agreement the Syracusans were also forced to allow Menon's mercenaries to settle within the city.

The entry of the exiled oligarchs and the mercenaries into the city was a sure recipe for political turmoil. This is quite possibly the result that the Carthaginians had intended, as a divided Syracuse could not effectively lead the Greek opposition. Once settled within the city, the mercenaries demanded to be made citizens. The granting of citizenship to outsiders was very rare in Greek cities and considered to be socially disruptive. It was also a policy that was carried out overwhelmingly by tyrants, as such new citizens would be beholden to the ruler.[3] In this case the mercenaries' demands met with even more resistance, as most were non-Greek Campanians from Italy. Not surprisingly the Syracusans refused the demands of the mercenaries and armed conflict broke out within the city. Eventually a committee of elder statesman managed to broker an agreement between the factions. The mercenaries were given time to sell up their property on the condition that they leave Syracuse and return to Italy.

After leaving Syracuse the mercenaries were welcomed into Messene as friends and allies. The Campanians betrayed their hosts, as their kinsmen had a century earlier at Entella, by seizing the city:

> After being admitted as friends and occupying the city, they first expelled or massacred the citizens and then took possession of the wives and families of the dispossessed victims, just as chance assigned them each at the time of the outrage. They next divided among themselves the land and all other property.[4]

The Campanian occupiers of Messene became known as the Mamertines, after Mamertus, their God of War.

In either 288 or 287, the democracy in Syracuse was again overthrown and Hicetas became the new tyrant of Syracuse. Coins minted by Hicetas show that unlike most of his contemporaries he did not adopt the title of king. Throughout Sicily tyrants seized power in a number of cities. One of these tyrants was Phintias who had seized power in Akragas and later annexed Gela and a number of other cities. The old rivalry between the cities was still there and war broke out between Hicetas and Phintias. Both sides pillaged one another's territory, causing great destruction. Eventually the two armies fought a battle somewhere near the modern city of Ragusa where Hicetas defeated Phintias. Made confident by his victory Hicetas then attacked the Carthaginians but was badly beaten at Terias River.

Perhaps as a consequence of this defeat, Hicetas was overthrown after nine years of rule and replaced as tyrant by Thoenon. It is usually considered that Hicetas, as an elected official of the democracy, had been another demagogue and Thoenon an oligarch, but as with so much of this period, this cannot be certain.

Perhaps one of the major consequences of the death of Agathocles was the loss of the Syracusan possessions in Italy. Without his strong leadership the Lucanians and Bruttians again began to put pressure on the Greek cities. Tarentum tried to fill the void left by Agathocles but was not powerful enough. In 283 Rome was at war with the Lucanians and Bruttians. In desperation, the Greek city of Thurii turned to them for help. The Romans placed a garrison in Thurii and defeated the Lucanians in battle. Locri, Croton and Rhegium soon followed suit and allied themselves with the Romans. The Roman successes in southern Italy meant the end of Syracusan power in the region forever. No longer could the rulers of Syracuse exploit the wealth of the Italian cities to contribute to paying for their armies.

Meanwhile in Akragas, Phintias had shown himself to be the worst sort of tyrant. He had forcibly relocated the people of Gela to a new city which he had named after himself. As a result, 'since he had shown himself a bloodthirsty murderer, all the cities subject to him came to loathe him and drove out their garrisons, the first to revolt being the people of Agyrium.' Diodorus again takes the opportunity to mention his native city. The revolt humbled the tyrant who 'changed his ways, and by a more humane rule held his subjects under control.'[5] Phintias later died while hunting wild boar, supposedly after dreaming that this would be his fate. He was succeeded by another Sostratus, most likely the grandson of Agathocles' old enemy of the same name who had sought refuge in Akragas. If so, it is possible that he too was a leader of the oligarchic faction.

War once again broke out between the new rulers of Syracuse and Akragas. Sostratus marched on Syracuse with an army of 10,000 men and soon captured the mainland part of the city. Thoenon, also with an army of 10,000 men was forced to retreat to Ortygia. As both armies were evenly matched it is difficult to understand how Sostratus managed to capture the city. The most likely explanation is that he was assisted by the supporters of his grandfather, personal relationships being so important in the politics of the Greeks. Once again Syracuse was at war with itself, which allowed the Carthaginians to seize control of most of Sicily.

As had become traditional in times of crisis, the Syracusans now looked abroad for support and a saviour. The traditional sources for such persons, Corinth and Sparta, were no longer willing or capable of providing any assistance. Since the rise of Macedonia under Philip and Alexander the Great, the era of individual Greek states being powers was over in the eastern Mediterranean. Those cities that had managed to cling to their freedom were too hard pressed fighting off the ambitious Macedonian kings to be interested in events in the distant west. There was, however, a potential saviour closer to home. Since 280, Pyrrhus, King of Epirus and

Agathocles' old ally, had been successfully fighting the Romans on behalf of the Tarentines.

Exhausted by their struggle and fearful of the advances of the Carthaginians the two contestants decided to send an embassy to Pyrrhus, with an invitation to come to Sicily. There is some evidence that this approach was a renewal of an earlier invitation made by Hicetas, perhaps after his defeat at Terias River.[6] Plutarch claims that the delegation was joined by representatives from Leontini and they: 'offered to put into his hands the cities of Akragas, Syracuse, and Leontini, and begged him to help them to drive out the Carthaginians and rid the island of its tyrants.'[7] This last request is unlikely, as all the delegates represented ruling tyrants. Plutarch has a tendency to exaggerate the anti-tyrant credentials of his heroes.

Pyrrhus of Epirus was one of those larger than life, mercurial characters that the wars of the Successors made possible. Epirus was a kingdom of the northwest of Greece, and included much of modern Albania. According to legend it was founded by Neoptolemeus, the son of the legendary hero Achilles. For much of its history it was a mainly rural kingdom and despised by the more urban Greeks to the south, who considered its population to be little more than barbarians.

Epirus had been drawn into the affairs of the newly emergent power of Macedon when Philip II had married the Epirot princess Olympias. She would become the mother of Alexander the Great. During his reign, 356–339, Philip completely reformed the Macedonian army. The infantry, who previously had been considered little more than a rabble, had been armed with a new weapon, a 6m-long pike, and taught to fight in close order. Held in two hands, the weapon projected about four metres from the holder, with the blades of the first five ranks reaching beyond the first rank. This gave it a huge advantage over troops armed with shorter weapons, including the Greek hoplite with his three metre long spear. Philip had also rearmed his cavalry with lances, about four metres long, replacing the shorter spears and javelins of most other cavalry, and turning them into genuine shock troops.

At some stage the kings of Epirus had reformed their army, which had also been considered to be a rabble, in the same manner as Philip. The most likely candidate was King Alexander of Epirus who had previously campaigned in Italy, 334–331, on behalf of Tarentum. This is not certain, but the reforms had certainly been carried out by the time of Pyrrhus' Italian campaign. In addition to these troop types, Pyrrhus' army also included another weapon new to the battlefields of the Greeks and Macedonians, the war elephant. The main advantages of the elephant were its size and the panic it induced in troops unfamiliar with it, especially cavalry, as their horses were afraid of the beasts. Its presence in Sicily would have a profound effect on his Carthaginian enemies.

Pyrrhus was born in 319, the son of Aeacides who became joint king of Epirus soon after Pyrrhus' birth. At this time the kingship of Epirus was divided and had largely become a plaything of various stronger powers, particularly the neighbouring Macedonian rulers. When he was three years of age Pyrrhus and his family were forced to flee the kingdom and he took refuge with the Illyrians, a non-Greek people to the north of Epirus.

In 307, after eight years of exile, Pyrrhus was returned to Epirus, probably as joint king, by an armed intervention of the Illyrian king, Glaucias. In 302 he was again driven from his kingdom by a rebellion of his subjects. He fled to seek refuge in Greece with Demetrius, who had married his sister a year earlier.

From there Pyrrhus accompanied Demetrius to join Antigonus the One-eyed in Asia. Antigonus and Demetrius were two of the foremost generals of the Successor period. Here he would have furthered his military education, especially in the rapidly developing art of siegecraft. Pyrrhus was present when Antigonus finally confronted his foes at the battle of Ipsus, the largest of the battles of the Successors, fought somewhere in Phrygia in 301. Pyrrhus is supposed to have won himself a enduring reputation for courage by fighting bravely during the battle. Antigonus is reputed to have observed that Pyrrhus would be the greatest general of his time if he survived long enough, a tribute to both his theoretical knowledge of military affairs and to his renowned personal courage. Later commentators would share Antigonus' opinion, with the great Carthaginian general Hannibal declaring 'that the foremost of all generals in experience and ability was Pyrrhus, that Scipio was second, and he himself third.'[8] With such a reputation there is little wonder that the Sicilians were keen to recruit him.

After Antigonus' defeat and death at Ipsus, Pyrrhus was sent to Egypt as a hostage by Demetrius. There he had been cultivated by Ptolemy as a useful asset in the ongoing struggles between the rival kings and married to his daughter. In 297 Ptolemy funded an expedition to return Pyrrhus to the throne of Epirus as a threat against the Macedonian king, Cassander.

Cassander soon after died and the throne of Macedonia was seized by Demetrius. In 288 Pyrrhus joined a coalition of kings which drove Demetrius out of Macedonia. As a reward Pyrrhus received half of the kingdom, with the other half going to Lysimachus. This agreement did not last and in 284 Pyrrhus was driven out of Macedonia by Lysimachus. Pyrrhus, like all his rival kings, was ruthlessly ambitious and always looking to expand his empire. At the end of 281, Pyrrhus, like his predecessor Alexander of Epirus, received an invitation to come to Italy to campaign on behalf of Tarentum against the increasingly acquisitive Romans. Earlier that year the Romans had invaded Tarentine territory and the war was going badly for the Greeks who were completely outmatched by the power of Rome. It is perhaps a sign of their desperation that they would once again risk calling in a foreign king, after their bad experiences with Alexander of Epirus and Cleonymus.

Pyrrhus, whose ambitions in Greece were limited by the power of Lysimachus, decided that the offer presented a new opportunity to expand his realm to include the wealthy cities of Italy. He could then use their revenues as a resource for further conquests. The extent of his ambition is best described in a conversation he had with his friend and chief diplomat Cineas. In this Pyrrhus described how defeating the Romans would be just a stepping stone along the road of conquest. Once the Romans were defeated he would take all Italy, Sicily and finally conquer Carthage. Then he would finally retire to a peaceful life of luxury. Cineas responded by pointing out that: 'Surely this privilege is ours already, and we have at hand, without taking any trouble, those things to which we hope to attain by bloodshed and great toils and perils, after doing much harm to others and suffering much ourselves.'[9]

Cineas was a follower of a new school of philosophy based on the teachings of Epicurus. As an ethical guideline, Epicurus emphasized avoiding pain, experiencing happiness and not inflicting pain on others. Happiness depended upon a person's simple needs, prudence in all things, friendship, kindness, a pain-free body and tranquillity of mind. Epicureans tended to avoid participating in politics since doing so often meant doing harm to others.

In many ways Epicurus' philosophy was a response to the rise of the tyrants and Macedonian kings, and the wars of destruction their ambitions had unleashed on the Greek world. Under such circumstances one could best avoid pain by seeking contentment in a life of seclusion. These ideals were in conflict with those of both democracy and aristocracy. Democrats despised citizens who did not participate in politics as being useless to the people. Greek and Roman aristocrats lived in a world where glory and reputation were attained largely by political advancement and military conquest. Both were essential for one's own reputation and one's heirs' position in society. Plutarch describes a debate between Cineas and the Roman Consul Fabricius where the latter scoffs at Epicurus' ideas: 'O Hercules, may Pyrrhus and the Samnites cherish these doctrines, as long as they are at war with us.'[10]

In 280 Pyrrhus and a force consisting of twenty elephants, 3,000 horse, 20,000 heavy infantry, 2,000 archers, and 500 slingers crossed over to Tarentum to join the 3,000 troops he had sent ahead. Most of the heavy foot would have been Macedonian and Epirot pikemen, although a few were mercenaries. Before agreeing to enter Italy, Pyrrhus had been able to drive a hard bargain and to make a number of demands on the Tarentines. They must pay the costs of the war, give him supreme command of the allied forces and, most importantly, allow him to place a garrison inside the city. In return the king promised to remain in Italy no longer than was necessary. Although Pyrrhus would, of course, decide how long this was to be.

In 280 Pyrrhus, with an army consisting of his own force and the allied Tarentines, defeated a Roman army at the Battle of Heraclea in southern Italy. Despite winning the battle, his losses, particularly among his own Epirot troops, were heavy. Pyrrhus commented after the battle that 'if we ever conquer again in like fashion, it will be our ruin.'[11] This is the origin of the modern expression 'Pyrrhic victory', although the ancient Greeks referred to them as Cadmean victories. Despite defeat, again the Romans refused to negotiate any settlement other than that Pyrrhus retreat completely from Italy.

Pyrrhus advanced on Rome, hoping that they would accept defeat and come to terms, as most Greek cities would have. He had, however, seriously underestimated both Rome's determination and power. The Romans called in all their detached forces and nearly trapped Pyrrhus before the heavily fortified city. He was forced to retreat back to Tarentum. Rome's ability to recover from defeat and raise new armies from its enormous manpower surprised many of its enemies. Cineas compared it to the legendary monster, the Hydra: 'since the consul already had twice as many soldiers collected as those who faced their enemies before, and there were many times as many Romans still who were capable of bearing arms.'[12] This was an ability that would continue to confound Rome's enemies for decades to come.

The next year Pyrrhus again attacked the Romans and defeated them in the Battle of Asculum, in Apulia. Although victorious, again his losses were heavy and he was wounded. Once again the Romans refused to negotiate any settlement other than Pyrrhus' retreat from Italy. In despair at being unable to achieve anything against the Romans, Pyrrhus returned to winter quarters in Tarentum. Pyrrhus' Italian campaign perhaps typifies the characterization of him in the ancient sources. He was able to win brilliant victories but unable to use them consolidate any lasting gains.

While Pyrrhus was wintering in Tarentum and pondering his next move, two opportunities for new conquests arose. Ptolemy Ceraunus, the new king of Macedonia, had died in battle against the forces of the invading Gauls. There also came the embassy from the Sicilians with their offer to place their cities under the command of Pyrrhus, provided that he drove the Carthaginians from the island. Plutarch claims that, 'Pyrrhus rated Fortune soundly because occasions for two great undertakings had come to him at one time and thinking that the presence of both meant the loss of one, he wavered in his calculations for a long time.'[13]

In the end the lure of the fabled wealth of Sicily proved far more attractive to Pyrrhus than a return to a Macedonia that had been recently devastated by an invasion of the Gauls. Pyrrhus possibly hoped, at least initially, that he could create a Sicilian kingdom, using the claims of his son, Alexander, a grandson of Agathocles. If the ancient sources are to be believed, Pyrrhus was already dreaming of emulating his former father-in-law Agathocles and invading Africa. As he told Cineas: 'For who could keep his hands off Libya, or Carthage, when that city got within his reach, a city which Agathocles, slipping stealthily out of Syracuse and crossing the sea with a few ships, narrowly missed taking?'[14]

As was his usual practice Pyrrhus sent Cineas to Sicily to prepare for his arrival. The Tarentines, learning of Pyrrhus' plans to move his operations to Sicily, were irate as his plan to abandon them. They demanded that he either continue the war against the Romans, the task for which he had been invited, or else withdraw completely from their territory. 'To this demand he made no very gracious reply, but ordering them to keep quiet and await his convenience, he sailed off.'[15] Pyrrhus had a well-deserved reputation for his lack of tact, a trait which would serve him badly in Sicily.

Pyrrhus ignored the demands of the Tarentines and ensured his continued control by imposing strong garrisons within the allied Italian cities, placing more than half of his Epirot troops in the cities. Such were the risks for the independent Greek *cities* when they invited foreign kings into their cities and allowed them to install a garrison. The Syracusans would be risking a similar fate by handing over command to Pyrrhus, but they most likely hoped that he would be another Timoleon, waging war for them and then conveniently retiring.

The Carthaginians did not remain idle while the Sicilians were making their offers to Pyrrhus. They dispatched a general, Mago, to the Romans, offering to send 120 ships to their aid. He addressed the Senate, saying that 'the Carthaginians were much concerned that they should be distressed by war in Italy from a foreign prince; and that for this reason he had been despatched to assist them; that, as they were attacked by a foreign enemy, they might be supported by foreign aid.'[16] It is probably as a result of this embassy that the Romans renewed their treaty with the Carthaginians for the final time. The terms of the pact included that:

If they make an alliance against Pyrrhus, both shall make it an express condition that they may go to the help of each other in whichever country is attacked. No matter which require help, the Carthaginians are to provide the ships for transport and hostilities, but each country shall provide the pay for its own men. The Carthaginians, if necessary, shall come to the help of the Romans by sea too, but no one shall compel the crews to land against their will.[17]

Having secured the new alliance, Mago then sailed to Tarentum and with:

With the cunning of a Carthaginian, went privately, a few days after, to Pyrrhus, as if to be a peace-maker from the people of Carthage, but in reality to discover the king's views with regard to Sicily, to which island it was reported that he was sent for; since the Carthaginians had the same reason for sending assistance to the Romans, namely that Pyrrhus might be detained by a war with that people in Italy, and prevented from crossing over into Sicily.[18]

The Carthaginians continued their efforts to build an alliance against Pyrrhus. They succeeded in making an agreement with the Mamertines of Messene. In an attempt to secure the straits between Italy and Sicily they launched an attack with their new allies the Romans on Rhegium, held by a garrison of Roman deserters. This attack failed, so instead the fleet was sent to Messene in order to guard against the expected crossing of Pyrrhus.

Before leaving Italy Pyrrhus had done all he could to secure his position in Italy. At the last minute he appears to have decided that as he had been invited to Sicily by a group of aristocratic tyrants, Alexander, the grandson of their old enemy Agathocles, might be a political liability rather than an asset. For the time being he left Alexander in command of the garrison of Locri. Pyrrhus probably sailed to Sicily with great expectations of finding easier conquests there than Italy had provided.

Chapter 17

Pyrrhus' Sicilian Campaigns

After he had brought under his power all Sicily with the exception of Lilybaeum, the one city the Carthaginians still held, he assumed the arrogance of a tyrant.

Dionysius of Halicarnassus 20.8

In the summer of 378 Pyrrhus sailed for Sicily with a fleet of sixty warships and transports from Tarentum. The historian Appian records his invasion force as including only his elephants and 8,000 cavalry.[1] The latter figure is improbable and is most likely the result of an error in copying Appian's text. The force is usually considered to have consisted of either 8,000 men in total or 8,000 infantry plus the cavalry. As Pyrrhus had left half of his Epirots in Italy, the remainder must have made up most of this force.

Meanwhile the Carthaginians had not been inactive. They had advanced on Syracuse with an army of 50,000 men and 100 ships. Once there they besieged the city and pillaged the countryside. The divided and exhausted Syracusans were unable to mount an aggressive defence. Despite having a fleet of 140 warships, presumably the remains of the fleet Agathocles had built to invade Africa, they lacked the will and resources to put to sea and combat the Carthaginian blockade. Instead they huddled behind their walls and 'pinned their hopes on Pyrrhus.'[2]

Pyrrhus sailed first to Locri. From there he evaded the Carthaginian fleet waiting at Messene by avoiding the Straits. He sailed further south and, emulating Timoleon, landed first at Tauromenium, where the local tyrant had already declared his allegiance to him. Next he sailed to Catane where the citizens welcomed him as a liberator and presented him with golden crowns. Here he disembarked his army and received reinforcements from the two cities, although this is unlikely to have been more than a few thousand men. Pyrrhus did not linger in either city but, hoping to catch the Carthaginians by surprise, marched on Syracuse.

Pyrrhus' rapid advance had caught the Carthaginians unprepared, and a part of their fleet, thirty ships, had been sent away. When Pyrrhus fleet sailed into the harbour prepared to do battle the overawed Carthaginians refused to engage. Pyrrhus landed on Ortygia and, as had been promised, accepted control of the island from Thoenon. Sostratus soon followed suit by handing over control of the rest of the city to the king. At this point all was going well, as 'Pyrrhus effected a reconciliation between Thoenon and Sostratus and the Syracusans and restored harmony, thinking to gain great popularity by virtue of the peace.'[3] The resources of a now united Syracuse were added to the king's forces. This included the fleet, the arsenal of Ortygia with its siege engines and artillery, perhaps the 20,000 troops that had been commanded by the rival tyrants and 'the money in the treasury'[4]

One of the ships of the Syracusan fleet was an enormous *enneres,* a 'niner', which Pyrrhus took as his own flagship. The active part of the Syracusan fleet, combined with the ships of the Tarentines would now have been more than a match for the 70 remaining Carthaginian vessels. Pyrrhus' swift capture of Syracuse caused the Carthaginians to withdraw both their fleet and army from the outskirts of the city without a fight. Many modern historians consider the retreat, given the Carthaginian superiority on land, to be the result of panic. It is, however, possible that the Carthaginians considered that without an effective blockade there was no point in continuing the siege. Perhaps they were also unwilling to risk their army in battle against the battle hardened Epirots, with their pikes, elephants and famous general, while also being threatened by the troops within Syracuse. It is also possible that the Carthaginians hoped that by avoiding battle they might later reach an agreement with Pyrrhus and avoid a full-scale war. If so, they had misread their man. Pyrrhus was never one to give up the chance of a possible conquest.

Pyrrhus had now secured his base for the coming campaigns. With the Carthaginians in retreat, delegations began to enter Syracuse from all the Greek cities offering to place themselves under Pyrrhus' command. As already promised, Heracleides of Leontini allied his city to Pyrrhus, thus giving him a further 4,000 infantry and 500 cavalry. Sostratus relinquished his control of Akragas and thirty other cities to Pyrrhus. He was proclaimed commander in chief of the Sicilian forces. At some point he also 'received the title of king of Sicily as well as of Epirus.'[5] Whether he took this title immediately or later, after he had won some victories over the Carthaginians, is a matter of much dispute. Although Pyrrhus had decided to leave his son, Alexander in Italy he later joined his father in Sicily and was appointed as his successor.[6]

Also debated is exactly what political powers were handed over to Pyrrhus by the Greek cities. Most likely Pyrrhus emulated Philip II of Macedonia and Antigonus the One-eyed by forming a military alliance under his command. The cities would swear oaths to the Gods, binding themselves to accept Pyrrhus' leadership in war and promising to supply agreed amounts of troops and money. Their freedom and autonomy would be guaranteed as long as they maintained their contributions. Failure to adhere to the provisions of the treaty could result in fines or intervention into the city's affairs. These last clauses could always be manipulated by the *hegemon* as an excuse to interfere in the affairs of the cities if he deemed it necessary.

Once affairs in Syracuse had been finalised, Pyrrhus marched to the city of Akragas. He was joined by a further 8,000 infantry and 800 cavalry from his allies, reputedly troops of equal ability to his Epirots. Encouraged by Pyrrhus' advance, the city of Enna expelled its Carthaginian garrison and allied itself with Pyrrhus. The reinforcements received from his Sicilian allies brought Pyrrhus' army up to a total of 30,000 infantry, 2,500 cavalry, and his elephants.[7]

The exact dating of the incidents in Pyrrhus' Sicilian campaign is difficult to determine precisely. Most likely events up to the gathering of his forces at Akragas had occupied much of 278. In either the autumn of 278, or the spring of the following year, Pyrrhus crossed the Halycus River and attacked Heraclea. Here the Carthaginians finally stood to defend their border. Pyrrhus stormed the city, capturing it from its Carthaginian garrison. He then seized the otherwise unknown town of Azones. From there he marched on Selinus, which came over to him without a fight.

Having secured the Greek cities of the south coast of Sicily, Pyrrhus prepared to strike against the Epicraty, territory inhabited by the Carthaginians and their traditional allies the Elymians. His strategy appears to have been to isolate and then attack the two major Carthaginian bases of Panormus and Lilybaeum. The Elymian cities of Halicyae and Segesta surrendered without resistance. Pyrrhus then marched on another Elymian city, Eryx, modern Erice. This city was held by a large Carthaginian garrison and occupied a naturally strong position, situated on a mountain 750 metres high. It stands on the coastal rout between Panormus and Lilybaeum. On top of the peak stood a famous temple to the Goddess of Love, where now stands a Norman castle. The city extended around the hill under the actual summit. The ascent to the city was long and steep on all sides. Here the Carthaginians again chose to stand their ground.

The city is roughly triangular in shape, with two sides protected by precipitous slopes. It is against the third side, which faces southwest, that Pyrrhus, and later the Arabs and Normans, must have launched their assaults. The remains of the walls on this side have been dated back to about 700, and are known as the 'Punic walls' due to the Phoenician writing still visible on some of the stones. Eryx was famous for being the site of one of the hero Hercules' 'Twelve Labours'. Hercules had, according to legend, killed the king of the Elymians in a wrestling match.

The garrison offered strong resistance and Pyrrhus was forced to bring up his engines and besiege the city. Eventually Pyrrhus determined the time was right for an assault. Pyrrhus lead the attack in person, according to

Diodorus, desiring to win high renown and vying to rank with Hercules.'[8]
Plutarch down-plays the heroic motive, merely stating that Pyrrhus 'made a
vow to Hercules that he would institute games and a sacrifice in his honour,
if the god would render him in the sight of the Sicilian Greeks an antagonist
worthy of his lineage and resources.'[9]

Pyrrhus was the first to mount the walls and, being easily recognizable
in his ornate armour, became the target of the Carthaginian defenders.
Pyrrhus fought heroically, pushing the defenders from the walls:

> Most he laid dead in heaps about him with the strokes of his sword. He
> himself suffered no harm, but was a terrible sight for his enemies to
> look upon, and proved that Homer was right and fully justified in
> saying that valour, alone of the virtues, often displays transports due to
> divine possession and frenzy.[10]

The city was taken by storm and secured with a garrison. After the capture
of the city, Pyrrhus made good on his promise, sacrificing to Hercules in a
magnificent fashion while putting on spectacles and athletic games.

Personal prestige and standing among one's peers was always of crucial
importance to the legitimacy of Hellenistic kings. The generation after
Alexander the Great, however, always stood in his shadow. Military prowess
was one of the most important methods of obtaining prestige, hence
Agathocles' boasting of his defeat over the Macedonians of Cassander.
Another method was to display personal valour on the battlefield. In
personally leading the assault on Eryx, and being the first man upon the
walls, it is possible that Pyrrhus was attempting to emulate Hercules'
Sicilian heroics, thereby boosting his reputation among the Sicilians. It is
also possible that he was trying to step outside of the shadow of Alexander
who claimed descent from Hercules. Alexander had also attempted to
outdo Hercules when he had assaulted the fortress of the Rock of Aornos.
He had been the first to set foot upon it, but had been driven back by the
defenders. Alexander only managed to capture Aornos after it had been
deserted by its garrison. In leading the successful assault on Eryx by storm,
Pyrrhus could claim not only to have equalled Hercules but possibly to have
outshone Alexander. It may have been as a result of this piece of self-
promotion that Pyrrhus was declared to be King of the Sicilians.

Pyrrhus next advanced on the city of Iaetia, which surrendered immediately. Panormus was now isolated and Pyrrhus took the city by storm. Next
he took the nearby fortress of Mount Herctae. This lay near the sea between
Eryx and Panormus, on the plateau of a high hill rising up from a plain and
occupied a position similar in strength to Eryx, being inaccessible from all
but one side. Polybius describes the strategic importance of this position
as it possessed 'a harbour very well situated for ships making the voyage
from Drepanum (Trapani) and Lilybaeum to Italy to put in at, and with an

abundant supply of water.[11] It would become an important Carthaginian base in their future war against the Romans.

Up to this point Pyrrhus' campaign had been a triumphant march through Sicily; winning over the Greek cities without a fight and storming a number of Carthaginian fortresses. The siege-train of the Syracusans and their skilled engineers had probably played an important role in these successes. This was just the sort of campaigning Pyrrhus had always excelled at, fast marching resulting in a decisive battle or an overwhelming assault on an enemy position. All of Carthaginian Sicily had fallen to Pyrrhus except for the Carthaginian's main base at the city of Lilybaeum, which was now isolated by land and reliant on supply by sea. The Sicilian dream of expelling the Carthaginians from the island looked only a single battle away.

Unfortunately Diodorus' full account of Pyrrhus' campaign, which may have been based on the work of the historian Hieronymous of Cardia or Pyrrhus' own memoirs, and therefore probably detailed and reliable, has been lost. The surviving summary of his work is brief and mostly lacking in detail. It describes a number of successful sieges but no battles against the Carthaginians.

Justin claims, however, that Pyrrhus 'fought many successful battles with the Carthaginians'.[12] He uses the Latin word *proliea*, which is generally applied to land or naval battles rather than the more exact *obsidio*, meaning siege. Although Justin is not the most careful of compilers, his precise use of language gives his statement some credibility. It is therefore possible that Pyrrhus had defeated the Carthaginians in a number of battles during this campaign which have been excluded from the summary of Diodorus.

With all of Sicily except Lilybaeum under control, Pyrrhus prepared to lay siege to the city. The defenders desperately prepared themselves for the coming struggle:

> The Carthaginians brought over from Libya to Lilybaeum a considerable army, and having control of the seas, they transported a large amount of grain, and engines of war and missiles in incredible quantities. Since most of the city is surrounded by the sea, they walled off the land approaches, constructed towers at short intervals, and dug a great ditch.[13]

This account presents one problem. How had the Carthaginians gained control of the sea? After taking control of Syracuse, Pyrrhus had access to a powerful fleet of about 200 warships. Unfortunately, our limited sources do not provide an answer to this question. Only a few months later Pyrrhus would order the Sicilians to build him a new fleet. The most likely explanation is that the Greek fleet had, at some stage been destroyed or suffered severe losses, either through defeat by the Carthaginians or by being caught at sea in a storm. Carthaginian naval supremacy would make it impossible for the Greeks to completely blockade the city.

The desperate Carthaginians sent so many reinforcements to Lilybaeum that they began to overflow the walls of the city. The ditch that was constructed to protect the walls was located about 25 metres from them, and could easily be protected by missile fire from the city. It was a considerable obstacle, being nearly 20 metres deep.[14] This ditch was cleared and re-used in the later siege by the Romans. Parts of it are still visible today and are occupied by parks and playgrounds.

Lilybaeum occupied a promontory, and was bounded by sea on two sides. The city was square in shape, with strong walls protecting the landward sides. The crucial position was where the two sides of the wall joined and this was the scene of much of the fighting. The harbour, much larger then than now, was protected by two breakwaters, the remains of which can still be seen.

Before the assault began, the Carthaginians sent an embassy to Pyrrhus to discuss peace and an alliance. They offered him a large amount of money and the use of their fleet. Although the conditions of the offer are not recorded, presumably the Carthaginians proposed to assist Pyrrhus in a future campaign in Italy. If so, the Carthaginians were prepared to betray their Roman allies in order to cling on to a foothold in Sicily.

Pyrrhus found the offer tempting, as his allies in Italy were losing ground to the Romans in his absence. With the assistance of the Carthaginians as allies and the resources of Sicily behind him, he could return to Italy and renew the war with Rome. This plan did not sit well with his Greek allies, however, who pressed him to reject the terms and drive the Carthaginians out of Sicily forever.

They pointed out that allowing the Carthaginians to hold Lilybaeum would give 'the barbarians a stepping-stone for an attack on Sicily.'[15] This was a lesson that had been learned just over a century earlier when Dionysius the Elder had failed to drive the Carthaginians completely from the island after his destruction of Motya. Two years later, the Carthaginians had recovered and were besieging Syracuse. Pyrrhus was finally convinced by the arguments of the Sicilians and replied to the ambassadors that, 'there could be no settlement or friendship between himself and them unless they abandoned all Sicily and made the Libyan Sea a boundary between themselves and the Greeks.'[16]

Pyrrhus began his operations by testing the defences with constant attacks by relays of troops. The Carthaginian defences were too strong and well provided with artillery. The defenders easily beat off these attacks. Pyrrhus was forced to settle in for a siege. In the normal manner of Hellenistic sieges this became partly a technological race as Pyrrhus was forced to construct siege engines larger and more powerful than those he had transported from Syracuse. He also began mining operations under the walls but these achieved little due to the rocky nature of the ground. For two months the siege continued, but Pyrrhus' forces made little impression against the formidable fortifications.

The Carthaginian defences and their control of the seas had proven to be too strong. Throughout his career Pyrrhus had always excelled at the quick assault and capture of a city but had shown a reluctance to maintain and press a difficult siege. With winter about to close in, Pyrrhus decided to follow the precedent of Dionysius the Elder and quit western Sicily with the job unfinished. As with Dionysius' decision, this would prove to be disastrous to his cause. Pyrrhus, ever the adventurer, had decided to embark on a new campaign. He would emulate Agathocles and invade Africa while still engaged with the Carthaginians in Sicily. Perhaps remembering the lessons of Agathocles' campaign, Pyrrhus thought it necessary to build a large navy in preparation for the invasion. Pyrrhus ordered the Greek cities to provide both the money and the crews for the new fleet.

Pyrrhus' siege of Lilybaeum was to be the high-water mark of his Sicilian campaign; from this point his popularity and authority would rapidly disintegrate. His lifting of the siege was seen as poor leadership and a breach of faith. Many may have remembered his earlier willingness to accept the Carthaginian offer of support for a return to Italy. Others might have accused him as acting like earlier tyrants, by not finishing off the Carthaginians when he had the chance in order to justify his continued authority. Like the Greeks of Tarentum, they strongly opposed his decision to launch a new campaign before finishing what he had promised. They quite correctly saw him as abandoning their needs for his own selfish interests.

The abandonment of the siege would prove to be a crucial decision on Pyrrhus' part. The history of the two previous centuries had shown that the Carthaginians were capable of using their vast resources to quickly recover. As his Sicilian allies had predicted, Lilybaeum would be used as a base for a new Carthaginian offensive on the island. It would have been far better for Pyrrhus to have continued the siege while the new fleet was being constructed.

In his distinguished biography of Pyrrhus, Garoufalias, who is an avowed admirer of the king, justifies his decision by claiming that Pyrrhus 'could not mount an efficient siege or capture the city without simultaneously blockading it from the sea as well.'[17] This is perhaps correct, but does not excuse Pyrrhus' decision to lift the siege while the new fleet was being constructed. Pyrrhus would have been better advised to have continued the blockade of Lilybaeum while the ships were being built.

Antigonus the One-eyed had shown what could be achieved through perseverance. He had begun his siege of Tyre in 315 without an effective navy. The fleet of his enemy Ptolemy was able to support and supply Tyre. Antigonus resolutely continued his siege of the city while he built new ships for his fleet. A year and a half later Tyre fell. It would remain an important part of Antigonus' empire for decades to come. If Pyrrhus had succeeded in taking Lilybaeum he would have secured the whole of Sicily. This would have left the Carthaginians without any secure port on the island. Although this would not have prevented any future expedition, the absence of a secure place to land would have made it a far more dangerous operation. In abandoning his siege and planning to invade Africa, Pyrrhus was living up to his reputation as an irresolute commander. Plutarch claimed that 'what he won by his exploits he lost by indulging in vain hopes, since through passionate desire for what he had not he always failed to establish securely what he had.'[18]

Pyrrhus' order to the Greeks to construct a new fleet was the catalyst for his sudden decline in popularity. His command was greatly resented by the Sicilian Greeks and probably breeched their treaty obligations. He now began to appear as no better than previous tyrants, issuing commands to subjects rather than dealing with allies. Plutarch states that when Pyrrhus had first arrived in Sicily he had treated the Greek cities with courtesy, 'by gracious intercourse with them, by trusting everybody, and by doing nobody any harm.' Now Pyrrhus demonstrated what accepting the rule of a king could mean to the independent Greek cities:

> Not dealing with the cities in an acceptable or gentle manner, but in a lordly way, angrily putting compulsion and penalties upon them ... he ceased to be a popular leader and became a tyrant, and added to his name for severity a name for ingratitude and faithlessness.[19]

Dionysius of Halicarnassus makes even stronger criticisms of Pyrrhus' new policies. According to him, Pyrrhus:

> Assumed the arrogance of a tyrant ... took away the estates of Agathocles' relatives and friends from those who had received them at that ruler's hands and presented them to his own friends, and he assigned the chief magistracies in the cities to his own shield-bearers and captains, not in accordance with the local laws of each city nor for the customary period, but as was pleasing to him. Lawsuits and controversies and all the other matters of civil administration he would in some cases decide himself and in other cases would refer them either for reversal or for determination to those who hung about the court, men who had an eye for nothing except making gains and squandering wealth in the pursuit of luxury. Because of all this he was burdensome to the cities which had received him and was hated by them.[20]

Pyrrhus, aware of the growing opposition to his leadership, attempted to crush the dissent by force. Using the excuse of the Carthaginian threat, he introducing garrisons into the cities, Taking a leaf from Agathocles' book, he also arrested his main opponents and 'put them to death, falsely alleging that he had discovered plots and treasonable acts.'[21] Pyrrhus had violated the Greek cities' freedoms in almost every possible manner, not even leaving them the façade of autonomy. Finally, he had committed the ultimate transgression of imposing garrisons upon them. Rather than rid themselves of their tyrants, the Greek cities had merely replaced them with a more demanding and powerful autocrat.

Pyrrhus had a reputation for having little interest in the art of government, believing that the only skills needed by a king were those pertaining to war and arms. He was also accused of being overly arrogant towards his social inferiors. His chief diplomat, Cineas, is portrayed as often persuading his king to adopt more moderate policies than those proposed by Pyrrhus' generals. Cineas vanishes from the sources after going to Syracuse prior to Pyrrhus' arrival. The most likely explanation is that he died sometime during the campaign. His absence appears to have removed all restraint from the king, who now followed his, and his generals', natural inclinations.

After abandoning the siege of Lilybaeum, Pyrrhus returned to the eastern end of the island. During his absence the Mamertines of Messene had been extorting tribute from the neighbouring Greek cities. Pyrrhus acted quickly against this new threat. He marched against the Mamertines and defeated them in battle, despite their reputation for being 'numerous and warlike', and destroyed many of their strongholds.[22] The victory may have briefly restored some of Pyrrhus' lost reputation. He did not, however, capture their stronghold of Messene and the Mamertines would continue to remain a threat to the Sicilians and source of destabilization to the entire island.

Pyrrhus' military power and his garrisons succeeded for a time in controlling the Greeks. Nevertheless, in the way of tyrants, the king began to suspect that his closest supporters, Sostratus and Thoenon, were plotting against him. Sostratus wisely took fright and fled but Thoenon was arrested and executed.

This was only the beginning of the executions. Pyrrhus now embarked on an all-too-familiar purge of anyone suspected of opposing him:

> He banished and put to death many who held office and many who had called him in to help in their disputes, partly because he was displeased with them, on account of remarks to the effect that he had become master of the state through their influence, and partly because he was suspicious of them and believed that just as they had come over to his side so they might go over to someone else.[23]

In response to this, the Greek cities ended their alliance and rose in open rebellion against the king. The Greek revolt against Pyrrhus gave the Carthaginians the necessary time to recover their position. They gave safe haven to the Sicilian political exiles. Reinforcements were sent from Africa and they 'took up the war vigorously' and 'harassed him so severely that he abandoned not only Syracuse but Sicily as well.'[24] The latter claim may be an exaggeration but the Carthaginian revival did much to undermine Pyrrhus' position. Many of the Greeks now took the opportunity to ally themselves with the Carthaginians, believing that their less intrusive rule was preferable to the constant financial demands and political interference of Pyrrhus. Some even sought the protection of their former oppressors the Mamertines, allowing them to increase their power.

With his Sicilian empire under threat, Pyrrhus received bad news from Italy. Ambassadors came from his Italian allies who claimed that 'they could no longer withstand the Romans, and that, unless he gave them assistance, they must submit.' Pyrrhus was now faced with war on two fronts, 'as the Carthaginians threatened him on one side, and the Romans on the other, it seemed hazardous not to transport a force into Italy, and more hazardous to withdraw troops from Sicily, lest the one should be lost by not receiving assistance, or the other by being deserted.'[25]

In an attempt to reduce the pressure on one front, Pyrrhus fought and won a battle against the advancing Carthaginians, but it appears to have been yet another Cadmean victory as 'though he had the advantage, yet, as he quitted Sicily, he seemed to flee as one defeated; and his allies, in consequence, revolted from him, and he lost his dominion in Sicily as speedily and easily as he had obtained it.'[26]

The situation in Italy gave Pyrrhus an excuse to quit Sicily without it appearing to be a flight from defeat. He had not, however, finished with the Sicilians. Before departing the island he pillaged their cities and left with a fleet of 110 warships, of which at least fifty must have been expropriated from the Sicilians. As he departed Sicily, Pyrrhus lost most of his fleet and plunder to the Carthaginians when defeated in a sea battle in the Straits.

Pyrrhus had failed in Sicily partly because of his own shortcomings but also for many of the same reasons that the tyrants had. Only force or the threat of a powerful outside enemy could impel the Greek cities to surrender some of their autonomy to a war leader. Once the immediate threat had passed they would revert to type, chaffing under the demands and restrictions imposed upon them and demanding a return of their freedoms. Pyrrhus' failure to defeat the Carthaginians completely had undermined legitimacy for his authority and he was unable to maintain it by force.

The fact that Pyrrhus was not a Sicilian may also have played a role in his rapid descent into unpopularity. As long ago as Hermocrates' conference in 424, the Sicilians, despite their rivalries, had shown that they did possess an amount of collective identity: 'above and beyond this we are neighbours, live in the same country, are girt by the same sea, and go by the name of Sicilians.'[27] Only Timoleon, who had voluntarily surrendered power, was able to overcome this prejudice. As with others before him, Pyrrhus appears to have underestimated the resources of Carthage. Whenever they were threatened with total expulsion from the island, they would open their abundant coffers to raise new forces.

Pyrrhus' campaign in Sicily had lasted from 278 until 276, but in the end it had achieved nothing and perhaps made things worse for the Sicilians. Their cities were once again divided and easy prey for the resurgent Carthaginians. The chaos of the last year of his rule had allowed the Mamertines to become an increasing threat to the Greek cities. Over the horizon, however, a new power was emerging that would soon force the Syracusans and Carthaginians to ally with one another against a common enemy. In a quote that is probably apocryphal, Plutarch states that as Pyrrhus sailed away from Sicily he said, 'my friends, what a wrestling ground for Carthaginians and Romans we are leaving behind us!'[28]

Chapter 18

The Rise of Hieron II

He was affable in his address, just in his dealings, moderate in command; so that nothing kingly seemed wanting to him but a kingdom.

Justin 23.4

Pyrrhus' withdrawal from Sicily in 276 had left the island in a state of great confusion. Many of the Greek cities had accepted Carthaginian rule, others had allied themselves with, or been subjugated by, the Mamertines. Syracuse and a few other cities, clung to their independence. Such a period of crisis inevitably created the opportunity for an ambitious individual to seize power as the next saviour of their city. From Pausanias we know that the next tyrant of Syracuse was Hieron, usually known as Hieron II so as not to confuse him with the fifth century tyrant of the same name. Hieron seized power in either 275 or 274. 'After the death of the earlier dictator Agathocles, Syracusan dictatorship sprouted again in Hieron son of Hieroncles, who took over control the year after the hundred and twenty-sixth Olympics [276].'[1]

Our sources for the twelve years after Pyrrhus' departure until the first invasion of the Romans in 264 are limited. All that survive are a summary of Diodorus, a brief description in Polybius that is mainly interested in the effect these events had on the Romans, and a few lines of Justin. There is, however, just enough detail, mostly from Polybius, to provide an outline of events.

Polybius has a good reputation as a cautious and painstaking historian. His work was designed to explain the rise of Rome and reconcile the Greeks to Roman rule. Polybius states that: 'the date from which I propose to begin my history is the 140th Olympiad [220–216 B.C.]'[2] The events leading up to the outbreak of the First Punic War – as the wars between Rome and Carthage are known – are therefore treated briefly as part of the summary of affairs preceding this date.

Some historians argue that Pyrrhus did not totally abdicate his rule over Syracuse, claiming that when he departed he left his son, Alexander, behind to continue his rule of the city. Hellenistic kings did not readily abandon their conquests and Pyrrhus would adopt a similar policy when he quit Italy a year later, leaving a garrison in Tarentum that had to be forcibly removed by the Romans in 272. Alexander vanishes from the sources for the three years between 275–272, taking no part in his father's campaigns in Greece and Macedonia. It is tempting to surmise that he remained in Sicily for part of this time as strong ties between the Epirot royal family and the Syracusan aristocracy survived Pyrrhus' withdrawal. Polybius records that: 'Nereis, the daughter of Pyrrhus'[3] was the mother of a later tyrant, Hieronymus (fl. 231–214). It is sometimes claimed that she was the daughter of Pyrrhus but the long gap between his death in 272 and the birth of her first son around 231 makes this unlikely. She was probably the daughter of Pyrrhus II, and therefore the great-granddaughter of both Pyrrhus and Agathocles. If Alexander did remain in Sicily he must have quit the city by 274, the latest possible date for Hieron's seizure of power.

In the aftermath of Pyrrhus' departure the war of the Syracusans, and their few remaining allies, against the Carthaginians and Mamertines continued. The Mamertines appear to have recovered from their defeat by Pyrrhus and to have been the big winners during this period. They had gained control of an area stretching as far as Halaesa to the west and inland as far as Centuripae. They are also recorded as campaigning as far as the southern coast of Sicily where 'they laid waste to Camarina and Gela.'[4] To the south their borders ended at the territory of Tauromenium, one of the surviving allies of Syracuse. Polybius describes their new position of power:

> The Mamertines (for this was the name adopted by the Campanians after their seizure of Messene) as long as they enjoyed the alliance of the Romans together with the Campanians who had occupied Rhegium, not only remained in secure possession of their own city and territory but caused no little trouble to the Carthaginians and Syracusans about the adjacent territories, levying tribute from many parts of Sicily.[5]

During a Syracusan campaign against the Carthaginians a dispute arose between the troops in the field and the government in the city. The army convened their own assembly and elected two generals from their own ranks, one of whom was Hieron. He was probably elected due to his distinguished service in the campaigns of Pyrrhus, during which 'he was presented by King Pyrrhus with many military gifts.'[6] On his return to the city, Hieron's position was confirmed due to his 'mildness and magnanimity' despite the Polybius' assertion that 'the Syracusans, though by no means inclined to approve camp elections.'[7]

Hieron, like Dionysius the Elder, believed that the usual democratic method of appointing a committee of generals to command expeditions led 'to quarrelling among themselves and introducing continual changes.' As

with many a would-be tyrant before him, he decided that a simpler command system was necessary, with one commander in charge of Syracuse's
armed forces. In order to ensure that person would be himself, Hieron
sought out political allies. He married the daughter of Leptines who 'had a
wider circle of dependents and enjoyed more credit than any other burgher
and had an especially high name among the common people.' Leptines
would also be able to protect Hieron's interests while he was away from the
city on campaign. Polybius ominously adds that: 'from his first measures
it was evident at once to all capable of judging that his ambition was not
limited to military command.'[8]

Polybius' account implies that Hieron began his career as one of a number
of elected generals. As the goodwill of the common people appears to be
important, and numerous generals were elected and given joint commands,
it appears probable that some sort of democratic government had returned
to Syracuse. With the military support of his troops and the political
support of Leptines, Hieron had most likely removed his colleague and
had himself elected to the post of *strategos autocrator*. Hieron's rise to
power, unlike that of Agathocles, was supposedly peaceful. He achieved his
ambition 'without killing, exiling, or injuring a single citizen.'[9] In the early
years of his reign, Hieron's major policy appears to have been the total
expulsion of the trouble-making Mamertines from Sicily. This was probably
his justification for seeking the position of *strategos autocrator*.

In 270, two years after their capture of Tarentum, the Romans decided
to complete their conquest of southern Italy by finally dealing with the
Campanian deserters who had mutinied and seized Rhegium. Hieron
assisted the Romans in their capture of Rhegium by supplying them with
grain when the army was suffering from a lack of supplies. The surviving
rebels were taken to Rome, were they were publicly scourged and beheaded.
Due to the nature of their crimes they were not allowed proper burial but
their bodies thrown out of the city to be eaten by stray dogs. Hieron's
motive in assisting the Romans is not hard to understand; with the fall of
Rhegium the Mamertines were now cut off from assistance from their
kinsmen in Italy. While the Roman siege of Rhegium was still underway the
Syracusans, under the command of Hieron, attacked Mamertine territory
in Sicily.

The Syracusan army included a force of veteran mercenaries described as
'disaffected' and 'turbulent and seditious.' This could mean many things.
They may have been in arrears of pay, demanding citizenship for their
services or not sufficiently loyal to Hieron. When the opposing armies
met near Centuripae, Hieron ordered an attack by the mercenaries but
deliberately held back the citizen forces while the isolated mercenaries were
massacred by the Campanians. Hieron then retired to Syracuse and 'he
himself enlisted a considerable number of mercenaries and henceforth
continued to rule in safety.'[10] In other words, Hieron raised a force of

mercenaries loyal to himself to act as his bodyguard and as a counter force to the citizen soldiers of Syracuse.

Polybius ends his account of the rise of Hieron by describing how he

> efficiently armed and trained the urban levies and leading them out engaged the enemy in the Mylaean plain near the river Longanus, and inflicted a severe defeat on them, capturing their leaders. This put an end to the audacity of the Mamertines, and on his return to Syracuse he was with one voice proclaimed king by all the allies.[11]

The surviving fragments of Diodorus contain no account of the events leading up to Hieron's victory against the Mamertines but do contain a more detailed narrative of the campaign. After Hieron's initial defeat by the Mamertines he returned with his newly trained army. He stormed Mylae, capturing and then enlisting 1,500 mercenaries. From there he marched south and destroyed the fortress of Ameselum, enrolling more captured mercenaries. Halaesa, Abacaene and Tyndaris all surrendered and 'eagerly welcomed' their liberator. With these victories Hieron isolated Messene and 'drove the Mamertines into a narrow area.'[12] With Messene directly threatened, the Mamertines, under the command of Cios, marched out and confronted Hieron at the river Longanus, located between Mylae and Tyndaris.

Fourth century vases show Campanian soldiers armed as hoplites and it is usually considered that they fought in a phalanx in a similar manner to their Greek neighbours. From 340, however, they were allies of the Romans and probably, over time, adopted the Roman method of fighting. The first century Roman historian Livy belittles their courage, claiming that: 'the Campanians brought to the help of their allies the prestige of their name rather than actual strength; enervated by luxury they were worsted by a people inured to the use of arms.'[13] It should be noted, however, that Livy consistently denigrates the character and courage of Rome's opponents. The Greeks considered the Campanians to be brave fighters, describing the Mamertines as 'warlike' (*machimos*).[14] Despite a reputation for treachery, they were much sought after as mercenaries by both the Sicilians and Carthaginians.

The traditional view is that, until the early fourth century, the Romans also fought armed with spear and shield in the phalanx formation. This formation proved too inflexible to deal with the ferocious charges of the Gaulish tribes who had invaded northern Italy and defeated the Romans in 390. It had also proved unsuitable when fighting the Italian hill tribes in their home territory of forests and mountains. The hill tribes, such as the Samnites and Lucanians, tended to fight in looser formations and smaller units. They preferred to shower their enemies with javelins from afar and give ground when pressed. Ambushes and skirmishing were their normal method of fighting, rather than a straight forward battle of close order spearmen. If such troops could be forced into open battle they would usually be beaten by the phalanx, but this was often difficult to achieve.

The Romans, after their experiences fighting against both the Gauls and hill tribes, adopted new tactics and equipment. They broke their infantry up into smaller units of about 120 men, called *maniples* (handfuls). These were more flexible and could manoeuvre to support one another. They also deployed in three lines of heavy infantry, rather than the traditional single line. The first line was now used to break up the enemy attack. It could then fall back through the gaps in the maniples of the second line, or be reinforced by them. The reserve lines could then renew the assault on the enemy.

The Romans also re-armed the troops of the first line, the *hastati*, with throwing spears, *pila*, and a new shield, the *scutum*. This was a longer and narrower shield, giving more protection to the wielder, but, unlike the hoplite shield, none to his neighbour. Troops so armed now fought more individually, with sword and shield, rather than as a phalanx. They also adopted more open and shallower formations. The attack would begin with a shower of thrown spears, followed up by a charge into contact using sword and shield. As some stage the second line, the *principes* was also rearmed with *pila*. The third line, the *triarii*, although maintaining the thrusting spear, also adopted the *scutum*. In front of the three lines of heavy infantry were the *velites*, light infantry skirmishers armed with javelins. Roman armies were made up of units known as legions which contained about 4,200 infantry and 300 cavalry.

Roman armies were generally well trained and drilled before they took the field. Discipline was tight, with numerous offences resulting in the death penalty. One such offence was sleeping while on guard duty. This is in sharp contrast to the Syracusans, whose sentries were constantly surprised while asleep, drunk or had deserted their posts to sleep in the comfort of the city. The Romans also appointed a very high number of officers which made control of the army much easier.

Unlike the phalanx of the Greeks, the Romans encouraged individual bravery, rewarding and promoting those who displayed valour in battle. Lendon argues that the reason that the Romans adopted the manipular formation was not for tactical reasons but to encourage this sort of aggressive, individual behaviour.[15] Aggression in command was also encouraged and rewarded. This meant that the Roman legions soon developed a reputation for ferocious behaviour on the battlefield.

Third century coins of the Mamertines continue to show figures armed as hoplites. It would therefore appear safer to infer that those fighting in Sicily still fought as spearmen in a single phalanx, using the tactics and equipment of their former Syracusan employers, rather than the new formation and arms of their Roman conquerors. The coming battle would therefore have been a traditional clash of two phalanxes. If so, it may have been the last battle fought in this manner in the western Mediterranean region.

The three century long era of the hoplite as the dominant type of infantryman on the battlefield was over. They had been replaced by the legions of Rome and the pike-armed infantry of the Macedonians. In Italy, the armies of the Greek cities had been unable to stand in open battle against the Romans; it was only the arrival of a brilliant general such as Pyrrhus – along with his pikemen and elephants – that had allowed them to win their two victories over the Romans at Heraclea and Asculum. These would be the only known victories by Greek or Macedonian armies over the Romans on the field of battle.

The Carthaginians would win battles in their later wars against the Romans but their victories were the result of superior tactics, taking advantage of their greater numbers of cavalry and/or the judicious use of elephants. Their infantry also proved incapable of defeating their Roman counterparts in a stand-up fight. Battles between the two would often be a race to see whether the Carthaginian mounted could defeat the Roman cavalry, and expose the flanks of their infantry, before the Roman infantry routed the Carthaginian foot.

The Syracusan army at Longanus River totalled 10,000 infantry and 1,500 cavalry. The Mamertines had 8,000 infantry and supposedly only forty cavalry, although this latter figure in the text may be corrupt. Prior to the battle, Diodorus records one of those stories of hubris that he finds so much satisfaction in relating:

> Cios assembled diviners to inspect the entrails, and after sacrificing, he questioned them about the battle. When they replied that the gods revealed through the victims that he would pass the night in the encampment of the enemy, he was overjoyed, thinking that he was to gain possession of the king's camp.[16]

As the two sides deployed for battle, Hieron decided to send a flank march, consisting of 200 exiles from Messene, 'men noted for their courage and deeds of valour' and 400 other chosen soldiers around the enemy army to attack their rear. The detached force's march would be screened by a nearby hill. Hieron sent another detachment to seize some high ground near the river. This force assisted the Syracusan cavalry in gaining the advantage in their clash with the enemy cavalry. Despite this, the battle was still in the balance when the Syracusan flanking force arrived and attacked the rear of the Mamertines. The new arrivals 'slew them with no difficulty, since they were fresh and the enemy were battle-worn, then the Mamertines, surrounded on all sides, took to flight, and the Syracusans, attacking in force, cut the whole army to pieces.'[17]

Cios fought desperately but was wounded and captured. He was carried alive to the Syracusan camp and treated by their doctors. Diodorus then relates how Cios: 'in accordance with the prophecy and the prediction of the soothsayers, had spent the night in the enemy's camp.' The Gods were not finished with him, however, as when captured horses were brought to the Syracusan camp, 'Cios, recognizing his son's horse, supposed that the youth had been killed. In his excessive grief he burst the stitches of his wounds and by his own death set the price at which he rated the destruction of his son.'[18]

After the battle Hieron laid siege to Messene. The surviving Mamertines approached him as suppliants, seeking terms of surrender. The Carthaginians were, however, not prepared to allow such a triumph by their traditional rivals to go unopposed. Their commander, Hannibal, was stationed with a fleet at Lipari. He sailed to Hieron supposedly to offer congratulations – presumably the two must have already made peace – but he was 'in reality seeking to outmanoeuvre Hieron by deceit.' Hannibal sent a force into Messene to reinforce the garrison. Hieron, no doubt seething in anger at the betrayal of the Carthaginians, 'abandoned the siege as hopeless and returned to Syracuse, having achieved a resounding success.'[19]

At some point during his rule Hieron took the title of king. According to Polybius he was hailed as such by the allies after his victory at Longanus River. The aftermath of such a notable victory would be the obvious time for such an acclamation. Diodorus describes him, however, as king prior to this victory and Polybius' passage may depict the allies accepting a title that the Syracusans had already bestowed. Even the date of the victory is uncertain, 269 appears to be the most likely but as late as 264 has been proposed.

Justin has a much briefer account of events leading up to Hieron's rise to power. He relates that: 'When Pyrrhus had withdrawn from Sicily, Hieron was made governor of it; and such was the prudence he displayed in his office, that, by the unanimous consent of all the cities, he was first made general against the Carthaginians, and soon after king.' His account does add useful information about Hieron's background: 'He was the son of Hieroncles, a man of high rank, whose descent was traced from Gelon, an ancient prince of Sicily. His extraction on the mother's side, however, was so mean as to be even dishonourable; for he was the child of a female slave.'[20] His date of birth is unknown but 308 is the most likely year.

Justin adds a physical description of Hieron: 'the handsomeness of his person was remarkable, and his bodily strength wonderful.'[21] Polybius relates admiringly that:

> Although he lived constantly in the midst of affluence, luxury, and most lavish expenditure, he survived till over ninety, and retained all his faculties, as well as keeping every part of his body sound, which

seems to me to testify in no slight measure, indeed very strongly, to his having led a temperate life.[22]

Hieron was the first tyrant of Syracuse to produce coins with his own likeness. Before the rise of the Macedonian kings the Greeks had thought such portrayals to be sacrilegious. The coins portray a handsome man, although some, presumably from later in life, do show a much fleshier face and neck. Perhaps he was not as immune to luxurious living as Polybius suggests.

Justin also relates the usual stories of prophecy and miraculous events that are habitually attributed to successful ancient rulers. As the bastard child of a female slave he was exposed by his father as a disgrace to his family, but bees for several days fed him with honey. His father was advised by soothsayers that this 'signified that sovereign power was foreboded to the infant, took him home again, and brought him up most carefully with the hope that he would attain the promised honour.' While at school a wolf stole from him his book. On his first campaign, 'an eagle settled on his shield, and an owl upon his spear'. All these omens 'indicated that he would be prudent in counsel, active in the field, and a king.'[23] This account is so similar to the tales surrounding the career of Agathocles that one must wonder if these portents were a Syracusan cliché or Justin has confused the two.

The position of the Mamertines had been made precarious by Hieron's victory and in their desperation, in 265 or 264, they sent an embassy to Rome requesting assistance. This embassy appeal would lead to the 'first crossing of the Romans from Italy with an armed force.'[24] In addition it would be the flashpoint that would cause the first armed conflict between Rome and Carthage.

Chapter 19

The Outbreak of the First Punic War

Now that Etruscan unrest had come to a standstill and affairs in Italy were perfectly peaceful, whereas the Carthaginian power was becoming ever greater, the Romans ordered both the consuls to make an expedition into Sicily.

Zonaras 8.9

There are two main accounts of events leading up to the outbreak of the first war between Carthage and Rome, those of Polybius and Cassius Dio. The conflict is known as the First Punic War. The second century AD historian, Cassius Dio, provides the more detailed account of these events. Although a careful researcher, the main criticism of his writing is that as a rhetorician he was prone to amend his sources if he believed the facts to be lacking in drama.

Much of Dio's work has been lost and exists only in fragments. His books for this period have mostly survived through the excerpts of Zonaras, a private secretary to the Byzantine emperor Alexis I. Despite these shortcomings the following account of events leading up to outbreak of the war will mainly follow Dio's and Zonaras' accounts due to their greater detail.

The Mamertine embassy came to Rome 'offering to surrender the city and begging for assistance as a kindred people.' Opinion in Rome was divided as 'the succour demanded being so obviously unjustifiable.' The Romans had recently punished the Campanians in Rhegium for crimes similar to those occupying Messene. Harder heads within the city had, however, begun to fear the growing power of Carthage. They argued that if the Carthaginians – who already controlled Libya, much of Spain, Sardinia and Lipari – were to gain control of all of Sicily: 'they would be most troublesome and dangerous neighbours, hemming them in on all sides and threatening every part of Italy.' It was therefore necessary to support the Mamertines in order to prevent the Carthaginians from building 'a bridge for crossing over to Italy.'[1] Those in favour of supporting the Mamertines could argue that however serious their other crimes had been, unlike those who had seized Rhegium, they were not deserters from Rome's armies.

The debate continued in the Senate for many days. Eventually the Senate refused to recommend legislation to send an army to support the Mamertines. The power to decide war and peace was, however, the responsibility of the *comitia centuriata*, an assembly of all citizens eligible for conscription into the army. The two annually elected senior magistrates of Rome, the Consuls, also served as its generals. Many who held the position considered their term in office to be a chance to enhance their reputation and increase their wealth through a successful campaign, this inclined them to actively seek battle whenever possible. The two Consuls decided to bypass the decision of the Senate and take the request of the Mamertines directly to the *comitia*.

The Consuls won over the assembly by pointing out the rich plunder that could be gained in a campaign fought in Sicily. The people voted in favour of the resolution and appointed one of the Consuls, Appius Claudius, to command the expedition. Appius was consul for 264 which gives the date for the campaign.

The Roman decision to send troops to Messene would have far reaching consequences. It began a series of three conflicts during which the Romans and Carthaginians would fight for the dominance of the region. The causes of the outbreak of these wars were as much debated among historians in ancient times as they still are today. In many ways the acquisitive and paranoid nature of ancient empires made conflict inevitable once they came into direct contact. Cassius Dio perhaps sums it up best when he argues that whatever were the justifications put forward by both sides:

> The truth was otherwise. As a matter of fact, the Carthaginians, who had long been powerful, and the Romans, who were now growing rapidly stronger, kept viewing each other with jealousy; and they were led to war partly by the desire of acquiring more – in accordance with the instinct of the majority of mankind most active when they are most successful – and partly by fear. Both sides alike thought that the one true salvation for their own possessions lay in obtaining those of others.[2]

All that was needed was for both sides to find an excuse for war. This had been provided by the Mamertines.

Appius was delayed in sending assistance to Messene. As a result, the Mamertines began to lose patience and 'under the spur of necessity, called upon the Carthaginians.'[3] They sent a fleet under the command of Hanno to guard the Straits and reinforce the garrison in the city. For some unknown reason, the fleet was stationed to the north of the city, at Cape Pelorus, rather than in the harbour of Messene. Hanno also managed to negotiate a peace between the Mamertines and Hieron.

Meanwhile Appius had sent ahead a small fleet under Giaus Claudius to establish a Roman presence in the city. Arriving at Rhegium, he observed that the larger Carthaginian fleet controlled the seas and decided not to risk a crossing with his ships. Instead he sailed across in a small boat to Messene to discuss the situation. Claudius claimed the Romans had come to free the city and that the Carthaginians should show good cause for their occupation or immediately withdraw. Soon afterwards, Claudius tried to force a crossing but was defeated and driven back to Rhegium, losing a number of ships. The first blows in the Punic Wars had been struck, but neither side could have predicted that the ensuing war would last twenty-four years.

Alarmed by the turn of events, 'Hanno, wishing to throw the responsibility for breaking the truce upon the Romans, sent to Claudius the captured triremes and was restoring the captives; and he urged him to agree to peace.'[4] Claudius refused his offer. After observing weather conditions in the Straits he managed to use a favourable wind and current to bring his fleet into Messene, before the Carthaginian fleet at Cape Pelorus could intervene. Encouraged by the presence of a Roman force within the city, 'the Mamertines, partly by menace and partly by stratagem, dislodged the Carthaginian commander.'[5]

The Carthaginians reacted in their usual way to military failure by crucifying their general and slaughtering all the Campanian mercenaries in their army. More practically, they commenced a blockade of Messene by land and sea. Next they approached their old enemy, Syracuse and 'when they had arranged a treaty of alliance, they agreed on joint attack on Messene.'[6] The alliance of such traditional foes would prove to be riddled with suspicion on both sides. The Syracusans marched to Messene and took up a position alongside the Carthaginians to complete the encirclement of the city. The two allies' camps were separated by an intervening mountain. This had the advantage of keeping the old rivals apart, thus reducing possible friction, but would make it difficult for them to support one another.

Appius, upon arriving at Rhegium, attempted to reach a negotiated settlement with the besieging forces. Perhaps in an attempt to divide the allies, Appius publicly announced that he would not make war on the Syracusans. Hieron replied by listing the crimes of the Mamertines and exposing both the cynicism and ambition of the Romans:

The Romans, harping as they did on *fides* [honour], certainly ought not to protect assassins who had shown the greatest contempt for good faith; but if, on behalf of men so utterly godless, they should enter upon a war of such magnitude, it would be clear to all mankind that they were using pity for the imperilled as a cloak for their own advantage, and that in reality they coveted Sicily.[7]

Appius' army is described as a 'strong force.' Although we are not told the size of his army it was probably the usual consular force of two legions plus allies; about 20,000 men. To this could be added the surviving Mamertines. If so, Appius would have outnumbered the Syracusans who were unlikely to have fielded more men than the 11,000 they had at Longanus River, but may have had less men than the combined forces of his enemies.

Once again, the poor position of the Carthaginian fleet at Cape Pelorus allowed the Romans to complete a night crossing and land in Sicily. Appius decided to take advantage of his surprise appearance and immediately attack the Syracusans. Hieron advanced his army to engage the Romans. Given the likely difference in numbers this would appear to have been unwise but perhaps Hieron was hoping to catch the Romans before all of their force could be deployed. The Syracusans' cavalry had the best of their encounter with the Roman cavalry but the Roman infantry won the day. Hieron retired to the safety of the mountains and then under the cover of night retreated to Syracuse.

Appius, learning of the Syracusan retreat, decided to attack the Carthaginians the next day. Reinforced by the Mamertines, the Romans assaulted the fortifications of the Carthaginians. The Carthaginian position, protected on one side by the sea and on the other by a marsh, was too strong and they drove the Romans back with a shower of missiles. Believing they had won the day the Carthaginians pursued the Romans onto more open land. The Romans rallied, wheeled about and routed the Carthaginians, who retreated back to their camp and dared not advance again for the remainder of the campaign. In these first two encounters on Sicilian soil, the Roman infantry had lived up to their reputation.

Appius decided to leave the Carthaginians bottled-up in their camp while he marched against Syracuse, pillaging the countryside as he went. Arriving at the city he made several assaults on the city but the walls of Dionysius proved strong. The Syracusans made occasional sallies out with mixed success. In one such skirmish, Appius was nearly captured. He escaped by offering to discuss terms with Hieron but: 'when the man came with whom he was to conclude the terms, he kept falling back unobtrusively, while conversing with him, until he had retired to safety.'[8]

Unable to make any impact on the fortifications of Syracuse the Romans soon began to run out of supplies. They also suffered the same fate as many other armies that had besieged Syracuse; disease broke out within their ranks. With the end of the year and the end of his term as Consul approaching, Appius abandoned the siege and retreated to Messene. There he left behind a garrison and returned to Italy.

This account of the first year of the war derives largely from Zonaras. Polybius' short description largely agrees with Zonaras' account. However, like most good historians, Polybius did enjoy nothing more than finding fault with the work of other historians. In this case, he criticizes the work of an earlier writer, Philinus, who provides an alternative account of the campaign. According to Polybius, Philinus claims that: 'the Romans reaching the city by sea, at once marched out against the Syracusans, but after being severely handled returned to Messene. They next sallied out against the Carthaginians and were not only worsted but lost a considerable number of prisoners.'[9] Polybius sarcastically observes that despite these victories Hieron decided to burn his camp, abandon all his garrisons and retire to Syracuse. The Carthaginians also inexplicably decided to disperse into garrisons and not face the Romans in the field. After the retreat of their enemies, the Romans were able to ravage the countryside unopposed and lay siege to Syracuse.

Polybius dismisses Philinus' account of the Roman defeats as 'full of inconsistencies and does not require a lengthy discussion.' He further claims that it is 'impossible to reconcile the two assertions,' that following their victories both the Syracusans and Carthaginians spent the rest of the year cowering behind their fortifications. He concludes that: 'we must therefore concede that Philinus's initial statements are false, and that, while the Romans were victorious in the engagements before Messene, this author announces that they were worsted.'[10]

Philinus was a citizen of Akragas, which was sacked by the Romans during the first Punic War. He later accompanied the Carthaginian general Hannibal during his campaigns in Italy during the Second Punic War (218–202). Polybius, although using Philinus as one of his two main sources for his account of the first war, accuses him of pro-Carthaginian bias. Given Philinus' background such partiality would not be surprising.

Polybius criticism of Philinus' account is plausible. It should be noted, however, that Polybius himself admired the Romans and the major purpose of his work was to reconcile the Greeks to Roman rule. He also admits that his other main source for this period, the Roman historian Quintus Fabius Pictor, was just as biased. 'Philinus will have it that the Carthaginians in every case acted wisely, well, and bravely, and the Romans otherwise, whilst Fabius takes the precisely opposite view.'[11] Unfortunately not enough of either writer's work survives to prove Polybius' assertions. If Polybius has dismissed Philinus' account, then he must have used the equally biased report of Fabius. This might explain why the minor defeat of the Romans at Messene and their failures before Syracuse are omitted from Polybius' narrative.

Diodorus records a different series of events. He claims that there was no battle between the Romans and the Syracusans, as after the Roman crossing: 'Hieron, thinking that the Carthaginians had treacherously permitted the crossing, fled to Syracuse.'[12] If Diodorus is correct the Syracusans, faced by a strong Roman army and suspecting their new allies – albeit traditional enemies – of treachery, had deserted the Carthaginians without a fight. Abandoned by their allies, the Carthaginians were defeated in battle. The

Romans pursued but failed to take the Carthaginian-held city of Echetla and withdrew to Messene. The siege of Echetla is also mentioned in Polybius' summary of Philinus, whom Diodorus cites as one of his sources.

Overall it would seem best to accept the account of Zonaras. To his narrative could be added the dispersal of the Carthaginian army to garrisons and the Roman failure at Echetla, recorded by Philinus and Diodorus. The differing descriptions of the battle between Hieron and Appius before Messene are the most problematic. It is tempting just to accept Polybius' short account: 'leading out his forces he drew them up in order of battle, the king of Syracuse readily accepting the challenge. After a prolonged struggle Appius was victorious and drove the whole hostile force back to their camp. After despoiling the dead he returned to Messene.'[13] This account largely agrees with that of Zonaras.

If we assume, however, a pro-Roman bias in this depiction, another interpretation of the battle is possible. Appius leads his army out to attack the Greeks. Hieron sends his cavalry forward to engage the Romans before they are fully formed up for battle. The Syracusans defeat the Roman cavalry but are then driven off by the advancing Roman infantry. Hieron, seeing the size of the advancing host, decides not to engage fully and retreats to the cover of the hills. He concludes that the Carthaginians have betrayed him by allowing the Romans to cross and by not supporting him in the battle. Believing his situation to be hopeless, Hieron retreats to Syracuse under the cover of night.

In effect, the battle, while little more than a cavalry skirmish, is a strategic victory to the Romans. Zonaras and Polybius exaggerate the size of the Roman victory. Philinus concentrates on the cavalry skirmish and claims a victory to the Syracusans. Diodorus decides that the affray does not deserve to be described as a battle. Ever-ready to denigrate the Carthaginians he claims that the retreat of Hieron is due to the treachery of his allies. Although this version of events can only be supposition, it does have the advantage of incorporating all the known details and takes into account the supposed biases of all our sources.

If Polybius' account is correct, Appius had been able to take advantage of the poor dispositions of the enemy and defeat their two armies separately. Years of mistrust and hostility had probably played a role in their inability to support one another and in the Syracusans' hasty abandonment of the Carthaginians. Diodorus has a more detailed account of events after Messene. In this the Romans pursued the Carthaginians south and besieged them at the city of Echetla, but were defeated and driven off with heavy losses.

The Romans had saved their new ally, the Mamertines, from destruction, but nothing of consequence had been decided. The following year, 263, the Romans, being at peace throughout Italy, decided to take the war in Sicily seriously. They voted to send both Consuls and an army of four legions plus allies, about 40,000 men, to Sicily.

The new Consuls took the city of Adranum by storm and began a siege of Centuripae. The presence of such a strong Roman army persuaded many of Carthage's allies to switch sides. While the Romans were encamped before Centuripae, envoys arrived from Halaesa and numerous other Sicilian cities offering to ally themselves with Rome. The Romans accepted their offers and, having secured their position in north-eastern Sicily, they advanced on Syracuse with the intention of once again besieging the city.

Hieron, considering Syracuse to be abandoned by its ally and facing a Roman army twice as large as previously, sent envoys to the Consuls to discuss a settlement. Unbeknown to Hieron, the Carthaginians had sent a fleet to assist Syracuse but it had not arrived before the completion of the treaty. The Consuls were keen to accept Hieron's offer

> for the sake of their supplies; for since the Carthaginians commanded the sea they were apprehensive lest they should be cut off on all sides from the necessities of life, in view of the fact that the armies which had previously crossed to Sicily had run very short of provisions.[14]

Peace with Syracuse would simplify operations for the Romans, as they could concentrate on fighting the Carthaginians with a secure base to their rear. For the remainder of the war, Syracuse, along with Messene, would be an important supply and naval base for the Romans.

The Romans agreed to a fifteen year peace with Syracuse on the conditions that they pay an indemnity of 100 talents and return any prisoners of war. Hieron was allowed to continue to rule Syracuse and those cities that had been subject to him: Acrae, Leontini, Megara, Helorus, Neetum and Tauromenium. From this list we can see just how far the power of Syracuse had fallen since the days of Agathocles. Since his death the Syracusans had lost their empire in Italy and undisputed leadership of the Sicilians. Without access to these resources and troops, Syracuse was forced to rely on its own means. Hieron now ruled only the traditional territory of Syracuse plus the cities of Leontini and Tauromenium.

Although a wealthy city, Syracuse could not hope to compete with the resources of either Carthage or Rome. Apart from its widespread trading interests, Carthage controlled large agricultural lands in Africa and Sardinia, and rich silver mines in Spain. The Romans controlled all of Italy south of Rome and had access to perhaps 272,000 men,[15] plus allies, liable for military service. Left to its own means, Syracuse could raise armies of less than 15,000 men, a far cry from the 35,000 men the democracy sent to relieve Gela and Agathocles had taken to Italy, or the 80,000 that Dionysius took to Motya. Such a small force could not compete in the field with the

20,000 men Appius brought to Sicily, let alone the 40,000 that came the following year.

In signing this treaty, Hieron was admitting that Syracuse was no longer a power to be reckoned with and could not oppose the regional super-powers of Rome and Carthage. Perhaps Hieron hoped that the two new enemies would exhaust themselves and thereby he could resurrect Greek power on the island. It had happened before under Dionysius, Timoleon and Agathocles. All had, however, faced only a single enemy, Carthage, which was hated by the other Greeks of the island.

Earlier Syracusan rulers had been able to take advantage of Carthaginian difficulties, or indifference, and the hatred of the Greeks towards them to recover lost ground. Unlike them, Hieron was caught in a vice between two more powerful states engaged in a life and death struggle. There would be no opportunity for recovery. Under Hieron Syracuse was to be relegated to the role of a subordinate ally of Rome. As Pyrrhus had supposedly predicted, Sicily was now a prize to be fought over by the Romans and Carthaginians.

Chapter 20

The Siege of Akragas

How, when, and for what reasons the Romans first took to the sea.

Polybius 1.20

After the defection of Hieron, the Carthaginians realized that they needed to send a strong force to Sicily. They raised a large army of mercenaries, mainly Ligurians, Gauls and Spanish. Akragas, the second largest Greek city, was chosen to become their base of operations against the Romans. In one way, the choice of Akragas was a poor one, as the city had no proper harbour and is situated over a kilometre from the sea. Once the Romans had completed their blockade of the city it would be impossible for the Carthaginians to bring in supplies by ship.

In 262, Rome again sent both Consuls, Lucius Postumius and Quintus Mamilius, to Sicily. Learning of the concentration of Carthaginian troops at Akragas they abandoned all other operations and, gathering their forces before the city, began their siege. The Carthaginian dominance of the seas meant that the Romans could not rely on supplies from Italy. As a result they sent out foragers to bring in the local harvest, which usually occurs in Sicily around August. The Carthaginian garrison launched a surprise attack while the Romans were dispersed across the countryside and killed many. Encouraged by their success the Carthaginians advanced on the Roman camp and attacked it while many of its defenders were still absent. Polybius describes the advantages the strict discipline of the Romans gave them in such situations:

> But on this occasion and often on previous ones it is the excellence of their institutions which has saved the situation for the Romans; for with them death is the penalty incurred by a man who deserts the post or takes flight in any way from such a supporting force. Therefore on this occasion as on others they gallantly faced opposites who largely outnumbered them, and, though they suffered heavy loss, killed still

more of the enemy. Finally surrounding them as they were on the point of tearing up the palisade, they dispatched some on the spot and pressing hard on the rest pursued them with slaughter to the city.[1]

After this clash both sides conducted their operations with more caution. The Roman commanders separated their force into two detachments. One moved to the west of the city to cut it off from supplies. The two camps were connected by a double line of fortifications: one facing inwards towards the city and the other outwards to guard against any attempts to relieve it. Forts were then constructed at intervals to strengthen the lines. A supply base was located at the village of Herbessus, about 30km to the northeast of the city.

In this period the Romans appear to have been somewhat behind the times in their siege techniques, not employing artillery or other engines. If a city could not be stormed, or betrayed, their usual method was to encircle it with a double line of walls. The city would then be starved into submission. The discipline of the Roman forces meant they excelled at this type of operation.

Both sides now settled in for the siege, which lasted for over five months. Eventually the Carthaginian garrison began to suffer from hunger. The commander, Hannibal, sent constant messages begging for assistance. Finally the Carthaginian government dispatched the forces they had recruited, 50,000 infantry, 6,000 cavalry and sixty elephants to Sicily under the command of Hanno. Elephants were a new element in Carthaginian armies, probably raised as a result of facing those of Pyrrhus a decade earlier.

Pyrrhus' elephants had been Indian elephants brought back from the east by Alexander the Great and his Successors. This source was no longer available to the armies of the west and they were a dwindling resource. Pyrrhus had used his small force as a reserve to be unleashed at decisive moments in a battle rather than in the usual method of spreading them out along the front of the battle line.

Indian elephants were not available to the Carthaginians so they solved this problem by capturing and taming the African forest elephant. This was not the African bush Elephant but a smaller animal, up to 2.5m tall at the shoulder. It was also smaller than the Indian elephant, which could be 3m tall at the shoulder, and was therefore a weaker beast. According to Polybius, who would have seen both, in clashes between the two, the African elephants: 'declined the combat, as is the habit of African elephants; for unable to stand the smell and the trumpeting of the Indian elephants, and terrified, I suppose, also by their great size and strength, they at once turn tail and take to flight before they get near them.'[2]

The smaller size of the African elephant was not a problem for the Carthaginians, however, as none of their enemies fielded elephants of any type. Pyrrhus' elephants had been improved by the addition of towers to the backs of the animals to protect and elevate the fighting crew, who had previously sat directly on the backs of the animals. Pyrrhus may have been responsible for this innovation and it was adopted by the Carthaginians.

After landing at Lilybaeum, Hanno marched to Heraclea. From this point on the two accounts we have of the campaign, those of Polybius and Zonaras, vary greatly. The following narrative mostly follows Zonaras' version, which is more detailed and appears to be more coherent than Polybius' brief summary.

From Heraclea, Hanno marched on Akragas, successfully ambushing a detachment of Roman cavalry along the way. After arriving at Akragas, he camped on a hill, about 2km from the Roman lines, to the west of the city. At first Hanno challenged the Romans to fight but as they were well supplied, they were content to starve the city out and refused to do battle. As a result both sides did little more than skirmish for the next two months.

The deadlock was broken when a group of men approached Hanno and offered to betray the Roman depot at Herbessus. The attack was a complete success and the Romans now found themselves cut off from supplies. They 'were as a fact both besieged and besiegers at the same time; for they were so hard pressed by want of food and scarcity of the necessities of life, that they often contemplated raising the siege'.[3] It was at this point that Hieron, 'who thus far had co-operated with them reluctantly, now sent them grain'[4] This must have been a dangerous operation in the face of the dominance of the Carthaginian fleet and cavalry. The Syracusans needed to use 'every effort and every device' in order to provide only a 'moderate amount of strictly necessary supplies.'[5] Hieron had probably been half hearted in his assistance up to now as he hoped that both sides would wear themselves out in a long siege. With the capture of Herbessus and the Romans facing imminent defeat, he chose – or was forced – to provide some supplies.

These moderate supplies may have held off starvation but were insufficient to keep the army fully fed. Hunger soon led to disease breaking out within the Roman ranks. These privations caused the Romans to become 'eager to run risks, while Hanno now showed hesitation, since their eagerness led him to suspect that he might be ambushed.'[6] Eventually the deteriorating situation within Akragas, where the garrison and civilian population of 50,000 were facing starvation, forced Hanno to accept battle. Hunger had forced both sides to break the stalemate and risk all in a decisive encounter. Given the length of the siege, the battle was probably fought early in 261. The Consuls would have been keen to fight before their replacements arrived and stole their chance for glory.

Diodorus records that the Roman force besieging Akragas numbered 100,000 but this figure includes the slaves and labourers employed in the construction of the Roman earthworks. An army of two Consuls usually numbered 40,000 and to this should be added their Sicilian allies. Hanno had brought to Sicily a force of 56,000 men and sixty elephants. Allowing for losses from skirmishes and disease it is likely that both armies consisted of about 50,000 troops. The Carthaginians may have outnumbered the Romans, as Zonaras claims, and would have had more cavalry.

None of our sources have left a detailed account of the battle. As with much of the campaign, there are two different accounts of events. Zonaras describes a battle fought late in the day near the Roman siege lines:

> Hanno now undertook to bring on a battle, in the expectation that Hannibal would fall upon the Romans in the rear, assailing them from the wall. The consuls learned his plan, but remained inactive, and Hanno in scorn approached their entrenchments; and they sent some men to lie in ambush behind him. When now, toward evening, he fearlessly and contemptuously led a charge, the Romans joined battle with him both from ambush and palisade.[7]

In the ensuing battle Hanno was defeated with heavy losses. A sally by Hannibal was also repulsed by troops left to guard the Roman lines. After the battle Hanno abandoned his position and retreated to Heraclea.

Frontinus' account of the battle largely agrees with that of Zonaras but with greater emphasis on the Romans ambushing Hanno:

> Every day the Punic chieftains drew up their line of battle directly in front of the fortifications of the Romans, while Postumius offered resistance by way of constant skirmishes, conducted by a small band before his entrenchments. As soon as the Carthaginian commander came to regard this as a matter of course, Postumius quietly made ready all the rest of his troops within the ramparts, meeting the assault of the force with a few, according to his former practice, but keeping them engaged longer than usual. When, after noon was past, they were retreating, weary and suffering from hunger, Postumius, with fresh troops, put them to rout, exhausted as they were by the afore-mentioned embarrassments.[8]

Polybius has a completely different account of the battle. He claims that both sides 'led out their forces to the space between the camps and engaged.'[9] The most likely site for an open battle of this type would have been on the plain to the west of Akragas. In such a battle the Romans would have formed up in their usual three lines of heavy infantry, with the *velites* ahead and what remained of their cavalry on the wings. Polybius relates that the Carthaginians adopted the unusual formation of placing their elephants in reserve behind a first line of infantry. The normal position for such troops was either ahead of the battle line, or on the wings were they could engage the enemy cavalry. Perhaps the Carthaginians were not yet confident in using their new weapons, or they may have been emulating

Pyrrhus who tended to form up his small number of elephants as a reserve behind each wing. The Carthaginians would also have placed their cavalry on the wings.

Polybius describes the battle as a straightforward encounter where both sides advanced and engaged in combat:

> [The fight] lasted for long, but at the end the Romans put to flight the advanced line of Carthaginian mercenaries, and as the latter fell back on the elephants and the other divisions in their rear, the whole Phoenician army was thrown into disorder. A complete rout ensued, and most of them were put to the sword, some escaping to Heraclea. The Romans captured most of the elephants and all the baggage.[10]

Only Diodorus gives any indication of losses. He states that there were two battles, during which Hanno 'lost 3,000 infantry, 200 cavalry, and had 4,000 men taken prisoner; eight elephants were killed and thirty-three disabled by wounds.'[11] He also records the Roman losses for the entire campaign as 30,000 infantry and 1,500 cavalry. If accurate, this figure must include those of the allied Greeks and labourers, otherwise the Roman army would have been all but destroyed.

If Diodorus is correct, however, it is possible that there were two battles, one around the entrenchments late in the afternoon, ending with the Carthaginians being driven off and a second, an encounter battle the next day. Otherwise Zonaras and Polybius must have used completely different descriptions of the battle. In this case, with such conflicting accounts, it is impossible to determine the exact course of the conflict around Akragas.

There are also diverse accounts of the aftermath of the battle. Polybius claims that during the night Hannibal and the Carthaginian garrison took advantage of the fatigue of the Romans to break out of Akragas and escape. The Romans later entered the undefended city. Zonaras instead relates that Hannibal and his garrison sought to escape the city but were attacked by the people of Akragas. Hannibal managed to escape but most of his troops were lost. Turning on the Carthaginians did not save the Akragantians as the Romans refused to pardon them. Both authors agree that the Romans sacked the city and sold its inhabitants into slavery.

Polybius relates that it was only after the news of the sack of Akragas reached the Roman Senate they decided to widen the scope of their ambitions in Sicily:

> In their joy and elation they no longer confined themselves to their original designs and were no longer satisfied with having saved the Mamertines and with what they had gained in the war itself, but, hoping that it would be possible to drive the Carthaginians entirely out

of the island and that if this were done their own power would be much augmented, they directed their attention to this project and to plans that would serve their purpose.[12]

The capture of Akragas also appears to have had a decisive impact on the thinking of Hieron. Up to this point he had been lukewarm in his support of Rome. The fall of the city convinced Hieron that the Romans would be victorious and from that point on he became a steadfast ally of Rome for the remainder of his long reign.

The Carthaginians responded to the defeat at Akragas by sacking their general Hanno. Fortunately for him, he was not crucified but instead stripped of his rights as citizen and given a heavy fine. He was replaced as commander by Hamilcar. Hannibal, the former commander of Akragas, was given command of the fleet and ordered to raid Italy in an attempt to divert Roman forces from Sicily but met with little success. Later in the year Hamilcar, reputedly 'a man superior in generalship to all his countrymen'[13] took command of the fleet and campaigned with more urgency. He ravaged parts of Italy and won back some of the cities in Sicily. The new Roman Consuls for 261 achieved little of note except for taking control of a few inland towns in Sicily which came over to the Romans voluntarily after the fall of Akragas. A stalemate now descended over the conflict:

> As the Carthaginians maintained without any trouble the command of the sea, the fortunes of the war continued to hang in the balance. For in the period that followed, now that Akragas was in their hands, while many inland cities joined the Romans from dread of their land forces, still more seaboard cities deserted their cause in terror of the Carthaginian fleet. Hence when they saw that the balance of the war tended more and more to shift to this side or that for the above reasons, and that while Italy was frequently ravaged by naval forces, Libya remained entirely free from damage, they took urgent steps to get on the sea like the Carthaginians.[14]

The first three years of campaigning in Sicily had demonstrated to the Romans the difficulties of campaigning overseas without the support of a fleet large enough to challenge that of the Carthaginians. In addition to being able to raid Italy and Sicily at will, as long as the Carthaginians controlled the seas the Roman forces in Sicily would continue to risk being cut off from supplies. The Romans decided, therefore, that they must build a fleet and challenge the Carthaginians at sea.

The Romans had long possessed a small fleet of triremes but since their conquest of southern Italy they had come to rely mostly on the fleets of their Greek subject allies. Nonetheless, naval technology had moved on since the era of the trireme and the standard warship was now a quinquireme, a 'five.' As Grainger observes, since the days of Dionysius the Elder: 'there was a competitive pressure on all sea-states to build more, bigger and better ships – a naval arms race that the like of which was perhaps not seen again until the early years of the twentieth century AD.'[15]

The Romans ordered the construction of a fleet of 100 quinquiremes and twenty triremes. This presented problems, as Polybius claims that: 'their shipwrights were absolutely inexperienced in building quinquiremes, such ships never having been in use in Italy, the matter caused them much difficulty.'[16] He goes on to claim that the Romans were fortunate in capturing a Carthaginian ship and using it as a template. The author may be over dramatic here, as their new Syracusan allies had been building quinquiremes for over a century and could have easily supplied the necessary plans and experience. What the Romans may have copied was the Carthaginians method of cutting timbers of standard dimensions, numbering them and sending a complete package, something like a modern flat-pack, to the ship-yard. As the Romans built their fleet in less than three months, presumably the instructions were much simpler than their modern counterparts. While the fleet was being constructed, the rowers began their training on benches set up on land.

Two centuries earlier the Corinthians and Syracusans, when faced by superior Athenian seamanship, had developed tactics to negate their enemy's advantage. They reinforced the prows of their ships and, defying convention, deliberately ran into the enemy vessels head first in order to grapple them and turn the sea battle into a contest of boarding actions. The Athenians preferred to exploit their skill to outmanoeuvre the enemy ships and ram them.

In order to negate the superior experience of the Carthaginians at sea, the Romans developed their own tactics. They invented an ingenious device. They fitted to the prow of their ships with a device known as a *corvus*, raven. The *corvus* was a pole 7m in height and 25cm in diameter, with an iron spike at the top. To this was attached a gangway just over a metre wide, enough room for two marines to charge across side by side, while protected by hand-rails. The *corvus* was held in some sort of pivot, allowing the Romans to swing them in any direction rather than just directly forward. When a Roman vessel approached an enemy ship the *corvus* was raised by a pulley and then dropped onto the deck of the enemy vessel where it stuck fast. The Romans packed their ships with extra marines, allowing them to capture the Carthaginian vessels in boarding actions.

The one disadvantage of the *corvus*, and the extra marines, was that it made the Roman ships heavier and therefore slower than those of the Carthaginians. The added weight on the deck also affected the balance of the ship and made it less stable in heavy seas. In the treacherous seas to the south of Sicily this would prove to be a deadly shortcoming.

Traditionally the Romans had referred to the western Mediterranean Sea as being the *mare clause*, 'closed waters,' of the Carthaginians. Once their new fleet was ready the Romans would take to the sea in earnest and challenge the Carthaginians in their traditional domain.

Chapter 21

The Roman Conquest of Sicily

Such then was the end of the war between the Romans and Carthaginians for the possession of Sicily, and such were the terms of peace. It had lasted without a break for twenty-four years and is the longest, most unintermittent, and greatest war we know of.

Polybius 1.64

While the Romans were building and training their fleet, the land war continued in Sicily. Hamilcar appears to have used a strategy of attrition, refusing to fight the Romans in the field and attempting to wear them out through defensive sieges and raids. Given the Romans' lack of sophisticated siege techniques this was largely successful, as they wasted seven months ineffectively besieging the heavily fortified but small inland town of Mytistratus.

In 260 the Romans were finally ready to engage the Carthaginians at sea. At first it did not go well. The Consul who had been entrusted with the land operations, Gnaeus Cornelius, was taken in by a Carthaginian ruse. He sailed his small fleet of seventeen ships to Lipari, where he had been tricked by false reports of a rebellion. The Carthaginians trapped him in the harbour. Gnaeus panicked and surrendered his force without a fight.

A few days later, however, the Romans would win their first naval battle. The bulk of the fleet, about a hundred ships, was sailing along the coast of Italy when Hannibal decided to observe and evaluate the new Roman navy. Taking fifty ships he encountered the Roman fleet and was quickly overwhelmed by their superior numbers. Hannibal escaped with only a small portion of his squadron.

When the other Consul for the year, Gaius Diulius, heard of his colleague's defeat, he took command of the fleet. Learning that the Carthaginians were ravaging the coast near Mylae, he immediately sailed against them. Despite their recent defeat, the Carthaginians, still commanded by Hannibal, were 'overjoyed and eager, as they despised the inexperience of the Romans.'[1] The Carthaginian fleet numbered 130 ships, their flagship was a seven captured from Pyrrhus, while the Romans had 120 ships.[2] Overconfident, Hannibal sailed directly at the outnumbered Romans, without bothering to manoeuvre or to maintain good order. The Roman *corvi* took the Carthaginians completely by surprise and they lost the ensuing battle and fifty ships, including their flagship. The reported surprise of the Carthaginians at the deployment of the Roman *corvi* appears unusual as the two sides had already clashed twice. Given the one-sided nature of the two earlier fights perhaps there had been no need, or opportunity, to deploy the *corvi*.

After the defeat at Mylae, Diodorus observed that 'no one is so shattered in spirit by defeat as are the Carthaginians.'[3] For the next two years they limited themselves to defensive actions but refused to take on the Romans in any major engagement at sea. The Romans, who 'contrary to all expectation, gained the prospect of success at sea their determination to prosecute the war became twice as strong.'[4] They decided to broaden the fighting by invading Corsica and Sardinia. Corsica was captured but the attempt on Sardinia failed. In Sicily, however, the fighting continued in a desultory manner with both sides capturing minor towns from each other but achieving little of significant value.

In 258 the Romans besieged the city of Camarina but were unable to capture it. On this occasion the Roman general decided to make use of the expertise of the Syracusan engineers and: 'having sent to Hieron for engines of war, bringing up a siege battery and making a breach in the wall. He captured the city, and sold into slavery most of the inhabitants.'[5] Polybius provides further detail, stating that the city fell only after they had brought up a 'siege battery and made a breach in the wall.'[6] With the fall of Camarina the Romans secured their hold on eastern Sicily as many further cities came over to them.

In 257 the Romans won another decisive naval victory, when they ambushed Hamilcar off Tyndaris. Despite this 'the land forces accomplished nothing worthy of mention, but spent their time in minor operations of no significance.'[7] Made confident by their victories at sea, the Romans decided on a more daring strategy to end the stalemate, they would emulate Agathocles and invade Africa. In order to achieve this objective, the Romans decided to build an even larger fleet. The Carthaginians, realizing they would eventually lose the war if they could not regain control of the sea, embarked on their own ship building programme. As a result of these decisions both sides

> threw themselves most thoroughly into the task of organizing naval forces and disputing the command of the sea ... The Romans, therefore, after making preparations as I said, for the coming summer, set to sea with a fleet of three hundred and thirty decked ships of war and put in to Messene.[8]

The Carthaginians, perhaps learning of the Roman intentions, threw all their efforts into building a new fleet of 350 ships. The Roman fleet was accompanied by the transports taking Regulus' invasion force to Africa. The best troops in the army were assigned to the warships in order to boost the numbers of marines in case the Carthaginians attempted to intercept the fleet. After leaving Messene the fleet sailed past Syracuse and westward along the southern coast of Sicily. The Carthaginians, seemingly aware of the Roman objective, were determined to prevent the invasion of their homeland. They sailed to Lilybaeum and then along the southern coast to Heraclea.

The two fleets clashed off Cape Ecnomus, east of Heraclea and near to the modern city of Licata. It was a huge battle, one of the largest naval battles ever fought. The Romans had 330 ships and 140,000 men, opposed to the Carthaginians' 350 ships and 150,000 men.[9] The Romans formed up their fleet in four squadrons. Two formed the vanguard but were angled back, a third was behind these protecting the transports, and the fourth in reserve. The Roman fleet was commanded by the Consuls for 256 Lucius Manlius and Marcus Regulus. They commanded the two forward divisions. The final formation was 'in the form of a simple wedge'[10] with the point facing the Carthaginians.

The Carthaginians, commanded by Hamilcar, formed a single line, with both wings overlapping the Roman formation. Both sides were attempting to take advantage of their natural strengths. The Romans with their heavier ships planned to smash through the Carthaginian line, whereas the Carthaginians hoped to use their faster ships to attack the flanks and rear of the Romans. The left wing of the Carthaginian line was angled forward along the shoreline.

The Romans began the battle by attacking the thin line of the Carthaginian centre. They obeyed Hamilcar's orders to fall back and delay contact. The first and second Roman squadrons pressed forward opening a gap between themselves and the third and fourth squadrons. When Hamilcar believed that he had drawn the Roman leading squadrons far enough away from the transports he ordered all the Carthaginian vessels to engage. The Carthaginian right attacked the Roman rearguard, their left fought the third squadron while their centre engaged the Roman vanguard. The encounter degenerated into three separate battles, all some distance from each other:

> The engagement that followed was a very hot one, the superior speed of the Carthaginians enabling them to move round the enemy's flank as well as to approach easily and retire rapidly, while the Romans, relying on their sheer strength when they closed with the enemy, grappling with the ravens every ship as soon as it approached, fighting also, as they were, under the very eyes of both the Consuls, who were

personally taking part in the combat, had no less high hopes of success.[11]

First to give way was the Carthaginian centre. Manlius pursued the fleeing enemy while Regulus turned to assist the rearguard who, hampered by guarding the Roman horse transports, were having the worst of the struggle. The Carthaginian right was overwhelmed and it too fled. Finally both Consuls, observing that the Roman third squadron was in difficulties, attacked the Carthaginian left. This was trapped against the shoreline and annihilated. The Carthaginians lost more than thirty ships sunk and sixty-four captured. Roman losses were twenty-four ships sunk.

Polybius claims that the major reason for the Roman victory was again their use of the *corvus*, which appears to have paralyzed the enemy, for: 'if the Carthaginians had not been afraid of the ravens and simply hedged them in and held them close to the land instead of charging, apprehensive as they were of coming to close quarters.'[12] The Roman commanders had also shown great tactical skill in co-coordinating their separate squadrons. They had obviously learned a lot in the six years since they had built their fleet.

After the battle the Romans pulled in to Sicily to repair their vessels and rest their crews prior to crossing to Africa. Like Agathocles before them, Romans landed on the eastern tip of Cape Bon. The fortress city of Aspis was first to fall after a brief siege and was garrisoned by the Romans. The city at Kerkouane, which had recovered from Agathocles capture, was also sacked by Regulus and this time was abandoned permanently. The Carthaginians, demoralized by news of the defeat at Ecnomus, failed to oppose the Romans and concentrated their forces around Carthage. As a result the Romans met no opposition as their plundered the rich farmlands of the cape:

> Setting out from it [Aspis], they ravaged the country and acquired cities, some of their own free will and others by intimidation; they also secured great booty, received vast numbers of deserters, and got back many of their own men who had been captured in the previous wars.[13]

While this was occurring, a message arrived from Rome with orders for one of the Consuls to return while the other remained with a force sufficient to end the campaign. Regulus, noted for his lack of wealth, decided to stay. No doubt he hoped to win further plunder. A force of 15,000 infantry, 500 cavalry and forty ships was assigned to him. These small numbers display a certain overconfidence on the part of the Romans. They appear to have badly underestimated the resources that Carthage could call upon in an emergency. Hamilcar, with 5,000 troops, returned to Africa and other forces were hastily raised.

Despite this, Regulus' forces were sufficient to defeat the Carthaginians at the battle of Adys. The battle took place in difficult terrain and, after a hard fought infantry fight, the Romans prevailed and captured the enemy camp. According to Polybius the Carthaginian defeat was largely 'owing to the incompetence of their commanders':

> Though their best hope lay in their cavalry and elephants, yet by quitting the level country and shutting themselves up in a precipitous place, difficult of access, they were sure to make it plain to their adversaries how best to attack them, and this is exactly what did happen.[14]

Importantly for later events, the unengaged Carthaginian cavalry and elephants were able to escape.

The Roman victory encouraged the Numidians to revolt and they joined in the pillaging of the countryside. The Carthaginians, after two serious defeats within the year, huddled in despair within the city expecting a Roman siege. Faced by another crisis they: 'sought out the sacrifices that had been omitted for many years, and multiplied the honours paid to the gods.'[15] The implication being that human sacrifice had fallen into disuse but, faced by destruction, they again resorted to sacrificing children to appease the gods.

Regulus, with his annual term of Consul coming to an end, hoped to win all the glory by bringing the campaign to an immediate end. He offered terms of surrender to the Carthaginians but

> since he was elated by his success and took no account of the vicissitudes of human fortune, dictated terms of such scope and nature that the peace framed by him was no better than slavery. Seeing the ambassadors were displeased at these terms, he said that on the contrary they should be grateful, for this reason, that inasmuch as they were unable to offer resistance either on land or sea in defence of their freedom, they should accept as a gift whatever concessions he might make.[16]

While the Carthaginians were debating Regulus' terms, a new group of mercenaries arrived from Greece. One of these was an experienced Spartan officer by the name of Xanthippus. He spent his time telling his friends, and anyone else who would listen, what the Carthaginian commanders had done wrong and how they should fix it. His self promotion earned him a hearing with the Carthaginian generals who handed over to him *de facto* control of the army. Once appointed, he spent the winter drilling the troops:

Drawing it up in good order before the city and even beginning to manoeuvre some portions of it correctly and give the word of command in the orthodox military terms, the contrast to the incompetency of the former generals was so striking that the soldiery expressed their approval by cheers and were eager to engage the enemy.[17]

Early in the new year, the Carthaginian commanders, accompanied by Xanthippus, advanced out of the city with an army of 12,000 infantry, 4,000 cavalry and nearly 100 elephants. They camped in open countryside close to Tunis. Regulus, expecting to be relieved at any time, was keen to give battle despite the flat terrain. This was one of the weaknesses of the Roman system, Consuls appointed for only one year were generally eager to give battle in order to win the glory, and the loot, for themselves.

The size of Regulus' force at the battle is not recorded but it must have been somewhat smaller than that which remained with him after Manlius' departure. It probably outnumbered the Carthaginian foot but was seriously deficient in cavalry. Xanthippus decided to engage the Romans on the flat plain between Carthage and Tunis. He gave the Carthaginians a lesson in how they should draw up their armies in order to take advantage of their usual superiority in cavalry and elephants, and inferiority in infantry. The elephants were spread out along the front of the army to cover the infantry formed up behind them in the centre. The cavalry, supported by the best mercenary infantry, was placed on the wings.

Regulus, alarmed at the numbers of elephants, drew up his infantry with the heavy infantry in a deeper formation than usual, probably by doubling the depth of his maniples. The few cavalry were divided between the wings and the *velites* skirmished in front of the heavy infantry. By shortening his line in this manner Regulus' allowed the Carthaginian cavalry to extend well beyond both his flanks.

As soon as the battle began, Xanthippus ordered his cavalry to attack the exposed flanks of the Roman line. They quickly routed the small numbers of Roman horse. Meanwhile the left of the Roman infantry managed to avoid most of the elephants facing them and broke the mercenary foot behind, pursuing them all the way to their camp. Along the rest of the infantry line, however, the Romans struggled against the elephants: 'pushed back when they encountered them and trodden under foot by the strength of the animals, fell in heaps in the *mêlée*, while the formation of the main body, owing to the depths of the ranks behind, remained for a time unbroken.'[18]

The battle was decided when the victorious Carthaginian cavalry began to the attack the rear and flanks of the now surrounded Roman right. The so far uncommitted infantry of the Carthaginian left joined the assault and the Romans broke. Most of the fugitives were cut down by the pursuing cavalry and elephants but Regulus and 500 others managed to escape only to be captured later. Two thousand survivors of the victorious Roman left managed to escape the battlefield and retreat to the safety of Aspis. The Carthaginians lost about 800 dead, mostly from among the mercenaries. Diodorus claims that it was Regulus' failure 'to guard against divine retribution' in refusing reasonable terms to the Carthaginians that caused his defeat, 'and in a short time he met with the punishment that his arrogance deserved.'[19]

The tactics used by Xanthippus would become a template for future Carthaginian commanders on how to best fight the Roman legions. Xanthippus soon displayed that he was also a keen student of Carthaginian politics and their mistrust of successful generals. After receiving a sizeable reward, he prudently sailed home. Zonaras relates, however, a different version of Xanthippus' fate. In this story, the ungrateful Carthaginians pursued his ship and sank it. 'Their reason for doing this was to avoid seeming to have been saved by his ability; for they thought that when once he had perished, the renown of his deeds would also perish.' Another version of Xanthippus' fate records that he took service in Sicily with the Sicels, led them to a victory over the Romans but was later murdered.[20]

The Carthaginian victory at Tunis had ended the immediate Roman threat to their city. Buoyed by their success, the Carthaginians decided to refit their remaining ships and build new ones. Soon they were able to put to sea with a fleet of 200 ships. In the early summer of 255 the Romans sailed for Africa with a fleet of 350 vessels under the command of the year's two Consuls, Marcus Aemilius and Servius Fulvius. They encountered the Carthaginian fleet near Carthage and easily defeated it, capturing 114 ships. After rescuing the surviving garrison at Aspis they sailed for Sicily. The fleet was struck by a wild storm off Camarina and here the Romans may have paid dearly for lack of stability of their ships caused by the extra weight of their *corvi*. The fleet was nearly destroyed:

> For of their 364 ships only 80 were saved; the rest either foundered or were dashed by the waves against the rocks and headlands and broken to pieces, covering the shore with corpses and wreckage. History tells of no greater catastrophe at sea taking place at one time.[21]

The disaster was blamed on the arrogance of the Roman Consuls who ignored the advice of their ships' pilots. Hieron once again makes a brief appearance in the record when he received 'the survivors hospitably, and having refreshed them with clothing, food, and other essentials, brought them safely to Messene.'[22]

The defeat of Regulus and the destruction of the Roman fleet breathed new life into the Carthaginian war effort. They sent reinforcements, including 140 elephants, under the command of Hasdrubal to Sicily and prepared another fleet of 200 warships. The Carthaginians were able to re-capture Akragas, perhaps due to treachery.

The Romans, despite the enormity of their disaster at sea, resolved to continue the war, for as Polybius observes: 'the Romans, to speak generally, rely on force in all their enterprises, and think it is incumbent on them to carry out their projects in spite of all, and that nothing is impossible when they have once decided on it.'[23] They resolved to build a new fleet and began the construction of 220 new ships. Within three months the fleet was built and in 254 they attacked and captured the major Carthaginian city of Panormus. The following year they successfully raided the African coast but lost another 150 ships in a storm. This time their resources were too stretched and they were unable to replace the losses.

As a result of these losses, the fleet of Syracuse was called into action and in 252 Hieron provided ships to Romans to capture the Carthaginian naval base at Lipari. The island was captured and the inhabitants massacred. The natural volcanic springs would later make the islands a popular tourist destination under Roman rule, as they are now.

With their fleet reduced, the Romans now relied on their army to win the war in Sicily. Although they won some minor victories, the war once again drifted into a stalemate as the Romans were apparently cautious about facing the large force of Carthaginian elephants in the open field. The apparent lack of fight among the Romans encouraged Hasdrubal to attempt to recover Panormus. In 251 he led an army against the city and ravaged the countryside in an attempt to persuade the Consul, Caecilius, to come out and fight.

Caecilius planned, however, to draw Hasdrubal onto a battlefield of his own choosing. He sent some of his light infantry out to skirmish with the Carthaginians while others were stationed in a trench in front of the walls of the city. Their supplies of missiles were constantly replenished. The rest of his infantry were led out of the gate opposite the enemy left wing. The drivers of the Carthaginian elephants 'anxious to exhibit their prowess to Hasdrubal and wishing the victory to be due to themselves, all charged those of the enemy who were in advance and putting them easily to flight pursued them to the trench.' Here Caecilius' careful preparations came into effect. The Romans poured 'a rapid shower of javelins' into the elephants, wounding many and throwing them into confusion. A stampeding elephant is just as much a danger to its own side as that of the enemy. The fleeing Carthaginian elephants 'turned on their own troops, trampling down and killing the men and disturbing and breaking the ranks.'[24] Caecilius then attacked the disordered Carthaginian troops and routed them with heavy losses.

A few Carthaginians escaped by swimming out to their fleet but most were killed in the pursuit. Caecilius captured 120 elephants by offering quarter to their handlers.[25] The animals were shipped of to Rome, no doubt to take part in the Consul's victory parade. The Roman crowds would develop a fondness for spectacles involving elephants and later the African forest elephant would be hunted into extinction to feed the arenas. Carthaginian possessions in Sicily were now reduced to a few isolated garrisons, the most important being the port cities of Lilybaeum and Drepanum.

The victory at Panormus encouraged the Roman government to increase their efforts and end the war in Sicily. They gathered a new fleet of 200 ships and, in 250, sent it to Sicily under the command of the new Consuls. Their orders were to capture the major Carthaginian base of Lilybaeum, for the Romans believed that 'if it fell into their possession it would be easy for them to transfer the war to Libya.'[26] There they joined the army and began the siege of the city.

The Carthaginian governments also realized the strategic importance of the city and threw all their efforts into its defence. The fighting was heavy but, like Pyrrhus before them, the Romans found the well fortified city a tough nut to crack. The Romans again suffered severely from supply problems until 'Hieron, the king of Syracuse, dispatched an abundant supply of grain, and gave them fresh courage to resume the siege.'[27] Although the Romans had a fleet stationed off Lilybaeum, due to the strong tides and winds they were unable to prevent Carthaginian supply ships from entering the harbour. Roman attempts to block the entrance failed due to the same conditions and the depth of the sea.

After the siege had dragged on for over a year, the Romans decided to break the deadlock by launching a naval attack on Drepanum. The Carthaginian commander, Adherbal, decided that it was better to risk a battle at sea rather than allow the Romans to blockade the port. He advanced his force out of the harbour on the opposite side to that of the Roman advance.

The Roman commander, Publius, was overconfident and did not expect the Carthaginians to come out and fight. His fleet had just begun to enter the port when he observed the Carthaginian vessels outflanking him. Attempting to give his ships more room in which to manoeuvre he ordered them to withdraw from the harbour. In the confined space the Roman vessels, with their nearly raised crews, fell into confusion as they collided with one another. Eventually they managed to get their ships into a rough line close to the shore. While the Romans had been desperately forming a line of battle, Adherbal had managed to outflank their left wing with five ships.

For once the Carthaginian fleet had the advantage:

They much surpassed the Romans in speed, owing to the superior build of their ships and the better training of the rowers, as they had freely developed their line in the open sea. For if any ships found themselves hard pressed by the enemy it was easy for them owing to their speed to

retreat safely to the open water and from thence, fetching round on the
ships that pursued and fell on them, they either got in their rear or
attacked them on the flank, and as the enemy then had to turn round
and found themselves in difficulty owing to the weight of the hulls and
the poor oarsmanship of the crews, they rammed them repeatedly and
sunk many.[28]

Adherbal had also placed the best of his infantry on board his ships and on
this occasion the Carthaginians were not at a disadvantage when it came to
boarding actions. The battle became a rout and Publius fled with about
thirty ships. The Carthaginians captured the remaining ninety-three Roman
vessels. Publius was later prosecuted and received a heavy fine.[29]

Soon after, the Romans suffered further a disaster at sea, with two more
fleets being destroyed by a storm of the southern coast as they attempted
to trap the Carthaginians. The Carthaginian pilots had more experience of
the area and the conditions. Anticipating the storm they prudently rounded
Cape Pachynus to shelter along the east coast. Polybius describes the stalemate that followed as the Romans: 'relinquished the sea, while continuing
to maintain their hold on the country. The Carthaginians were now masters
of the sea and were not hopeless of regaining their position on land.'[30]

This stalemate would last for seven years as the Romans continued
unsuccessfully to press the siege of Lilybaeum. The Carthaginians appointed
a new commander Hamilcar Barca (Thunderbolt), the father of the famous
general Hannibal who would later invade Italy during the Second Punic War.
Hamilcar continued the earlier strategy of refusing battle but harassing
the Romans with raids and ambushes from his base on Mount Herctae.
If the Carthaginians believed that they could force Rome to terms with
this strategy, they had underestimated the resolve of the Romans, whose
idea of making war was to continue fighting until the enemy was completely
defeated.

Such a war of attrition was costly to both sides but it was the
Carthaginians who began to feel the pinch first. In 244 the Carthaginian
government decided to cut costs by demobilizing a large part of their navy.
Sensing a chance to break the deadlock the Romans built yet another fleet.
The ongoing cost of the war had meant that there was no money left in
the public treasury for such an outlay. Instead the rich among the Romans
funded the project themselves on the understanding that if they won the
war they would be repaid from the booty. In 242 a fleet of 200 ships sailed
to Sicily under the command of the Consul, Lutatius.[31] Unopposed at sea,
he laid siege to Drepanum and spent the time drilling his crews.

Caught unawares, the Carthaginians were forced to launch a new fleet or
risk losing Sicily. They dispatched a hastily raised force of 250 warships
under the command Hanno to Sicily. Lutatius stationed his force at the
Aegates Islands off Lilybaeum and prepared to intercept the Carthaginians

as they approached the city. Although the sea was rough when the Carthaginians approached, Lutatius decided to engage the Carthaginian vessels while they were still laden with men and supplies for the crossing. This time the advantage was with the well trained crews of the Romans, for the Carthaginian ships: 'being loaded, were not in a serviceable condition for battle, while the crews were quite untrained, and had been put on board for the emergency, and their marines were recent levies.' The Roman fleet easily won the battle, sinking fifty ships and capturing seventy.[32]

The Roman victory at the Aegates Islands was decisive. The Carthaginians were without a fleet and no longer had the capacity to build another. The Romans dominated the seas and the Carthaginians were no longer capable of sending supplies to their few surviving garrisons. The government sent a message to Hamilcar Barca giving him full power to negotiate peace. Lutatius offered the following terms:

> There shall be friendship between the Carthaginians and Romans on the following terms if approved by the Roman people. The Carthaginians to evacuate the whole of Sicily and not to make war on Hieron or bear arms against the Syracusans or the allies of the Syracusans. The Carthaginians to give up to the Romans all prisoners without ransom. The Carthaginians to pay to the Romans by instalments in twenty years 2,200 Euboean talents.[33]

The government at Rome did not accept these terms and sent a delegation to Sicily to make amendments. They reduced the term of payment by one half, added a thousand talents to the indemnity, and demanded the evacuation by the Carthaginians of all islands lying between Sicily and Italy. Cassius Dio adds that they also 'forbade them to sail past Italy or their allied territory abroad in ships of war, or to employ any mercenaries from such districts.'[34] The Carthaginians had little choice other than to accept the terms and after twenty-four years the war was finally over.

Chapter 22

The Death of Hieron II

Quintus Lutatius became consul and departed for Sicily, where with his brother Catulus he established order throughout the island; he also deprived the inhabitants of their arms. Thus Sicily, with the exception of Hieron's domain, was enslaved by the Romans.

Zonaras 8.17

The First Punic War had inflicted enormous losses on both sides in resources and manpower. In the naval fighting alone: 'the Romans lost in this war about seven hundred quinquiremes, inclusive of those that perished in the shipwrecks, and the Carthaginians about five hundred.'[1] The Romans, as the victors, were in a much stronger position to recover as they shared the belief that in war the loser should pay the costs of the winner. In addition to the Carthaginian tribute they would also be able to exploit the resources of their new province, Sicily.

By defeating Carthage, the Romans had achieved their major aim of the war, driving the enemy out of Sicily and seizing most of it for themselves. Hieron was allowed to maintain control of the south-eastern corner of the island, from Tauromenium to Camarina, but the rest of Sicily became a Roman province ruled by a governor. Sicily was Rome's first overseas conquest and, as such, its cities were not absorbed into Rome in the same way as the Italian communities had been nor were large colonies of Roman settlers sent to the island. According to Appian, Rome 'levied tribute on the Sicilians, and apportioned certain naval charges among their towns, and sent a praetor each year to govern them.'[2] The exploitation of Sicily's riches would encourage the Romans to seek further conquests, for as Cicero astutely observed, Sicily was: 'the first who taught our ancestors how glorious a thing it was to rule over foreign nations.'[3]

Due to the services rendered by Hieron during the war, Syracuse and its possessions were, in 241, spared the fate of their fellow Sicilians. In gratitude for his support during the war, Hieron was made a permanent ally of Rome and freed from paying tribute. In the peace treaty, the Carthaginians were explicitly forbidden from making war against Syracuse.

The twenty-three years of peace that followed the end of the First Punic War allowed Syracuse to enjoy another period of prosperity. This era is only sparsely recorded as the ancient historians tended to be more interested in dramatic events, such as war, rather than the humdrum of day to day life. One record, although perhaps not an unbiased one, of the peace and prosperity of Syracuse during this period is recorded by Hieron's court poet Theocritus:

> *And fair and fruitful may their cornlands be!*
> *Their flocks in thousands bleat upon the lea,*
> *Fat and full-fed; their kin, as home they wind,*
> *The lagging traveller of his rest remind!*
> *With might and main their fallows let them till:*
> *Till comes the seedtime, and cicadas trill*
> *(Hid from the toilers of the hot midday*
> *In the thick leafage) on the topmost spray!*
> *O'er shield and spear their webs let spiders spin,*
> *And none so much as name the battle-din!*
> *Then Hieron's lofty deeds may minstrels bear ...*
> *Of Sicel Arethuse, and Hieron's fame.*[4]

Hieron is recorded as having ruled moderately. He brought in laws governing the collection of tithes on agricultural produce which were still in operation a century and half later when they were violated by the Roman governor Verres. Despite accepting the title of king, he avoided wearing regalia and such was his popularity that he could appear in public without a bodyguard. According to Polybius, he was so admired that he ruled: 'undisturbed by plots, and he kept clear of that envy which is wont to wait on superiority. Actually on several occasions when he wished to lay down his authority, he was prevented from doing so by the common action of the citizens.'[5] Whether these offers were genuine or not cannot be determined two millennia later. It should be remembered, however, that Agathocles also reputedly offered to stand down on several occasions.

The period of peace and prosperity after the end of the war allowed Hieron to build many new public buildings and works, within both Syracuse and its subject cities. In order to demonstrate his status as a king, Hieron had to display his wealth on the international stage. Examples that are recorded are: the portraits of him painted at Olympia to celebrate his victories in the chariot races and the lavish presents he sent to Rhodes after it was devastated by an earthquake. To ensure his self promotion, his gift to Rhodes included a group of statues 'representing the People of Rhodes being crowned by the People of Syracuse.'[6] Perhaps the most expensive piece of royal self-promotion was an enormous ship that Hieron sent, full of grain, to Ptolemy of Egypt. It was a floating palace which included a temple and banqueting hall with mosaic floors. It was propelled by twenty banks of oars and a crew of 600 sailors. To build it, Hieron had 'caused such a number of trees to be cut down on Mount Aetna as would have been sufficient for sixty triremes.'[7]

The most important power for Hieron to impress was of course Rome. In 237 Hieron visited Rome, where he made himself popular by attending the games and distributing a large quantity of grain to the people. Later the Romans demonstrated their high regard for Hieron by giving him gifts from their spoils taken in wars against the Gauls and Illyrians.

Like most Hellenistic monarchs, Hieron tried to impress others by attracting famous men of learning and literature to his court. The most renowned of these was the mathematician and engineer Archimedes. Few details of Archimedes' life survive. He was born in Syracuse in about 287 and was a relative of Hieron. At some stage during his career Hieron is supposed to have 'persuaded him to turn his art somewhat from abstract notions to material things, and by applying his philosophy somehow to the needs which make themselves felt, to render it more evident to the common mind.'[8]

Perhaps the most celebrated of these tasks is the tale recorded by the Roman scientific writer, Vitruvius, about the golden crown. Hieron suspected that a goldsmith contracted to make a golden crown had cheated the king by replacing some of the metal with the much cheaper silver. He gave Archimedes the task of proving the fraud. Famously, Archimedes is supposed to have solved the problem in the baths, realizing that the same weight of different materials displace different amounts of water. He immediately 'leapt out of the vessel in joy, and, returning home naked, cried out with a loud voice that he had found that of which he was in search, for he continued exclaiming, in Greek, '*eureka*', (I have found it out).'[9]

Archimedes then alternately placed the crown, an equal weight of gold and of silver in the same container filled with water and measured the amount that ran out. When the amount displaced by the crown was found to be less than that of the gold but more than that of the silver, he had his proof that the goldsmith had stolen some of the gold. The unfortunate manufacturer was no doubt punished in an extremely painful manner.

Alas, the story is unlikely to be true. The specific weights of gold and silver are so close that with small weight of a crown the difference in the amounts of water displaced would be too small to measure accurately within the range of experimental error. Nonetheless, Archimedes may have been able to solve the problem using his own 'Law of Buoyancy' and 'Law of the Lever' in the following manner:

Suspend the wreath from one end of a scale and balance it with an equal mass of gold suspended from the other end. Then immerse the suspended wreath and gold into a container of water. If the scale remains in balance then the wreath and the gold have the same volume, and so the wreath has the same density as pure gold. But if the scale tilts in the direction of the gold, then the wreath has a greater volume than the gold, and so its density is less than that of gold. It must then be an alloy of gold and some lighter material.[10]

Perhaps more importantly to Hieron's needs and the security of Syracuse, Archimedes was also placed in charge of the defences of the city. In this capacity supervised the manufacture of war engines; improving designs and as well as inventing new ones. Archimedes also improved the fortifications of the fortress guarding the important pass of Euryalus, leading up to the Epipolae, to such a state that it was considered impregnable. The impressive and picturesque remains of this stronghold can be visited at *Castello Eurialo* in the outer suburbs of modern Syracuse. Although Syracuse may have enjoyed two decades of peace and prosperity after the First Punic War, the same cannot be said of either Rome or Carthage. The Romans were faced with a revolt of the Falisci, a people who lived to the north of Rome. This they easily crushed and destroyed their capital. The Carthaginians faced a much more formidable challenge; a revolt of their mercenaries was joined by both their Libyan subjects and Numidian neighbours.

The revolt began when the mercenaries and Libyan troops from Sicily were evacuated to Carthage and demanded their pay. As a result of the war and the reparations due to Rome, Carthage was hard pressed to meet their demands. The Carthaginians hoped to bargain down the amount owing. They gathered the troops at a city named Sicca (Le Kef), about 170km inland, and made a part payment. There the soldiers, remembering the lavish promises Hamilcar had made to them during the war, calculated 'the total pay due to them, all to their own advantage, and having arrived at a most exorbitant result, submitted that this was the sum they should demand from the Carthaginians.'[11] They rejected the Carthaginian offer of a reduced amount and 20,000 of them marched on the city, camping at Tunis.

Here, one of their commanders from Sicily whom they trusted, Gesco, managed to negotiate settlement with a number of the nationalities individually. This process broke down when a runaway Roman slave, a Campanian named Spendius, believed he would be returned to his master and executed. He was joined by a Libyan, Mathos, who believed that if the foreign mercenaries departed the Libyans would be at the mercy of the Carthaginians. At an assembly of the army, they convinced most of the troops to join them and murdered any opposition by having them stoned to death before they could speak. The troops seized Gesco and his pay chests by force. 'From this time forward they were at open war with

Carthage, having bound themselves by certain impious oaths contrary to the principles recognized by all mankind.'[12]

Being short of funds, and denied Libyan manpower, it was difficult for the Carthaginians to quickly raise an army to oppose the rebellion. Meanwhile the native Libyan population rebelled and 70,000 of them joined Mathos. Some of the Numidian rulers also allied themselves with rebels. Carthage was cut off from the interior; the cities of Utica and Hippacritae were besieged. A relief force sent to Utica was ambushed and defeated by the rebels. At this point the situation looked grim for Carthage.

The Carthaginians appealed for help from overseas and Hieron sent them a gift of grain. Polybius explains this as an astute move to prevent Rome gaining an easy victory:

> The stronger power should not be able to attain its ultimate object entirely without effort. In this he reasoned very wisely and sensibly, for such matters should never be neglected, and we should never contribute to the attainment by one state of a power so preponderant, that none dare dispute with it even for their acknowledged rights.[13]

At this point Hamilcar Barca was appointed sole commander of the Carthaginian forces. He demonstrated the same abilities he had in Sicily, outmanoeuvring and harassing the larger enemy forces. Hamilcar also used diplomacy to buy off sections of the disparate alliance. Becoming desperate, the rebels tortured Gesco and other Carthaginian prisoners to death and promised to do the same to any new captives. Hamilcar responded by having captured enemies trampled to death by his elephants, a punishment copied from the Successor kings. Atrocities on both sides soon escalated. Eventually Mathos and Spendius were captured and crucified. In 237 the Libyans surrendered on terms and the revolt was finally crushed.

After the conclusion of the war Hamilcar Barca was sent to Spain to expand Carthaginian territory. Although Carthage was forbidden by its treaty with Rome to send forces east, there was no such prohibition to it campaigning in Spain. Over the next two decades Hamilcar and his successors were successful in building a large empire in Spain. This increased Carthaginian wealth and power and made a new war with Rome inevitable.

During Carthage's war with the mercenaries, Rome had behaved in accordance with the treaty. This attitude soon changed. Rome took advantage of another mercenary revolt in Sardinia to claim the island contrary to their agreement with Carthage. The Carthaginians objected and made preparations to crush the revolt. The Romans declared that this was a hostile act and declared war on Carthage. In no state to fight Rome again, the Carthaginians capitulated. They surrendered Sardinia and agreed to pay another 1,200 talents. Polybius believed that the Roman action was 'contrary to all justice, and merely because the occasion permitted it.'[14]

It was the cause of great bitterness in Carthage and may have been the catalyst for their expansion in Spain.

Rome kept a watchful eye on Carthage's expansion in Spain. In 231 they sent a delegation to Hamilcar to question him about Carthage's ambitions. Hamilcar played on their own greed, telling them that the campaigns were necessary if Carthage was to be able to pay the indemnity owed to Rome. Rome's attention was then occupied by an attack of the Gauls of northern Italy. The reason for this war was Gaulish resentment of the Roman policy of planting colonies on their land. The attack quickly collapsed and in 226 the Romans again turned their attention towards Spain as they realized, 'that they had hitherto been asleep and had allowed Carthage to build up a powerful dominion.'[15] The threat of a new war with the Gauls forced the Romans to postpone confrontation with Carthage. A treaty was made which limited Carthaginian expansion to south of the River Ebro. The war with the Gauls continued until 218 when they surrendered to Rome and agreed to yield further land for Roman colonization. The Romans were now free to turn their full attention towards Carthage and its new empire in Spain.

The leadership on both sides was ready for a fresh trial of strength; all that was needed was a flashpoint. This was provided by the people of the Spanish city of Saguntum which had allied itself with Rome sometime after the treaty of 226. In 221, Hannibal, the son of Hamilcar Barca, became commander in Spain. In successive campaigns in 220–219 he pushed Carthage's control further inland and north, defeating many of the tribes up to the Ebro.

At the same time a dispute broke out between Saguntum and a Spanish tribe allied with Hannibal. According to Polybius: 'Hannibal tried as far as he could to keep his hands off this city, wishing to give the Romans no avowed pretext for war, until he had secured his possession of all the rest of the country, following in this his father Hamilcar's suggestions and advice.'[16] The Saguntians, fearing an attack by Hannibal, requested aid from Rome. They sent a delegation to Hannibal warning him not to attack their ally. Saguntum actually lies south of the River Ebro and Hannibal could claim that he was not violating the treaty of 226. This may have been a specious argument on Hannibal's part. For, as Goldsworthy has astutely pointed out, although Carthage had been forced to promise not to go north of the river, there is no real 'foundation for the common assumption that the Romans bound themselves not to intervene south of the Ebro.'[17]

In 219 Hannibal attacked Saguntum, and after a siege of eight months, captured the city. The Romans did nothing to aid their ally but early in 218 they sent a delegation to Carthage with an ultimatum that Carthage disown Hannibal's action and surrender him for punishment or prepare for war. The Carthaginians refused, stating that all the treaties they had ever made with Rome had been worthless. At that moment one of the Roman delegates

> gathering up his toga, said, 'Here we bring you war and peace, take which you please.' He was met by a defiant shout bidding him give whichever he preferred, and when, letting the folds of his toga fall, he said that he gave them war, they replied that they accepted war and would carry it on in the same spirit in which they accepted it.[18]

Polybius claims convincingly that the Carthaginians were willing to go to war again because they

> could ill bear their defeat in the war for Sicily, and ... they were additionally exasperated by the matter of Sardinia and the exorbitancy of the sum they had been last obliged to agree to pay. Therefore, when they had subjugated the greater part of Iberia, they were quite ready to adopt any measures against Rome which suggested themselves.[19]

Thus the Carthaginians wished to re-establish themselves as a major power in order to revenge themselves on Rome. The Romans had, somewhat belatedly, decided they needed to stop Carthaginian expansionism before it became a threat to Rome. Polybius adds that Hamilcar Barca had personal motives, believing that he had been unconquered in Sicily during the first war and yearned to inflict revenge on the Romans. This ambition had been passed onto his son Hannibal who, before he accompanied his father to Spain, had, at his father's insistence, sworn 'never to be the friend of the Romans.'[20]

The Carthaginian response was exactly as the Romans had expected. Prior to the dispatch of the delegation they had already made plans to carry out the war aggressively. They had raised 70,000 troops and a fleet of 240 warships. One Consul was ordered to Spain, another sent to Sicily to prepare to invade Africa and a third force was sent north to reinforce the garrison of 22,000 men already guarding the frontier with the Gauls.

Unlike the first war, however, the Romans were faced by an enemy willing to be just as aggressive as themselves. The Carthaginians had realized that their previous strategy of wearing the Romans down had failed because of Rome's determination to throw every last resource into the war. This time they resolved to take the fight to the Romans. Hannibal would invade Italy, ally with the Gauls and attempt to reduce Rome's resources by turning her allies against her.

In the spring of 218, Hannibal left Spain with an army of 102,000 men and thirty-seven elephants. Despite numerous clashes and hardships, he marched across Gaul and crossed the Alps. In the autumn he arrived in northern Italy with a much reduced army of 26,000 men and a few elephants. Hannibal was quickly able to raise a further 8,000 troops from his Gaulish allies. The news shocked the Senate who immediately recalled their army from Spain to join the garrison in northern Italy. Once there, the Romans demonstrated their usual aggression by attacking the Carthaginians. In the ensuing Battle of Trebia, fought in December 218, Hannibal demonstrated his tactical brilliance by heavily defeating a Roman army of about 40,000 men.

Hannibal then advanced south and over the next two years destroyed two more Roman armies at the battles of Lake Trasimene (217) and Cannae (216). Hannibal's strategy began to work as many of Rome's subjects, particularly in southern Italy, rebelled and joined Hannibal. In addition, King Philip V of Macedonia, alarmed by brief Roman incursions into Illyria and western Greece in 229 and 219 and encouraged by Rome's defeats, declared war in 217.

One Roman ally, however, remained loyal. Despite Rome's defeats, Hieron of Syracuse remained steadfast in his support. At the start of the war the Carthaginians had sent ships to the Aeolian Islands. Three had been caught by the currents and drifted south to the Straits of Messene. Hieron launched twelve ships which captured the Carthaginian vessels. From the prisoners he learnt that the Carthaginians had sent a fleet to western Sicily in an attempt to capture Lilybaeum if possible, if not to seek support from Carthage's old allies. Hieron passed this information to the Romans who strengthened their defences and drove off the Carthaginian expedition.

When the Consul appointed to take command in Sicily, Sempronius, arrived with his army at Messene in 218 he was greeted by Hieron

his fleet fully equipped and manned, and went on board the consul's vessel to congratulate him on having safely arrived with his fleet and his army, and to wish him a prosperous and successful passage to Sicily. He then described the condition of the island and the movements of the Carthaginians, and promised to assist the Romans now in his old age with the same readiness which he had shown as a young man in the former war; he should supply the seamen and soldiers with corn and clothing gratis.[21]

Hieron accompanied Sempronius to Lilybaeum with his fleet but then returned to Syracuse, where he remained until his death. The loyalty that Hieron displayed to Rome is often cited as a demonstration of his political foresight and ability to pick a winner. This may be true. It may, however, also have been a simple recognition of realpolitik. With a Roman garrison already on the island, the approach of a Consul with an army of 36,000 men and a fleet of 170 ships would have left Hieron with little real choice. Where he did show good judgement was in remaining loyal to Rome after the removal of Sempronius' army and Rome's three massive defeats by Hannibal. Not only did Hieron remain loyal, but Syracuse sent both men and grain to Rome after the defeat at Lake Trasimene. The even more catastrophic defeat of the Roman army at Cannae in 216 did not change Hieron's mind. In one of the last acts of his life, in response to a Roman call for urgent assistance, 'Hieron, the one man whom Rome could fall back upon,'[22] sent money and six months' supply of grain.

The date of Hieron's death is not recorded but it was probably late in 216. He was reputed to have been in his ninety-second year and had ruled Syracuse for sixty years. During his rule, Hieron had come to accept that Syracuse was no longer a major power. After an initial alliance with the Carthaginians against the Mamertines, a partnership doomed by centuries of mistrust, he had eventually thrown in his lot with Rome. Following this decision Syracuse had enjoyed a period of security and prosperity lasting nearly half a century. Syracuse was the only Sicilian city to maintain its freedom and autonomy after the Roman victory in the First Punic War.

Nevertheless events after his death, including the destruction of his entire family, are sometimes used as evidence to claim that 'throughout his reign Hieron depended on a pro-Roman oligarchy, while the commons were basically hostile.'[23] It does appear that Hieron, during his reign created 'a great council of the nation', which Livy refers to as a 'Senate.'[24] This would infer that it was some sort of aristocratic body set up to be independent of and above the assembly of the people. This council ceased to be called or have any authority after Hieron's death.

In general, although not exclusively, the democrats in cities, particularly those of the Greeks, were anti-Roman, whereas the wealthy were in favour of alliance with Rome. This preference is explicitly acknowledged by Livy:

> In Croton there was neither unity of purpose nor of feeling; it seemed as though a disease had attacked all the cities of Italy alike, everywhere the populace were hostile to the aristocracy. The senate of Croton were in favour of the Romans, the populace wanted to place their state in the hands of the Carthaginians.[25]

Notwithstanding this, the views of the ancient writers, themselves aristocrats who accepted Roman rule, are unanimously approving of Hieron. Polybius sums up Hieron's reputation among later Greeks forced to live under the rule of Rome:

> For during a reign of fifty-four years he kept his country at peace and his own power undisturbed by plots, and he kept clear of that envy which is wont to wait on superiority ... and having conferred great benefits on the Greeks, and studied to win their high opinion, he left behind him a great personal reputation and a legacy of universal goodwill to the Syracusans.[26]

Chapter 23

Hieronymus and the War with Rome

Hieronymus, who was but a boy and hardly likely to use his own liberty much less his sovereign power with moderation.

Livy 24.4

During his life Hieron had fathered three legitimate children: a son, Gelon, and two daughters. Gelon had married Nereis, a princess of the royal family of Epirus. He was remembered for his loyalty to his father but died shortly before him, at the age of fifty. Gelon had fathered two sons, the eldest, Hieronymus, was only fifteen years of age at the time of Hieron's death. The ancient Greeks had a truism regarding the families of tyrants: the first ruled effectively and was sometimes popular, the second clung to power by using force and the third was hopelessly debauched. By dying, Gelon had avoided his fate but Hieronymus is described by the ancient authors as the very personification of a third generation tyrant.

Brought up in the wealth and privilege of Hieron's court, Hieronymus was encouraged by guardians and friends to indulge in 'every kind of excess.'[1] Hieron was well aware of his grandson's character and in the last months of his life, as Agathocles had before him, attempted to end the tyranny and restore freedom to the Syracusans. Exactly what is meant by this is not clear; possibly Hieron wanted to restore the democracy or, more likely, create an oligarchy. His plan was opposed by his two daughters who were determined that their nephew Hieronymus should succeed to the kingship. This would allow their husbands, Andranodorus and Zoippus, to rule as regents for the boy. For Hieron it proved to be

> no easy matter for a man in his ninetieth year, subject night and day to the coaxing and blandishments of two women, to keep an open mind and make public interests predominant over private ones in his thoughts. So all he could do was to leave fifteen guardians for his son, and he implored them on his deathbed to maintain unimpaired the loyal relations with Rome which he had cultivated for fifty years, and

to see to it that the young man, above all things, followed in his foot-steps and adhered to the principles in which he had been brought up.[2]

After Hieron's death, the assembly approved his instructions and the council of fifteen was appointed to act as regents.

Where Hieron had eschewed the trappings of royalty, Hieronymus emulated Dionysius the Elder by parading around the city dressed in purple, wearing a diadem, surrounded by bodyguards and riding a chariot drawn by white horses. Despite being only fifteen years old he was soon hated and feared for his pomp, arrogance to his fellow citizens, lust and cruelty. This last trait was encouraged by his uncles who soon terrorized most of the council of regents into resigning or fleeing. Soon the fifteen had been reduced to three: his two uncles and their last remaining opponent, Thraso.

This was a crucial time for Syracuse. Following the defeat of the Romans at Cannae it looked very much like Hannibal could defeat Rome. Many of Rome's allies saw this as an opportunity to throw off the Roman yoke. Not surprisingly, many in Syracuse believed that it was now time to end the alliance with Rome and recover Syracuse's dominant position in Sicily. This faction was led by Andranodorus and Zoippus. Thraso was the leader of the pro-Roman faction and soon the three were involved in a struggle for supremacy. This is how Livy portrays the factionalism in the Syracusan court but he may have been analyzing events from a Roman perspective. Internal Syracusan politics and ambitions may have been equally or more important.

A conspiracy to murder the king was soon hatched. One of the conspirators was unmasked by an informer and tortured for further information. He named Thraso as the ringleader of the plot. Livy claims that Thraso was 'an innocent man, and falsely accused'[3] but as he was defending a supporter of Rome his testimony may not be impartial.

Hieronymus, however, believed the accusations and Thraso was tortured to death. If Livy is correct in his portrayal, 'the one link with Rome had now gone.'[4] The anti-Roman faction sent an embassy to Hannibal who responded by sending back two envoys, Hippocrates and Epicydes, the grandsons of a Syracusan who had gone into exile in Carthage after being involved in the murder of Agathocles' sons. Perhaps they were the grandsons of Arcesilaus who had been so confident about the survival of his children.

The Roman commander of Sicily, Appius Claudius, sent an embassy to Hieronymus in an attempt to hold the Syracusans to their alliance. The Romans were met with derision and mockery over their defeats at the hands of Hannibal. Such outbursts had never intimidated Roman representatives and they 'said that they would come back to him when he had learnt to receive embassies seriously, and, after warning him, rather than asking him, not to abandon their alliance lightly, they departed.'[5] Suspecting that

Hieronymus was leaning towards an alliance with Carthage the Romans strengthened their garrisons along the Syracusan border.

The Syracusans decided to investigate further the possibility of an alliance with Carthage. Hieronymus sent an embassy to Carthage to negotiate a treaty on the basis that: 'the Carthaginians were to assist him with land and sea forces, and after expelling the Romans from Sicily they were to divide the island so that the frontier of their respective provinces should be the river Himera, which very nearly bisects Sicily.'[6]

While this was occurring, Hippocrates and Epicydes captivated Hieronymus with ripping yarns of Hannibal's campaigns and battles. They also flattered him by reminding him that he was descended not only from Hieron but also from Pyrrhus, and therefore had inherited the right to rule over the whole of Sicily from both sides of his family. Through their toadying they won over Hieronymus to such an extent that 'he paid no heed at all to anyone else, being naturally of an unstable character and being now rendered much more feather-brained by their influence.' Hieronymus, full of self-importance, sent a second embassy to Carthage to alter the terms of their alliance 'affirming that the sovereignty of the whole of Sicily was his by right, demanding that the Carthaginians should help him to recover Sicily and promising to assist them in their Italian campaign.' These new terms were agreed to by the Carthaginians:

> Though they now clearly perceived in its full extent the fickleness and mental derangement of the young man, [they] still thought it was in many ways against their interests to abandon Sicilian affairs, and therefore agreed to everything he asked, and having previously got ready ships and troops they prepared to send their forces across to Sicily.[7]

The Carthaginians were probably prepared to accept any terms to win Syracuse as an ally. Once the Romans had been defeated, existing treaties could always be renegotiated or broken.

The Romans, learning of the pact with Carthage, sent another embassy to Hieronymus protesting about the breach of their treaty with Hieron. Hieronymus called a meeting of his advisors to discuss the matter. Most were too frightened to speak against the king but a few were more candid and spoke in favour of renewing ties with Rome. Hieronymus was, however, too far under the sway of Andranodorus, Hippocrates and Epicydes and decided on war with Rome. In attempt to buy time, he told the Roman delegation that he would adhere to the treaty if they returned all the tribute, grain and gifts given by Hieron to Rome and recognized his right to rule all of Sicily east of the Himera River. These terms would never be agreed by the Romans and both sides prepared for war.

Hieronymus raised an army of 17,000 men and advanced to Leontini in preparation to attack the neighbouring Roman garrisons. Opposition to

Hieronymus' rule was not yet over. A new plot to assassinate him had been hatched among those who wanted an end to the tyranny as well as peace with Rome. With the connivance of one of his bodyguards, Hieronymus was murdered while walking the streets of Leontini. He was so unpopular that his body was left abandoned and lay unburied in the street. Diodorus sums up the traditional view of his rule:

> As a result the youth, keeping company with flatterers who courted him, was led astray into luxurious living, profligacy, and despotic cruelty. He committed outrages against women, put to death friends who spoke frankly, summarily confiscated many estates, and presented them to those who courted his favour. This behaviour brought in its train first the hatred of the populace, then a conspiracy, and finally the downfall that usually attends wicked rulers.[8]

Polybius cautions, however, that Hieronymus was merely

> a boy when he succeeded to power, and lived only thirteen months after. In this space of time it is possible that one or two men may have been tortured, and some of his friends and some of the other Syracusans put to death, but it is hardly probable that there was any excess of unlawful violence or any extraordinary impiety.[9]

After Hieronymus' assassination, some of the revolutionaries remained in Leontini to secure the support of the army and mercenaries while others raced to Syracuse to prevent Andranodorus from seizing the vacant throne. They were too late, however, and Andranodorus had occupied the fortress of Ortygia and the public granary. Polybius' account of events after the assassination only survives in fragments and from here on it is necessary to rely largely on Livy for a description of events down to the fall of Syracuse. Livy wrote, however, to celebrate the history and victories of Rome. He therefore tends to consider the events in Syracuse from a largely Roman perspective.

The leaders of the revolution, Theodotus and Sosis, rode through the city, displaying the blood-soaked purple cloak and diadem of the king, calling the citizens to arms and promising the end of the tyranny. Those citizens without weapons stripped the temples of the arms of the Gauls and Illyrians which the Roman people had given to Hieron. They did so promising the gods to use the consecrated arms only in the defence of their freedom. The garrison of the granary joined the revolt and surrendered their charge to the rebels.

The next morning the people gathered in an assembly. Here the more conservative politicians urged mediation rather than armed confrontation. A delegation was sent to Andranodorus to discuss terms. At first he was inclined to reach an agreement until his wife, Demarta, a daughter of Hieron, reminded him of the advice given to Dionysius the Elder, that a tyrant should be dragged from office by his feet, not walking out on them. She advised her husband to delay making an agreement while he recalled Hieronymus' mercenaries from Leontini, promising them a substantial payment to remain loyal to the tyranny. Andranodorus, however, lacked the steel of his wife. The next day he addressed the assembly and promised to surrender power but first sought to arrange the safety of himself and his family. He explained to the people that he

> felt misgivings, when once the sword was drawn, as to how far the thirst for blood might carry you, whether you would be content with the death of the tyrant, which amply secures your liberty, or whether everyone who had been connected with the palace by relationship or by official position was to be put to death as being involved in another's guilt.[10]

Andranodorus then surrendered Ortygia, the stronghold of the tyranny. The next day an election was held for the magistrates of the new government. Livy calls these magistrates *praetors*, the second most important magistrates in Rome after the two consuls. From his account it most likely that what he describes is the office of general. Traditionally the Syracusan democracy annually elected fifteen generals. Andranodorus was chosen but most of his colleagues came from the ranks of the tyrannicides. The election of generals by the assembly would imply that a democracy had been restored. The majority of tyrannicides on the board of generals indicates, however, that the aristocratic faction, cashing in on their popularity gained from the murder of Hieronymous, were in the ascendancy.

The people also voted to once again tear down the walls of Ortygia, that imposing symbol of tyranny. Hippocrates and Epicydes, who had remained in Leontini, approached the new magistrates and asked that they be given an escort and allowed to leave Sicily. The newly elected generals, perhaps glad to be rid of any possible rivals, agreed.

This request was only a delaying tactic, as Hippocrates and Epicydes were scheming to bring down the new government and return the pro-Carthaginian faction to power. Pretending to be hiring their agreed escort, they set about recruiting their own force, mostly deserters from the Roman fleet, mercenaries and the desperate poor. The two set about undermining the aristocratic faction, by accusing them of 'secretly plotting and contriving to bring Syracuse under the suzerainty of Rome under the presence of renewing the alliance.'[11]

Such accusations would be easily believed, as it was generally the oligarchic factions within most cities who supported an alliance with Rome and the democrats who opposed it. The oligarchs admired Rome's constitution which had in its assemblies the outward appearance of a democracy while rigging its voting system to thoroughly favour the rich. They in turn preferred their subject allies to be ruled by oligarchies.

Although Livy tends to see Syracusan politicians as simply for or against Rome the real nature of politics in the city appears to have been far more complicated. Politics in a Greek democracy were always labyrinthine and while there were probably numerous intertwined factions, three emerge clearly from the sources. There was an oligarchic faction that favoured renewing the alliance with Rome. Centred on Andranodorus was a pro-Carthaginian clique that wanted a return to the tyranny. There was also a radical democratic faction that wanted to break the alliance with Rome and was falling under the influence of the Carthaginian agents Hippocrates and Epicydes.

Andranodorus was constantly being nagged by his wife to seize power while the city was in turmoil, with the mercenaries still loyal to him and the Carthaginians willing to give support. Finally he decided to move and hatched a plan to use his mercenaries to murder the other members of the government and re-take Ortygia. He recruited his nephew Themistus who leaked the plot to a friend, Ariston, an actor by profession. Ariston, 'thought that his country had the first and strongest claim on his loyalty,'[12] and exposed the plan to the magistrates. They immediately had Themistus and Andranodorus arrested and summarily executed.

A crowd gathered and demanded to know the details of the executions. One of the magistrates was tasked with explaining the actions. He gave details of the immediate plot but went on to denounce the crimes and anti-government actions of Hieronymus' surviving family. The magistrates then proposed a motion that the entire royal family should be exterminated. The people enthusiastically agreed, 'to put them all to death, men and women alike, in order to uproot completely the tyrant stock.'[13]

Executioners were sent out and the families, including the children were massacred. The only survivor was Zoippus who had been sent on an embassy to Egypt and had remained there when he learnt of Hieronymus' death. His wife, Heraclia fled with her young daughters to the sanctuary of an altar within her home. She claimed that she had hated Hieronymus and begged the executioners to spare them and let them join her husband in exile. When she saw that her appeal had made no impact she instead pleaded that her daughters be spared. This too made no impression on the executioners who dragged her from the altar and killed her. The two daughters, covered in their mother's blood, tried to escape into the street but were cornered by the executioners and killed.

Revulsion at the butchering of the families of the plotters soon caused a change of heart in the city. People began to denounce the generals and demanded that an election be called immediately to fill the vacant positions of Andranodorus and Themistus. Perhaps the *demos* had begun to suspect that the executions were a plot by the pro-Roman oligarchs. When the elections were called, members of the assembly – to the surprise of many – nominated Epicydes and Hippocrates. Later events would show that the two were prepared to institute revolutionary reforms and had probably done a deal with the radical democrats. At first the generals tried to ignore the nominations, but the crowd, infiltrated by the deserters, became increasingly strident in their support. At last, the generals 'powerless before a unanimous assembly, and dreading a seditious outbreak, they declared them to be duly elected.'[14]

Despite this, most members of the government were still attempting to avoid open war with Rome. Envoys had gone to Appius Claudius to arrange a ten day truce and renew the treaty of alliance. The Romans, anxious at the turn of events in Syracuse, had anchored a fleet of 100 ships just to the north of Syracuse. The possible defection of Syracuse could not have come at a worse time for Rome. After his victory at Cannae, Hannibal had marched south. Much of the important region of Campania, many of the Greek cities of southern Italy, and the Bruttians of south-western Italy had defected to Hannibal. If Sicily also fell then Hannibal would no longer be isolated from Carthage by the Roman bases on the island. Instead he would have secured his line of communication and supply back to his home city.

In 214 the Romans sent the newly appointed Consul, Marcellus, with a strong force to ensure they retained control of Sicily. Part of Marcellus' force would consist of two legions, 10,000 men, survivors of the defeat at Cannae. These men were in disgrace for fleeing the battlefield and had been banished to Sicily. They begged Marcellus to restore them to the legions so they could redeem themselves. He referred their request to the Senate who replied that 'the Roman commonwealth had no need of men who were cowards; if, however, as it appeared, Marcellus wished to use them, they were to receive from their commander none of the customary crowns or prizes for valour.'[15] The Syracusan delegation was directed by Appius to meet the newly arrived Marcellus. After listening to them, he was prepared to avoid war and dispatched an embassy to Syracuse.

The Carthaginians had also realized that the turmoil in Syracuse was their best chance to recover Sicily. They sent a fleet to the island. When news of its arrival off Cape Pachynus reached Syracuse, Hippocrates and Epicydes were encouraged to launch their coup. They roused their supporters by claiming that Syracuse was about to be betrayed to the Romans. Such accusations would have appeared justified when Appius brought the Roman fleet into the Great Harbour to support the partisans of Rome. Witnessing the arrival of the Roman vessels, the people of Syracuse raced down to the port to oppose any attempt to land.

An assembly was held to discuss the emergency. The discussion was heated and the outbreak of civil war seemed imminent when one of the leading citizens, Apollonides, addressed the assembly, pointing out how crucial their decision was:

> We must then do our very utmost to secure unanimity. Which alliance will be the more advantageous to us is a much less important question, and much less depends upon it, but still I think that we ought to be guided by the authority of Hieron in choosing our allies rather than by that of Hieronymus; in any case we ought to prefer a tried friendship of fifty years' standing to one of which we now know nothing and once found untrustworthy. There is also another serious consideration – we can decline to come to terms with the Carthaginians without having to fear immediate hostilities with them, but with the Romans it is a question of either peace or an immediate declaration of war.[16]

Livy describes Apollonides as free from 'party spirit,' which his 'speech gave it all the greater weight.' This is hardly an impartial observation, as the speech was clearly pro-Roman. The generals gathered to discuss the proposal and agreed that 'there appeared to be no possible means of carrying on a war with Rome' and decided to send an embassy to Marcellus to make peace.[17]

A few days after the decision was made, a delegation came from Leontini requesting a garrison be sent to the city as protection from possible Roman raids. The dominant pro-Roman faction saw this as a chance to rid the city of their opponents. Hippocrates was ordered to Leontini with a force of 4,000 mercenaries. This was a poor decision on the part of the pro-Romans, as they could no longer control Hippocrates. He used his freedom of action to raid the Roman province and wiped out one of their garrisons. Appius responded in kind by destroying one of the Syracusan border forts.

Marcellus sent an ultimatum to Syracuse, saying that the peace had been broken and they must exile Hippocrates and Epicydes or face war. Epicydes fled to Leontini where he discovered that there was great anger over the Roman raids. He convinced the people to secede from Syracusan control. The Syracusans then disavowed the actions of Hippocrates and told the Romans that they: 'may carry on war with them without any infringement of their treaty with us, nor shall we stand aloof in such a war, if it is clearly understood that when they have been subjugated they will again form part of our dominions in accordance with the terms of the treaty.'[18]

Marcellus' army stormed Leontini with their first assault. Hippocrates and Epicydes abandoned the city and fled to the Herbessus to the west of Syracuse. A Syracusan army of 8,000 men had been advancing towards Leontini to assist the Romans when they were told of its capture. The messenger claimed, falsely, that the population had been butchered and the city sacked. In reality only the Roman deserters among the mercenaries had been executed.

The claim, however, further strengthened the hand of those opposed to Rome. The Syracusan troops were outraged at the supposed massacre and refused to advance any further. The generals hoped to avoid a mutiny and retreated to Megara Hyblaea. Learning that the two Carthaginian agents had escaped to Herbessus, the Syracusan generals decided to advance on that city, capture them and hopefully put an end the disorder.

Hippocrates and Epicydes decided that their only chance of survival was to surrender to the Syracusan soldiers. As luck would have it, the first soldiers they met were 600 Cretan mercenaries that Hieron had sent to fight for Rome. They had been captured by Hannibal, treated well by him and returned to Sicily to serve under Hieronymus. They were, therefore, well disposed towards their former officers and joined them. More of the army began to show their support. The Syracusan generals demanded that the outcasts be immediately arrested but the Cretans, and some others, closed ranks around the pair. Unwilling to see an open breach in the army, the generals again retreated to Megara Hyblaea and informed Syracuse of the situation.

Hippocrates sent out his Cretan supporters to block the roads and intercept any of the messengers from the generals to or from Syracuse. They captured one message addressed to Marcellus in which the generals in Syracuse had candidly written:

> You have acted rightly and properly in not sparing a single Leontine, but all the mercenaries are making common cause and Syracuse will never be at peace as long as there are any foreign auxiliaries either in the city or in our army. Do your best, therefore, to get into your power those who are with our generals in camp at Megara and by their punishment secure liberty at last for Syracuse.[19]

Hippocrates read out the message to the mercenaries who then turned on the Syracusan component of the army. The generals fled and the rest were in danger of being massacred when Epicydes and Hippocrates ordered the mercenaries to stand down. They believed that the Syracusans would be of more use as hostages or allies. An agent was sent into Syracuse to spread the tale of the Roman destruction of Leontini.

Their agent relayed a vivid account of the supposed massacre which caused the Syracusans to shut their gates and put the city onto a state of alert. Anti-Roman feeling was strong among the people but 'a few of the aristocracy were anxious to guard against a nearer and more pressing danger,'[20] their political opponents. Hippocrates and Epicydes advanced to a position just outside the city and began to contact their supporters within, calling on them to join in defending their land against the depredations of the Romans.

The Syracusan generals attempted to dissuade the people, reminding them that not so long ago Hippocrates and Epicydes had been the sycophants of the tyrant. The supporters of the brothers would not listen and threw open one of the gates. The generals who opposed Hippocrates and Epicydes and their supporters were hunted down and murdered. The pair were clearly playing the role of demagogues, as the next day they opened the prisons and freed the slaves throughout the city. These joined those described as a 'motley crowd,' most likely the poorer citizens in the assembly. Their supporters re-elected Hippocrates and Epicydes as generals and thus, according to Livy, Syracuse, 'after its short-lived gleam of liberty, fell back into its old bondage.'[21] This is of course the opinion of a Roman aristocrat, as many of the people of Syracuse would have seen it as the end of the rule of the oligarchs and their foreign supporters.

Plutarch claims that Hippocrates was tyrant of Syracuse and has Marcellus accuse the Syracusans that 'they had elected those very tyrants for the purpose of going to war.'[22] It is tempting to believe that at this time one, or both, were elected as *strategos autocrator*. Livy, however, again uses the expression, *praetor*, general, to describe the positions of Hippocrates and Epicydes. At no time does Livy use the words *tyrannus*, his usual expression for the Greek tyrants, to describe their offices. The most likely conclusion that can be drawn is that they were two of a number of elected generals, theoretically equal to their peers, and under the control of the assembly. Nonetheless, their popularity and personal entourage of mercenaries probably ensured that they had the deciding opinion on most matters.

Livy's account, that of a Roman aristocrat who would have despised Carthage and the *demos*, portrays the brothers simply as agents of Carthage who play on the gullibility of the mob. From the accounts of their rise it is obvious, nonetheless, that there was genuine fear of both Roman domination, and the political designs of their oligarchic supporters, among the people of Syracuse. Most likely Hippocrates and Epicydes used these anxieties, as other tyrants before them had, for their own purposes but this makes such fears no less real.

When the Romans learned of the political change in Syracuse they immediately marched on the city. Marcellus, as had many attackers before him, made his headquarters on the hill of the Temple of Zeus to the south of the city. Another embassy was sent to Syracuse but Hippocrates and Epicydes denied it access to the city. Openly displaying their hostility, they insisted on meeting the envoys outside the walls. The Roman spokesman demanded that the killers of their friends be handed over and the former government restored. Epicydes refused their demands and reminded them of the strength of the walls of Syracuse: 'if you provoke us to war you will learn by experience that to attack Syracuse is not quite the same thing as attacking Leontini.' With these words he left the envoys and closed the gates.[23] The siege of Syracuse had begun.

Chapter 24

The Fall of Syracuse

He himself, however, as he looked down from the heights and surveyed the great and beautiful city, is said to have wept much in commiseration of its impending fate, bearing in mind how greatly its form and appearance would change in a little while, after his army had sacked it.

Plutarch, *Marcellus* 19

The Romans, made over confident by their success at Leontini, believed that they would easily capture Syracuse. As soon as they had brought up their artillery they began simultaneous attacks by land and sea. The land attacks concentrated on the main northern gate to the city known as the Hexapyla. Marcellus led a squadron of sixty ships, packed with archers and slingers, to attack the seawall of Achradina to the north of the Little Harbour. Eight other vessels were lashed together in pairs to enable them to carry towers.

The ancient sources all credit Archimedes as being the driving force behind the effective defence of Syracuse. During his years in charge of the fortifications he had packed 'the walls with artillery of every kind, according to the requirements of the different positions.'[1] As the Romans attacked, Archimedes directed the larger engines, throwing huge stones, to concentrate on the doubled vessels. Meanwhile smaller catapults, firing darts from loopholes lower in the walls, shot directly at the other ships. Livy describes another type of engine, generally known as 'Archimedes Iron Hand,' designed to cripple those vessels that managed to get alongside the walls:

A huge beam swinging on a pivot projected from the wall and a strong chain hanging from the end had an iron grappling hook fastened to it. This was lowered on to the prow of a ship and a heavy lead weight brought the other end of the beam to the ground, raising the prow into the air and making the vessel rest on its stern. Then the weight being removed, the prow was suddenly dashed on to the water as though it had fallen from the wall, to the great consternation of the sailors;

the shock was so great that if it fell straight it shipped a considerable amount of water.[2]

Polybius adds that the controller, once he had 'made fast the opposite end of the machine, and by means of a rope and pulley, let the chain and hand suddenly drop from it.'[3] Rorres and Harris, who constructed a model of the device, report that securing the machine was essential 'if counterweights were used, as the entire structure would collapse if the ship were suddenly released from its equilibrium position without supporting the opposite end of the lever beam. Indeed, this collapse occurred several times in our laboratory simulations when we forgot to do what Polybius described.'[4]

There has been much modern scepticism regarding this weapon, largely based on the descriptions of later, twelfth century, writers who exaggerated the effect, claiming that the ships were lifted completely out of the water and dropped. Rorres and Harris' reconstructions have shown that the Iron Hand does work if operated in the manner described by both Livy and Polybius. They report that its basic mechanism was merely 'an extension of the use of existing machines and devices. It may have been a modified crane such as was used at docks for loading and unloading ships.' Nor did it need to be too big an engine due to the limited stability, height and length of a quinquireme. The ship only needed to be lifted a small amount for the stern to draw water or, if caught by the side, for the ship to capsize.[5]

A simpler modification of the existing cranes also allowed the Syracusans to drop rocks of over 200kg in weight onto the Roman ships and siege equipment. Another weapon attributed to Archimedes was the use of a mirror, or bank of mirrors by which in an

incredible manner he burned up the whole Roman fleet. For by tilting a kind of mirror toward the sun he concentrated the sun's beam upon it; and owing to the thickness and smoothness of the mirror he ignited the air from this beam and kindled a great flame, the whole of which he directed upon the ships that lay at anchor in the path of the fire, until he consumed them all.[6]

Numerous modern tests have shown this to be completely impractical, if not impossible.[7]

The massed fire of the Syracusan artillery forced Marcellus to call off the attack. He tried again at night and, under the cover of darkness, some ships made it to the walls, only to be destroyed by Archimedes' devices. Marcellus admitted defeat and called off the attack. Appius' land attack met no better success as 'his men while at a distance were mowed down by the shots from the mangonels and catapults.'[8] No doubt there were other competent engineers in Syracuse, but the ancient writers were fixated on the brilliance of individuals such as Archimedes and attributed the successful defence to him alone. Such attitudes are demonstrated by Polybius' claim that: 'Such a great and marvellous thing does the genius of one man show itself to be when properly applied to certain matters.'[9]

So effective was the Syracusan artillery that for the following eight months of the siege the Romans never again attempted to take the city by storm. According to Plutarch: 'the Romans became so fearful that, whenever they saw a bit of rope or a stick of timber projecting a little over the wall, ' "There it is," they cried, "Archimedes is training some engine upon us," and turned their backs and fled.'[10] The Romans were forced to adopt their old strategy of blockading the city and attempting to starve it into submission.

While the siege was deadlocked, Marcellus took a part of the army to campaign beyond Syracuse in order to force the submission of its subject cities and any others that had gone over to the Carthaginians. Megara Hyblaea was taken by assault and destroyed as an example to the rest. This proved effective as the nearby cities of Herbessus and Helorus immediately surrendered.

Events in Sicily did, however, encourage the Carthaginian army to send an expedition of 23,000 men and twelve elephants to the island under the command of Himilco. He quickly captured the traditional Carthaginian strongholds of Heraclea and Akragas. This in turn raised the confidence of those cities which had not yet surrendered to Rome and encouraged others to revolt.

As the Carthaginian army advanced towards Syracuse, Hippocrates evaded the blockade with 8,000 men in an attempt to join them. Marcellus, who had failed to save Akragas and knew nothing of the advancing Syracusan army, encountered them by accident. The Syracusans, also unaware of the enemy, were in the process of setting camp. Marcellus was first to react and immediately attacked. The Syracusans were caught out of formation and largely unarmed. The infantry surrendered, while Hippocrates and the cavalry managed to escape and later joined Himilco. Marcellus returned to Syracuse but his victory dissuaded, for a time, any more cities from joining the revolt.

Himilco advanced on Syracuse and made camp about 12km from the city. At the same time, a Carthaginian fleet of fifty-five ships entered the Great Harbour. The arrival of the Carthaginian forces raised hopes within the city that the blockade would soon be lifted. The Romans, however, landed reinforcements at Panormus which succeeded in eluding Himilco and reinforced the army around Syracuse. With their limited forces, the Carthaginian commanders in Sicily began to despair that they would not be able to break the Roman siege. The fleet, outnumbered two to one by the Romans, withdrew to Africa. Himilco, also inferior in numbers, 'saw that the enemy were in great strength and safe within their lines round Syracuse he marched away, not caring to waste time by looking on in idleness at the investment of his allies.'[11]

Himilco decided that his force could better be used in encouraging more cities to defect from Rome. In this he met with some success. The population of Morgantina, a Roman supply depot, rebelled and drove out their Roman garrison. Other cities also joined the rebellion. The hatred of foreign garrisons in cities, and the limitations on freedom and autonomy they imposed, is clearly demonstrated by the remarks of the magistrates at Enna when they demanded that the Roman garrison withdraw:

> The city and its stronghold are under our authority; if as free men we accepted the Roman alliance we did not hand ourselves over to be kept in custody as slaves. We think it right, therefore, that the keys of the gates should be given up to us; the strongest bond between good allies is to trust one another's loyalty; it is only if we remain friends with Rome voluntarily and not by constraint that your people can feel grateful to us.[12]

The hegemonic powers which imposed such garrisons had a completely different view. They believed that such demands were treason and could be punished as such. The Roman commander responded with brutal counter-measures. He surrounded the unarmed men of the city while they were in an assembly and killed them all. The city was then thoroughly sacked. For this action the garrison was rewarded by Marcellus who allowed them to keep the plunder from the city. Marcellus approved the act, 'thinking that, by the terror thus inspired, the Sicilians would be deferred from any longer betraying their garrisons.'[13] This was a serious miscalculation on his part. As news of the massacre spread throughout Sicily, it was considered an impious and murderous outrage and many of those cities that had been wavering in their loyalty went over to Carthage. After the massacre, Marcellus constructed a new camp at Leon, to the north of Syracuse, and went into winter quarters.

At the start of the next spring Marcellus was unsure whether to concentrate his efforts on completing the siege of Syracuse or to continue the blockade with a reduced force and attack Akragas. The situation before Syracuse looked unpromising, as the city could not be taken by direct assault and was being supplied from the sea by the Carthaginians. Marcellus decided to attempt the most efficient way of taking a city, by internal treachery. He sent some of the Syracusan aristocratic exiles to make contact with their friends inside the city. Marcellus promised that if they could arrange the surrender of the city they would be 'free and live under their own laws.'[14] This expression was probably a euphemism for being subject allies of Rome under an oligarchy.

Security within the city was tight and for a while no messages could be sent. Eventually a slave belonging to one of the exiles pretended to be a deserter and was allowed into the city. The traitors arranged a method of contact where they could leave the city under fishing boat nets and secretly enter and leave the Roman camp. The plot was betrayed to Epicydes and the eighty men involved were arrested and tortured to death.

Soon after, another opportunity presented itself to Marcellus. A Spartan acting as an emissary for Philip of Macedonia, now also at war with Rome, had been captured by the Romans while travelling to Sicily. Epicydes was anxious to ransom him and Marcellus agreed. At that time the Romans were keen to seek the alliance of the cities of Greece against Macedonia and Marcellus would be hoping to secure the Spartans' good will. The exchange took place outside of the northern walls. One of the Roman delegates seized the chance to do some reconnaissance. He counted the number of rows of stones in the wall and estimated their size. From this he was able to calculate the approximate height of the wall. This proved to be lower than it had appeared to the naked eye.

Marcellus conducted further observations but it was found that because of its lower height it was strongly guarded by the Syracusans. At this stage an act of treachery finally came to the aid of the Romans. A deserter from within the city brought news that a festival of Artemis was about to be celebrated for three days within the city and Epicydes had distributed free wine to the people.

The Romans decided to take advantage of the opportunity and launch an attack during the festival. A select force of 1,000 of the fittest men was ordered to attempt an assault at the low point of the walls during the night, when hopefully the guards would be drowsy from their celebrations. Everything went as planned, the Romans managed to sneak up unobserved under the cover of darkness and gained a foothold on the walls unopposed. Once the breach had been made the Romans seized the Hexapyla with little opposition. Some of the guards were asleep, others were 'either stupid with wine after their revels or were drinking themselves drunk.'[15] Once the gate was secured the Roman detachment sounded their trumpets and attacked, spreading confusion and fear throughout the surrounding area. Some of the Syracusans rushed to arms but were easily beaten off, others fled in terror. Syracuse was such a large city that many were able to sleep through the night in blissful, drunken ignorance.

At daybreak the Romans were able to enter through the gate with their main force. What little Syracusan opposition which remained on the Epipolae was easily brushed aside. Epicydes advanced out of Ortygia, thinking that only a small breach had been made. When he saw that the most of the heights were occupied by the Romans he retreated rapidly to Achradina, fearing that his opponents in the city might shut the gates behind him.

When Marcellus looked down from the heights, he observed that Syracuse was

> the fairest city of the time, he is said to have shed tears at the sight, partly through joy at his great achievement, partly at the memory of its ancient glories. He thought of the Athenian fleets which had been sunk in that harbour, of the two great armies with their famous generals which had been annihilated there, of all of its many powerful kings and tyrants, above all, of Hieron, whose memory was so fresh, and who, in addition to all his endowments of fortune and character, had distinguished himself by his services to Rome. As all this passed through his mind and with it the thought that in one short hour all he saw round him would be burnt and reduced to ashes.[16]

Remembering these past glories, Marcellus supposedly decided to make one last attempt, through the exiles, to avoid the destruction of the city. More practically, he might have hoped to avoid having to storm the still formidable fortifications of the inner city. Achradina and Ortygia were mostly held by the Roman deserters and, knowing that there would be no mercy for them, they refused to allow the messengers to approach. Once more Syracuse was divided between hostile forces but this time one of them was a foreign invader.

The Romans held all of the Epipolae except for the fortress guarding the pass of Euyralus. This was the only access point to the heights from the west. Marcellus was keen to take it in order to prevent an attack from this direction by the Carthaginians. One of the exiles was sent to discuss terms of surrender with the garrison commander, an Argive named Philodemus. Hoping that Himilco and Hippocrates would come to the aid of the city, Philodemus kept putting off the Roman advances. Marcellus finally gave up his attempts to get the garrison to surrender.

While this was happening, envoys came to him from the areas of Tyche and Neapolis, which lie between the Epilpolae and Achradina. They begged him to spare their inhabitants from destruction. Marcellus' officers advised him to reject the appeals and 'many of them actually urged that the city should be burned and razed to the ground.' This proposal he rejected but faced by the insistence of his men, 'much against his will, and under compulsion, he permitted booty to be made of property and slaves, although he forbade his men to lay hands on the free citizens, and strictly ordered them neither to kill nor outrage nor enslave any Syracusan.'[17] Seeing the Roman occupation of these areas, without any opposition from Epicydes or reaction from the Carthaginians, Philodemus despaired of relief and decided to back the winning side. He handed over the reputedly impregnable fortress without a blow being struck.

With the capture of the fortress, Marcellus was free from the fear of any attack on the Epipolae from outside the walls. He built three new camps in the suburbs around Achradina and determined to starve the final Syracusan stronghold into submission. Realizing that without outside intervention Syracuse would be lost, the Carthaginians reinforced the remnant of their fleet in the Great Harbour. Himilco and Hippocrates advanced in a final attempt to break the siege. They constructed a camp to the south of the city.

Messages were exchanged with Epicydes and a combined attack on the Roman positions was agreed. Hippocrates made an attack on the old Roman camp to the south of the city, probably on or around the temple of Zeus, while the Carthaginian fleet landed troops to prevent its reinforcement from the city. At the same time Epicydes sallied out from Achradina to attack Marcellus. All of the attacks were easily defeated by the Romans, as 'the excitement which the enemy caused was much more alarming than the fighting.'[18] The only result was to cause the Romans to strengthen their positions.

The Romans once again settled into their blockade which dragged on into the autumn. This season was always unhealthy around Syracuse due to the marshes to the south. The large numbers of people packed in and around the city did not improve matters. Plagues broke out which affected everybody. 'Deaths and funerals were a daily spectacle; on all sides, day and night, were heard the wailings for the dead.'[19] The death toll was high but particularly so among the Carthaginians who were camped to the south and were notorious for the poor sanitation of their camps. Their Sicilian allies deserted them to escape the disease. Both their commanders, Hippocrates and Himilco, died and so many succumbed that the army disintegrated. Marcellus removed his garrison of the southern fort into the city where shade and shelter helped to reduce the death rate among the afflicted.

After they had withdrawn from Syracuse, the Sicilian allies of Carthage reinforced their army and again advanced towards Syracuse. The Carthaginians still nursed hopes of destroying the Roman army while it was bogged down before Syracuse. They raised a new fleet, under Bomilcar, of 130 warships and 700 cargo vessels, to break the blockade. Unfavourable winds prevented the fleet from rounding Cape Pachynus. Bomilcar sent the transports back to safety at Heraclea while he remained at Pachynus. Epicydes, fearing that the Carthaginians would abandon their rescue attempt, sailed out of the city to impress upon Bomilcar the urgency of the situation.

In true Roman fashion, Marcellus, although having fewer warships, decided to confront Bomilcar's fleet and sailed to Cape Pachynus. Bomilcar was unwilling to engage as the Romans had the advantage of the easterly wind despite Epicydes' entreaties for him to fight. When the wind dropped, Bomilcar sailed offshore in an attempt to round the point. The Romans sailed aggressively straight at the Carthaginian fleet and Bomilcar appears to have lost his nerve. Instead of engaging the Romans, he set sail and fled to

Tarentum, which had recently rebelled in favour of Carthage. The supply ships were ordered back to Africa. Epicydes, 'finding all his hopes suddenly crushed,'[20] did not dare risk sailing back to besieged Syracuse. Instead he deserted his command and retired to Akragas to await events.

Abandoned by the Carthaginians, many of the remaining Sicilians in revolt against Rome realized that all was lost and sent envoys to Marcellus to seek terms. Marcellus offered peace on the following conditions: 'that all that had been included in the king's dominions should belong to Rome, and that all else was to be retained by the Sicilians together with their liberty and their laws.'[21] This sounds far too lenient, more likely Marcellus imposed the usual Roman terms, that the cities could maintain some autonomy in their internal affairs but would pay tribute to, and be allies of, Rome. The Sicilians sent a delegation to the remaining Syracusan commanders in an attempt to get them to accept the same terms. Meanwhile they decided not to rely on diplomacy and persuaded their friends within Syracuse to assassinate their generals.

The coup was a success and the three leading generals were murdered. The rebels then called an assembly to discuss the Roman offer. They asked why the Syracusans should continue to suffer now that the enemies of Rome, Hippocrates and Epicydes, no longer ruled the city. Now, they claimed, was the time to make peace and deliver Syracuse from tyranny. The suggestion was met with approval and perhaps relief by the people.

The Syracusans sent a delegation to Marcellus. The leader of the Syracusan embassy claimed that it was Hieronymus and his creatures Hippocrates and Epicydes who had made war on Rome, not the Syracusan people. He reminded Marcellus of the great deeds done by Hieron in support of Rome. If Marcellus accepted their surrender he would have the glory of capturing the greatest of the Greek cities, a triumph that had eluded both Athens and Carthage. Marcellus was inclined to accept their surrender on terms but once again the vexed question of the deserters in Syracusan service raised its ugly head. Although not recorded it is certain that Marcellus, as was the usual Roman policy, would have insisted on the surrender of these traitors.

The deserters, fearing correctly that they were about to betrayed, convinced the other mercenaries that they too would share the same fate. They in turn rebelled against the new government, murdering the generals and citizens alike. Once in control they elected six of their own generals, three to command in Achradina and three on Ortygia. After things had settled down, however, the mercenaries began to realize that the deserters had duped them.

Marcellus decided to take advantage of this split and approached one of the commanders of Achradina, a Spaniard named Moericus. He sent to him an agent who was also Spanish and had just arrived from Spain. Since 215 the Romans had made steady inroads into Carthaginian controlled Spain. Many of the Spanish tribes had decided to ally themselves with Rome in order to throw off Carthaginian control. The agent convinced Moericus that if he threw in his lot with Marcellus he could use Roman influence to obtain a high position in his homeland. Moericus agreed to betray his position.

In order to divert suspicion as to his true intentions, Moericus convinced his fellow commanders to put an end to the frequent exchange of envoys between the two sides. He also got them to agree to a clear delineation of areas of command. Livy states that Moericus received the area 'from the fountain of Arethusa to the mouth of the Great Harbour.'[22] This area is, however, on the western side of Ortygia. Either Livy is incorrect in his original claim that Moericus commanded in Achradina, or there had been a major reshuffle of commands.

The fountain, Fontana Aretusa, still exists and papyrus plants grow in its waters. South of Syracuse is the only site outside of Egypt where papyrus grows wild. The original plants, a closely guarded monopoly of the Ptolemies, were a gift from Ptolemy II to Hieron II and were first propagated in the fountain. The Syracusans believed that the fountain derived from the Alpheius River in the Peloponnesus which runs past the sanctuary of Olympia. The river is supposed to run 500km under the sea before it reappears at Syracuse.

Now that he had a traitor within the walls, Marcellus determined to take the final Syracusan stronghold by force. He launched a dawn attack against Achradina, while ships were sent to land at Moericus' area. Most of the garrison of Ortygia marched to support their comrades fighting to defend the walls of Achradina. Moericus and his men joined the Romans and they soon overran the few remaining troops guarding Ortygia. Once he learned that Ortygia had fallen, Marcellus sounded the retreat as he did not want the main part of his army to enter Ortygia and plunder the royal treasury. Later he would be disappointed to find that the famous treasury had largely been stripped by the various rulers after Hieron.

The recall of the attackers allowed the deserters to somehow escape the city. With the deserters gone and Ortygia captured, further resistance by the remaining Syracusans and mercenaries still under arms would be suicidal. They sent an embassy to Marcellus offering to surrender, the only condition being that he spare their children. Marcellus, no doubt exasperated by the collapse of all the previous offers, replied:

> The crimes committed against the people of Rome during these last few years by those who have held Syracuse quite outweigh all the good services which Hieron rendered us during his fifty years' reign. Most of these, it is true, have recoiled on the heads of those who were guilty of them, and they have punished themselves for their breach of treaties far more severely than the Roman people could have wished. I have been for three years investing Syracuse, not that Rome may make the

city her slave, but that the leaders of deserters and renegades may not keep it in a state of oppression and bondage.[23]

Despite these words Marcellus was determined that the Syracusans should be made to pay for abandoning Rome and the inconvenience of their three years of resistance. The gates to Achradina were opened by those seeking peace. The Romans entered, seized the royal treasury and Achradina was given over to be plundered by his soldiers. Unlike the earlier agreement with the citizens of Tyche and Neapolis, the citizens received no guarantee for their safety and many were killed by his rapacious soldiers. Only the houses of the friends of the Romans were saved. Marcellus gave orders that Archimedes should be spared but as the soldiers approached him he was engaged in creating a geometric design. Archimedes, engrossed in his drawing and feeling a tug at his arm

> not knowing who it was that pulled him, said to the man: 'Stand aside, fellow, from my figure.' But as the other kept on pulling, he turned, and recognizing him as a Roman cried out: 'Let somebody give me one of my machines.' The Roman, in terror, immediately killed him, a decrepit old man, but marvellous for his works.[24]

Marcellus buried the dead mathematician in his family tomb. The unfortunate killer was either executed or banished. Despite Archimedes' fame, Cicero, a century and a half later, claims that he found the tomb to be neglected and forgotten by the Syracusans.

During the course of the Roman siege the city, reputedly the largest and most beautiful of the Greeks, had been completely stripped bare of its wealth. According to Livy, Marcellus

> removed to Rome the ornaments of the city, the statues and pictures in which Syracuse abounded; they were, it is true, spoils taken from the enemy and acquired by the laws of war, but that was the beginning of our admiration for Greek works of art, which has led to the present reckless spoliation of every kind of treasure, sacred and profane alike.[25]

The Syracusans never forgave Marcellus for the sacking of their city. Two years later, 'while Marcellus was serving as Consul for the fourth time, his enemies induced the Syracusans to come to Rome and accuse and denounce him before the senate for terrible wrongs which they had suffered contrary to the terms of surrender.' Marcellus, quite rightly, replied that 'they had suffered nothing except what men whose city has been taken by storm in war cannot possibly be prevented from suffering,'[26] not surprisingly the prosecution failed.

Despite the sack, Marcellus was correct: the Syracusans had got off relatively lightly by the standards of their time. The Romans had breached the walls by force and the usual fate of cities so captured was for all the men to be slaughtered and the women and children sold into slavery.

With its capture by the Romans in 212,[27] Syracuse, five centuries after its foundation, had ceased to be an independent state. It would be incorporated into the Roman province of Sicily and be ruled by a Roman governor. The age of tyrants of Syracuse had come to an end.

Epilogue

The fall of Syracuse did not end the conflict in Sicily. Fighting would continue until 210, when the main Carthaginian base, Akragas, fell to the Romans by treachery. The remaining cities still opposed to Rome soon surrendered, giving Rome complete control of all of Sicily. Epicydes, having abandoned Syracuse, also fled from Akragas and returned to Carthage.

Marcellus, the conqueror of Syracuse had returned to Rome in late 211 to be elected Consul. Despite his success, Marcellus' political enemies were able to humiliate him by denying him a triumph – a parade for the most successful of generals. Instead they forced him to accept a lesser honour, an ovation, claiming that he had left Sicily still to be conquered. Further embarrassment was caused when he was allocated the province of Sicily but the Sicilian allies successfully blocked his appointment. They had not forgiven his sack of Enna and wholesale plundering of Syracuse, despite Plutarch's claim that: 'the blame for these was thought to belong to the sufferers rather than to the perpetrators.'[1] Marcellus would continue to command in Italy but would later be ambushed and killed by Hannibal.

The Second Punic War would continue until Hannibal was recalled to Africa and defeated at the Battle of Zama in 202. Carthage finally surrendered in 201. This time the conditions were harsh. Carthage lost all its overseas possessions, its fleet was reduced to ten triremes and a tribute of 10,000 talents was imposed, to be paid over fifty years as a constant reminder of its defeat.

Despite these terms, Carthage once again recovered largely under the political leadership of Hannibal. The Romans were, however, a vengeful people, and particularly harboured grudges against those who had the temerity to invade Italy. They continually hounded Hannibal until he was forced to flee Carthage. He finally committed suicide in Bithynia in 183, at the age of seventy. Hannibal's final words were: 'Let us relieve the Romans from the anxiety they have so long experienced, since they think it tries their patience too much to wait for an old man's death.'[2]

The death of one old man was not enough to satisfy many Romans. Nothing would allay their fears until Carthage was totally destroyed. In

149, on the most spurious of reasons, Rome would once again go to war with Carthage. In 146 the city would be sacked and destroyed. The 50,000 survivors of the siege were sold into slavery. It was claimed, although by later historians, that the ground was symbolically sown with salt so that nothing could ever grow there.

The Carthaginians had not been the first invaders of Italy to experience Rome's revenge. During the Third Macedonian War (171–168), the Molossians, the tribe of Pyrrhus, had supported Macedonia against Rome. The Romans conquered Molossia in 167 and remorselessly pillaged the country, enslaving 150,000 of its inhabitants. Central Epirus was devastated and depopulated. It remained a wasteland for over a millennium.

The Syracusans were perhaps fortunate that they had lost their Italian empire before the Romans had come to southern Italy, or they may have shared a similar fate. As it was, Syracuse was incorporated into the Roman province of Sicily. The Romans were mostly interested in Sicily as a source of grain. Gradually the land would be commandeered by rich Romans, who would found large estates (*latifundia*) that were worked by slaves captured in Rome's later campaigns of conquest. The masses of slaves on the island and the dispossession of the native farmers would lead to major slave uprisings in 139 and 104. As was the case with other provinces, exploitation of Sicily would become extreme in the later decades of the Roman Republic. Ambitious politicians would accumulate huge debts in their attempts to be elected to the chief positions in Rome. Those who succeeded would be awarded provinces to govern and would recoup their losses by abusing their positions and stealing from their subjects.

The most famous example of this is brought to light by the famous case prosecuted by Cicero, where the Sicilians sought compensation for the crimes of their governor, Verres. They accused him of taking bribes, plundering the artworks of both individuals and temples, and overtaxing the population. This would normally have been accepted as usual behaviour by a governor but Verres probably overstepped the mark when he accepted bribes to allow the Messenians to avoid their naval duties and unlawfully crucified a Roman citizen. Against all expectation the jury found him guilty. He was fined and sent into exile.

Under the empire Syracuse would become one of only six Sicilian cities granted the privileged status of *colonia* with some citizens being granted full Roman citizenship. Most of Sicily was not granted such rights until the third century AD. During this time Syracuse would recover and become a leading commercial hub and the administrative centre of the Roman governor. Little is known of its history during this period.

In 468 Sicily was captured by the Vandals, sold to the German ruler of Italy, Odoacer, and recaptured by the Byzantines in 535. During the ninth century AD, the Arabs would conquer Sicily with Syracuse being one the last cities to fall in 878. The Arab conquest marked the beginning of the end for Syracuse as the premier city of Sicily. Thereafter Palermo, the old Carthaginian city of Panormus, would be made their capital, becoming one of the most splendid cities in the Arab world. After the Normans had taken the island, Palermo would remain the leading city of Sicily.

Today Syracuse is a city of about 120,000 people, which occupies much the same area as it did in ancient times. It is still a working port but its main industry is tourism – a legacy of its Greek heritage. To the south of the city are the remains of the Temple of Zeus which is currently a locked archaeological site. When I visited the area there were numerous holes in the fence and the site looked like it was often used for partying by the local youth. To the west of the city are the spectacular ruins of the fort designed by Archimedes, the *Castello Eurialo*. Most guidebooks claim admission to the site is free but, be warned, this is not the case.

In Syracuse the two main attractions are the *Parco Archaeological Della Neapolis* and Ortygia. The park contains the ruins of the Greek and Roman theatres and a huge temple built by Hieron II. The main attraction is, however, the Garden of Paradise which occupies the site of the old quarries. It was here that the survivors of the Athenian expedition were starved to death and the tyrants kept their prisoners. This includes the Ear of Dionysius, a cave where the acoustics are so good that guards could listen to the prisoners' conversations. Most tour guides are keen to prove that this claim is genuine.

Ortygia is at the heart of modern Syracuse and is described as a living museum to all the epochs of the city. One can walk the streets knowing that one is following not only in the footsteps of the tyrants but such scholars as Plato and Archimedes. The Fontana Aretusa, the site of the Roman landing, is still there along with its papyrus plants. At the end of a long day it is a good place to sit and gaze across the waters of the Great Harbour, just as the Syracusans have done for over twenty-seven centuries.

Notes

Preface

1. Diodorus was a citizen of the town of Agyrium in Sicily and probably wrote his history between the years 56–26 BC. It covered events, in forty books, from legendary times prior to the Trojan War until the beginning of Caesar's campaigns against the Celts. Unfortunately those books covering events after 301 have been lost and exist only in summaries, 'fragments', by later historians. Diodorus' value as an historian came under stinging attack by the German scholars of the nineteenth century, but in more recent times his reputation has been largely rehabilitated. He is now generally seen as a competent historian who read widely and produced his own work. His major weakness, which shall be seen often, is a tendency to moralize and look for signs of divine justice.
2. Plutarch (c 46–120 AD) is best known for his biographies which compared the paired lives of famous Greeks and Romans. Although invaluable, these works have their limitations, for, as Plutarch readily admits, he was a biographer not an historian. Plutarch's many biases will be discussed in the relevant chapters.
3. Justin's work was an anthology, excerpted from the earlier work of the historian Pompeius Trogus, 'omitting all that was not pleasurable to read or did not supply a moral lesson.' The date of composition is hotly disputed, with the period 144–230 AD being the most likely.
4. Polybius was a Greek general and historian of the first century BC. While a hostage of the Romans, he wrote a history to explain the rise of Rome to his fellow Greeks.
5. Livy (59 BC–17 AD), was a Roman aristocrat and historian who wrote a monumental history of Rome, *Ab Urbe Condita Libri*, 'Chapters from the Foundation of the City,' covering the period from the earliest legends of Rome, well before the traditional foundation in 753 BC, through the reign of Augustus. It was meant to glorify Rome's past, comparing it to the preceding years of civil war, and convince the Romans to return to their old virtues.

Chapter 1

1. Diodorus 16.5. The phrase was popular in antiquity being repeated by Aelian, *Varia Historia* 6.12 and Plutarch, *Dion* 7, 10.
2. Plato, *The Seventh Letter*.
3. Plutarch, *Pyrrhus* 9.
4. Plutarch, *Timoleon* 1.
5. Plutarch, *Dion* 1.

6. Plutarch, *Dion* 3.

7. Plutarch, *Comparison of Dion and Brutus* 3.

8 Plutarch, *Comparison of Dion and Brutus* 4.

9. Plutarch, *Dion* 8.

10. Plutarch, *Dion* 37.

11. Plutarch, *Dion* 47.

12. Diodorus 16.6.

13. Diodorus 16.17.

14. Cornelius Nepos (c. 100–24 BC) was a Roman writer of Gallic origin born in Cisalpine Gaul not far from Verona. He was a very popular author but appears to have been more interested in style than accuracy.

15. Nepos *Dion* 1. See also Plutarch, *Comparison of Dion and Brutus* 3.

16. Plutarch, *Dion* 8–9.

17. Justin 21.2. The eye disease may have been a result of his hobby of woodwork which he took up in his youth as a politically harmless pastime.

18. Diodorus 15.76.

19. Justin 21.1.

20. Plutarch, *Dion* 6.

21. Nepos *Dion* 1.

22. Plutarch, *Dion* 6.

23. Plutarch, *Dion* 7.

24. Plutarch, *Dion* 7.

25. Plato, *The Seventh Letter*.

26. Plutarch, *Dion* 7.

27. Plutarch, *Dion* 9–10.

28. Plato, *The Republic* 6. It has been argued that, by the time of his second visit to Syracuse, Plato had despaired of cities accepting philosophers as their rulers and had lowered his expectations getting them to adopt laws which a philosopher could approve. See Porter, WH. *Life of Dion* (New York, 1979) pp. 71–3.

29. Kenny, A, *An Illustrated Brief History of Western Philosophy*, (Malden, 2006) p. 46.

30. Plato, *Statesman*.

31. Plato, *Statesman*.

32. Plutarch, *Moralia* 827.

33. Porter, p. xvii.

34. Plato, *The Seventh Letter*.

35. Plutarch, *Dion* 11.

Chapter 2

1. Plutarch, *Dion* 11.

2. Plutarch, *Dion* 12.

3. Plutarch, *Dion*, 13

4. Plutarch, *Dion* 13.

5. Diodorus 16.6; Plutarch, *Dion* 14; Nepos *Dion* 4.

6. Plutarch, *Dion* 15.

7. Plutarch, *Dion* 16.

8. Diodorus 16.5.

9. Diodorus 16.5.

10. Justin 21.1–2.
11. Nepos *Dion* 3.
12. Plutarch, *Dion* 18.
13. Plato, *The Seventh Letter*.
14. Plato, *The Seventh Letter*.
15. Plutarch, *Dion* 18. Scylla and Charybdis were mythical sea monsters that supposedly inhabited the Straits of Messina. Scylla was described as having six heads perched on long necks and ate sailors who came too near. Charybdis had a single gaping mouth that sucked in huge quantities of water and belched them out creating gigantic whirlpools.
16. Plato, *The Seventh Letter*.
17. Plato, *The Seventh Letter*.
18. Plato, *The Seventh Letter*.
19. Plato, *The Seventh Letter*.
20. Diodorus 16.9; Aelian Plato, *Varia Historia* 6.12
21. Nepos, *Dion* 5.

Chapter 3

 1. Aelian *Varia Historia* 12.60.
 2. Plutarch, *Dion* 27.
 3. Plutarch, *Dion* 28.
 4. Plutarch, *Dion* 30.
 5. Diodorus 16.12.
 6. Diodorus 16.12.
 7. Plutarch, *Dion* 31.
 8. Plutarch, *Dion* 32.
 9. Diodorus 16.16.
10. Plutarch, *Dion* 32.
11. Plutarch, *Dion* 33.
12. Plutarch, *Dion* 34.
13. Diodorus 16.16.
14. Plutarch, *Dion* 35.
15. Plutarch, *Dion* 37.
16. Waterfield, R, *Why Socrates Died Dispelling the Myths* (London, 2010) p. 22. For a more detailed description of how such groupings worked see pp. 21–3
17. Plutarch, *Dion* 37–9.

Chapter 4

 1. Diodorus 16.17.
 2. Diodorus 16.18.
 3. Diodorus 16.19.
 4. Plutarch, *Dion* 41.
 5. Plutarch, *Dion* 44.
 6. Plutarch, *Dion* 44.
 7. Plutarch, *Dion* 44.
 8. Plutarch, *Dion* 47.
 9. Plutarch, *Dion* 49.
10. Plutarch, *Dion* 49.

11. Plutarch, *Dion* 49.
12. Plutarch, *Dion* 50.
13. Plutarch, *Dion* 52.
14. Plutarch, *Dion* 53.
15. Xenophon, *Constitution of Lacedaemon* 8; Aristotle, *Politics* 2.7.5.
16. Nepos, *Dion* 7.
17 A talent was about 26kg of silver, so the bribe was about 500kg. The best way to assess the real value of the bribe is that it was about 200 years pay for a mercenary hoplite.
18. Plutarch, *Dion* 57.
19. Nepos, *Dion* 10.
20. Some modern scholars tend to reject this accusation as unlikely and a part of a campaign to blacken Hicetas' reputation. Although the latter may well be correct, I can see no good reason to dismiss the claim as false. See for example: Talbert, RJA, *Timoleon and the Revival of Greek Sicily, 344–317 B.C* (Cambridge, 1974) p. 87 and Westlake, HD, *Timoleon and his Relations with Tyrants* (Manchester, 1952) pp. 11–12.

Chapter 5

1. Athenaeus, *The Deipnosophists* 11.119
2. Plutarch, *Dion* 54; Plato, *Epistle 6* 333.
3. Polyaenus 5.4. Polyaenus was a Macedonian by birth. He wrote for and dedicated his book on the stratagems of war to the emperor Marcus Aurelius (161–180 AD).
4. Plato, *Epistle* 8354C
5. Athenaeus, *The Deipnosophists* 12.58.
6. Justin 21.3.
7. Plutarch, *Timoleon* 1
8. Athenaeus, *The Deipnosophists* 12.58.
9. Justin 21.1.
10. Cicero, *Tusculan Disputations* 5.21. Translated by CD Yonge at: http://thriceholy. net/Texts/Tusculan2.html#V
11. Plutarch, *Timoleon* 1.
12. Diodorus 16.67.
13. Plutarch, *Timoleon* 2.
14. Talbert, p. 53.
15. Plutarch, *Timoleon* 1.
16. Xenophon, *Anabasis* 6.1. Translated by H G Dakyns at: http://ebooks.adelaide. edu.au/x/xenophon/x5an/index.html
17. Plutarch, *Timoleon* 3.

Chapter 6

1. Plutarch, *Timoleon* 33.
2. Talbert, pp. 1, 5.
3. Polybius 12.25, 12.23.
4. Nepos, *Timoleon* 2; Diodorus 16.67.
5. Plutarch, *Comparison of Timoleon and Aemilius* 2.
6. Bosworth, B, 'History and Artifice in Plutarch's Eumenes', in Stadter, PA, *Plutarch and the Historical Tradition* (London, Routledge, 1992.) p. 80.

7. Plutarch, *Timoleon* 3.
8. Aristotle, *Politics* 5.6; Xenophon, *Hellenica* 7.4.6.
9. Plutarch, *Timoleon* 4.
10. Plutarch, *Timoleon* 4.
11. Nepos, *Timoleon* 1.
12. Diodorus 16.65.
13. Diodorus 16.65.
14. Plutarch, *Timoleon* 5.
15. Plutarch, *Timoleon* 3.
16. Talbert 131; Salmon, JB, *Wealthy Corinth: a History of the City to 338 BC* (Oxford, 1984), pp. 385–6.
17. Diodorus 16.65.
18. Plutarch, *Timoleon* 7.
19. As proposed by Talbert pp 56–57.
20. Plutarch, *Timoleon* 9.
21. Plutarch, *Timoleon* 10.
22. Plutarch, *Timoleon* 11.
23. Plutarch, *Timoleon* 13.

Chapter 7

1. Diodorus 16.68.
2. Westlake, pp. 17–28.
3. Talbert, p. 99
4. Talbert, p. 108.
5. Diodorus' chronology throughout Book 16 is confused. The dating of the events of Timoleon's campaign is therefore open to much debate among scholars. This is particularly the case with the Battle of Crimisus, which Diodorus assigns to the years 340/39, but is dated by historians anywhere from 341 to 338, with the earlier date the most popular. I find none of the arguments totally convincing and will therefore, by default, follow Diodorus' chronology and date the battle to 339. For a full discussion of the problems see Talbert, pp. 44–51.
6. Diodorus 16.69.
7. Diodorus 16.69. Plutarch, *Timoleon* 17, has the same number of ships but 60,000 soldiers. The figures for the number of soldiers are usually discredited by modern commentators who claim that they most likely record the numbers all the Carthaginian forces in Sicily rather than just those sent to Syracuse. See for example: Talbert, pp. 62–63 and Westlake, pp. 29–30. It does, nonetheless, equal the number of men who crossed to Sicily with Mago and there must have already been garrison troops on the island. It would seem reasonable that Mago would bring all available forces to win a prize as important as Syracuse.
8. Plutarch, *Timoleon* 17.
9. Plutarch, *Timoleon* 16.
10. Plutarch, *Timoleon* 17.
11. Plutarch, *Timoleon* 18.
12. Plutarch, *Timoleon* 19.
13. Plutarch, *Timoleon* 20.
14. Plutarch, *Timoleon* 20.
15. Plutarch, *Timoleon* 22.

16. Justin 21.4.4; Aristotle, *Politics* 1307a; Orosius 4.6.20
17. Westlake, p. 30.
18. Talbert, p. 81.
19. Plutarch, *Timoleon* 22.
20. Plutarch, *Timoleon* 22.
21. Diodorus 16.69.
22. Westlake, pp. 33–4.
23. Diodorus 16.70.
24. Justin 21.5.
25. Plutarch, *Timoleon* 22.

Chapter 8

1. Plutarch has Timoleon capturing Messene twice (*Timoleon* 20 and 34). The first time is prior to his capture of Syracuse and the latter when he describes the overthrow of the tyrant Hippo. His later description of the removal of Hippo may in fact belong here.
2. Plutarch, *Timoleon* 24.
3. Diodorus 16.73.
4. Plutarch, *Timoleon* 25.
5. Livy 10.28.
6. Diodorus 16.78.
7. Talbert, pp. 69–74.
8. Polyaenus 5.12.3
9. Polyaenus 5.12.1; Plutarch, *Timoleon* 26; Diodorus 16.79.
10. Plutarch, *Timoleon* 27.
11. Plutarch, *Timoleon* 27.
12. Plutarch. *Timoleon* 27.
13. Plutarch. *Timoleon* 28.
14. Plutarch. *Timoleon* 28. Plutarch has the initial fight lasting much longer with the Greeks only prevailing after the thunderstorm struck. Again I have preferred Diodorus' account. The normal depth for a hoplite phalanx was eight, although it could range from four to sixteen. The Thebans had already successfully used a phalanx fifty deep. It is unlikely, however, that the Carthaginians were emulating this tactic. Instead they had been forced to adopt this formation by the nature of the river crossing.
15. Diodorus 16.79.
16. Diodorus 16.80.
17. Diodorus 16.80.
18. Diodorus 16.80.
19. Diodorus 16.81.
20. Diodorus 16.81.
21. Diodorus 16.81. Plutarch places the sending of the embassy somewhat later, after the sending of a new Carthaginian force to Sicily and the defeat of Hicetas and Mamercus. It is not impossible that several embassies were sent.

Chapter 9

1. Diodorus 16.82; Plutarch, *Timoleon* 30.
2. Plutarch, *Timoleon* 28.

3. Diodorus 16.81.
4. Plutarch, *Timoleon* 30.
5. Plutarch, *Timoleon* 30.
6. Plutarch, *Timoleon* 31.
7. Plutarch, *Timoleon* 30.
8. Plutarch, *Timoleon* 31. The exact location of the Damurius River is unknown but it probably ran into the sea in Syracusan territory north of the city.
9. Plutarch, *Timoleon* 33.
10. Diodorus 16.81.
11. Plutarch, *Timoleon* 34.
12. Polyaenus 5.12.2.
13. Justin 22.1.
14. Diodorus 16.82.
15. Diodorus 16.83; Plutarch, *Timoleon* 35.
16. For a full discussion of the evidence see Talbert, pp. 146–160.
17. Diodorus 16.82.
18. Plutarch, *Timoleon* 35.
19. Plutarch, *Timoleon* 37.
20. Polybius 12.23.
21. Plutarch, *Timoleon* 39.

Chapter 10

1. Diodorus 21.17.
2. Plutarch, *Pericles* 28.
3. Polybius 12.15.
4. Diodorus 21.17
5. Justin 22.1.
6. Polybius 12.15: 'Nor can I approve the terms in which he speaks of Agathocles, even if that prince were the most impious of men. I allude to the passage at the end of his story in which he says that Agathocles in his early youth was a common prostitute, ready to yield himself to the most debauched, a jackdaw, a buzzard, who would right about face to anyone wished it.'
7. Diodorus 19.3.
8. Justin 22.1.
9. Diodorus 19.3.
10. Diodorus 19.3.
11. Perhaps the two of the most notable examples of such behaviour are the brothers Tiberius and Gaius Gracchus. Although members of one of the most distinguished Roman families they led the movement for land reform at the end of the second century. Tiberius was beaten to death by a patrician mob. Nonetheless his brother continued his reform programme and a decade later suffered a similar fate.
12. Justin 22.1.
13. Diodorus 19.4.
14. Diodorus 19.4.
15. Justin 22.1.
16. Diodorus 19.6.
17. Justin 22.2.
18. Diodorus 19.5.

19. Diodorus 19.6.
20. Diodorus 19.6.
21. Diodorus 19.61. For a full discussion of what may have been meant be 'freedom' and 'autonomy' see: Champion, JR, *Antigonos' Policy of Freedom for the Greeks*, Slingshot 248 (2006), pp. 20–4. The most important promise was not to impose a foreign garrison.
22. Ployaenus 5.72.
23. Justin 22.2.
24. Polyaenus 5.38.
25. Diodorus 19.6. Diodorus' version of events is somewhat different to that of Polyaenus. He omits the oligarch's plot, stating that Agathocles had used the age-old ruse of claiming falsely that there was a plot against him 'because of his sympathy for the common people.' Similar claims had been used successfully by the earlier tyrants, Peistratus of Athens and Dionysius the Elder.
26. Diodorus 19.6–7.
27. Diodorus 19.7.
28. Diodorus 19.8. Polyaneus (5.3.7) records the number of exiles as 5,000.
29. Diodorus 19.9. Agathocles, did, however, adopt the title of king nine years later, although he refrained from wearing its symbol, the diadem.
30. Polybius 9.23.
31. Diodorus 19.9.
32. Diodorus 19.9.
33. Diodorus 20.63.
34. Plutarch, *Moralia* 176.

Chapter 11
1. Diodorus 19.65.
2. Diodorus 19.70.
3. Diodorus 19.71.
4. Diodorus 19.71.
5. Justin 22.3.
6. Diodorus 19.72.
7. Polyaenus 5.15.
8. Diodorus 19.102.
9. Diodorus 19.103. This brutal action was designed to ensure that they could never serve as sailors or rowers again. Sometimes only the thumb, or the right hand, was amputated. The practice had become common in the final years of the Peloponnesian War as both sides desperately sought to win control of the sea. It does seem pointless on this occasion to inflict the punishment on the crews of neutral vessels.
10. Diodorus 19.103.
11. Diodorus 19.104.
13. Diodorus 19.106.
14. Diodorus 19.107.
15. Diodorus 19.107.
16. Diodorus 19.107. By suggesting alternative reasons for his actions, Diodorus is likely to be recording the motives given by different sources, both for and against Agathocles.

17. Diodorus 19.108.
18. Diodorus 19.108.
19. Diodorus 19.108.
20. Diodorus 20.4.
21. Diodorus (13.114) records an example of the terms the Carthaginians might impose: 'the inhabitants of Selinus, Akragas, and Himera as well as those of Gela and Camarina may dwell in their cities, which shall be unfortified, but shall pay tribute to the Carthaginians; the inhabitants of Leontini and Messene and the Siceli shall all live under laws of their own making.' According to Diodorus (14.65) some Greeks found their own tyrants harsher masters than the Carthaginians, who even if they 'defeat us in war, they would only impose a fixed tribute and would not prevent us from governing the city in accordance with our ancient laws.'
22. Diodorus 19.110.
23. Polyaenus 6.41; Justin 21.3.
24. Diodorus 20.3.

Chapter 12
1. Diodorus 20.4; Polyaenus (15.3.5) has a slightly different version, claiming: 'he ordered a proclamation to be made, that whoever wished to be excused from the expedition might go ashore, and take with him whatever property he had on board. All those who took advantage of the proclamation, he ordered to be executed as traitors and cowards.'
2. Justin 22.5.
3. Justin 22.5.
4. Diodorus (19.72) records Agathocles as earlier preparing 'a store of weapons and missiles of all kinds', perhaps for just such a situation.
5. Diodorus 20.5.
6. Justin 22.6.
7. Frontinus 1.12.9.
8. Diodorus 20.7.
9. Diodorus 20.7. This more cynical motive is repeated in Polyaenus 15.3.5 and Justin 22.6: 'the means of flight being taken away, they might understand that they must either conquer or die.'
10. Justin 22.5.
11. Diodorus 20.8.
12. Diodorus 20.8.
13. Justin 22.6.
14. Justin 22.5.
15. Diodorus (20.8) gives the distance from Tunis to Carthage as 2000 stades nearly 400 kilometres. This probably is a result of a corruption of Diodorus' text.
16. Diodorus 20. 10; Justin 22.6. For the population of urban Carthage see Fields, N. *Roman Conquests: North Africa* (Barnsley, 2010) p. 4.
17. Diodorus 20.10.
18. Diodorus 20.11.
19. A fragment of the Roman general and historian, Arrian (*PSI XII 1284*), describes these tactics in a battle fought a decade earlier between two of the Successor generals. When the infantry phalanx of Neoptomus was attacked by the cavalry of Eumenes, they: 'advanced in close battle order to make the most fearful

impression with those behind them ... firing javelins in order to throw back the assault of the cavalry.' A translation of the fragment by Walter Goralski can be found in the journal: *Ancient World* 19 (1989)

20. Diodorus 20.12.
21. Diodorus 20.13; Justin, 22.6. 6; Orosius, 4.6.25.
22. Diodorus 20.13; Herodotus, 1.66.
23. Diodorus 20.14.

Chapter 13
1. Justin 22.7.
2. Diodorus 20.17.
3. Tillyard, HJW, *Agathocles* (Cambridge, 1908) p. 124.
4. Diodorus 20.29.
5. Diodorus 20.29.
6. Tillyard, p. 136.
7. Cicero, *On Divination* 1.24. Largely repeated by Valerius Maximus 1.7. ext. 8 Cicero translated by WA Falconer at: http://penelope.uchicago.edu/Thayer/E/Roman/Texts/Cicero/de_Divinatione/1*.html
8. Tillyard p 135.
9. Diodorus 20.32.
10. Diodorus 20.33.
11. Diodorus 20.34. Although the veracity of the mutiny should not be doubted, too many of its details are similar to the accounts of Alexander the Great's murder of Cleitus the Black for the story to be taken literally.
12. Diodorus 20.34.
13. Diodorus 20.40. Justin (22.7) claims that is was Ophellas who made the first approach as he was 'grasping, with extravagant hopes, at the dominion of all Africa' and proposed the division of spoils.
14. Diodorus 20.42.
15. Justin 22.7. Tillyard maintains throughout his work that Bomilcar was the leader of the peace party within Carthage and had been in treasonous contact with Agathocles throughout the war. He argues (p. 155) that the death of Bomilcar was the turning point in the war as: 'The disloyal party in Carthage would not dare to raise its head for many years after such a blow, and the hands of the Senate were strengthened for a more resolute conduct of the war.' This argument is pure supposition based largely on Justin's claims that Agathocles and Hamilcar had been in league when Agathocles had seized power in Syracuse. No doubt there were those within Carthage who favoured a peaceful settlement. There is, however, far too little known about of the internal politics of Carthage to draw any firm conclusions as to their identity. Nor is there any real evidence to suggest that Bomilcar was anything other than an ambitious opportunist.
16. Diodorus (20.55) claims that Utica had revolted but there is no record of having been captured. Here I prefer the testimony of Polybius (1.82) who states that Utica 'had gallantly held out during the invasion of Agathocles' and had 'never had on any occasion given the least sign of hostility to Carthage.'
17. Diodorus 20.54.
18. Appian, *Punic Wars* 110.
19. Diodorus 20.55.

Chapter 14

1. Diodorus (20.56) gives a figure of 82,000 for the number of Syracusan infantry but with the city so reduced this figure is impossible to believe. Most likely a mistake in copying the text has occurred.
2. Diodorus 20.57.
3. Diodorus 20.62.
4. Talbert, pp. 167–8.
5. Diodorus 20.62. A similar criticism of the Akragantians is made at 16.84. These claims by Diodorus are often interpreted as general comparison of the inferior fighting ability of citizen hoplites compared to the superiority of mercenaries. Yet here there is no evidence that this Syracusan army was wholly or even partly composed of mercenaries. It is more likely that for some reason Diodorus had a particular contempt for the people of Akragas and their reputedly decadent lifestyle.
6. Justin 22.8.
7. Polyaenus 5.3.3.
8. Diodorus 20.63.
9. Justin 22.8.
10. Plutarch, *Moralia* 176, 'as he was besieging a city, some from the walls reviling him, saying, Do you hear, potter, where will you have money to pay your soldiers! – he gently answered, I'll tell you, if I take this city.' Diodorus 20.63, 'once when he was besieging a certain not inglorious city and people from the wall shouted, "Potter and furnace-man, when will you pay your soldiers?" he said in a way, "when I have taken this city."'
11. Diodorus 20.65.
12. Diodorus 20.68; Justin 22.8.
13. Justin 22.8.
14. Polybius 7.2.
15. Miles R *Carthage Must be Destroyed* (2010) p. 154.
16. Diodorus 20.70.

Chapter 15

1. Diodorus 20.71. The knucklebones were probably bone plated whips.
2. Diodorus 20.77.
3. Diodorus 20.78.
4. Diodorus 20.79.
5. Diodorus 20.79. The amount of grain received was about 7,600 tonnes.
6. Justin 22.8.
7. Polyaenus 5.3.2. Polyaenus records the number executed as 10,000.
8. Plutarch, *Pyrrhus* 12.
9. Diodorus 20.89.
10. Plutarch, *Demetrius* 17–18.
11. Diodorus 20.54.
12. Justin 23.1.
13. Plutarch *Moralia* 557. See also *Moralia* 176, where a similar answer was given to the people of Ithaca, home of Odysseus, when they complained of a raid by Agathocles' troops.
14. Diodorus 21.2.

15. Diodorus 21.4.
16. Plutarch, *Pyrrhus* 10.
17. Plutarch, *Demetrius* 25. Of the other kings only Lysimachus took serious offence, as treasurers were generally eunuchs.
18. Diodorus 21.15.
19. Justin 23.2
20. Diodorus 21.8.
21. Diodorus 21.16. He cannot have been as young as Diodorus implies as he had been commanding troops in Italy six years earlier. His father had died eighteen years prior, after being absent in Africa for four years, so twenty-two is his lowest possible age. Presumably he was in his mid-twenties and therefore under the age of thirty, the normal age at which Greeks were considered mature enough to command. Being the king's grandson had no doubt helped his advancement.
22. Justin 23.2.
23. Justin 23.2.
24. Diodorus 21.16.
25. Diodorus 21.16
26. Diodorus 21.16.
27. Diodorus 21.16.
28. Cicero, *Treatise on the Republic* 3.43. Translated by F Barnham at: http://files.libertyfund.org/files/546/Cicero_0044-01_EBk_v5.pdf
29. Cicero, *Verres* 2.4.112. Translated by CD Yonge at: http://www.perseus.tufts.edu/hopper/text?doc=Perseus%3Atext%3A1999.02.0018%3Atext%3DVer.%3Aactio%3D2%3Abook%3D2%3Asection%3D2

Chapter 16.

1. Justin 23.2.
2. Diodorus 21.18.
3. For a full discussion see: Champion J, *The Tyrants of Syracuse: War in Ancient Sicily Volume I: 480–367 BC* (Barnsley, 2010) pp. 34–5 and Lomas, K, 'Tyrants and the polis: migration, identity and urban development in Sicily', in *Ancient Tyranny* (Edinburgh, 2006), pp. 95–118.
4. Polybius 1.7.
5. Diodorus 22.2.
6. Diodorus 22.6: 'they once again invited King Pyrrhus to come to Sicily.'
7. Plutarch, *Pyrrhus* 22.
8. Plutarch, *Pyrrhus* 8. Pyrrhus' position in the top three varies depending on the source, see also: Plutarch, *Flamminius* 21; Appian, *Syrian Wars* 10; Livy 35.14.
9. Plutarch, *Pyrrhus* 14.
10. Plutarch *Pyrrhus* 20.
11. Zonaras 8.3.
12. Plutarch, *Pyrrhus* 19. The Hydra was a giant serpent that possessed nine heads. Each time a head was cut off it grew two more. It was killed by Heracles as one of his Twelve Labours.
13. Plutarch, *Pyrrhus* 22.
14. Plutarch, *Pyrrhus* 14.
15. Plutarch, *Pyrrhus* 22.
16. Justin 18.2.

17. Polybius 3.25.
18. Justin 18.2.

Chapter 17

1. Appian, *Samnite Wars* 28
2. Diodorus 22.8
3. Diodorus 22.8.
4. Dionysius 20.8. Dionysius claims that the number of Syracusan ships handed over was 200 but this probably an error for the total of the combined fleet.
5. Justin 23.3.
6. Justin 23.3 states that: 'he destined for his son Helenus the kingdom of Sicily, as an inheritance from his grandfather (for he was the son of Agathocles's daughter), and to Alexander that of Italy.' Justin has clearly made an error here as Helenus was not the son of Lanassa. Most historians believe that he has transposed the names and it was Alexander who was made his heir in Sicily. For a full discussion see: Garoufalias, P, *Pyrrhus , King of Epirus* (London, 1979), pp. 104, 396–7 n. 47.
7. Plutarch, *Pyrrhus* 22. Diodorus 22.9 records only 1,500 cavalry but this is only 300 more than those supplied by Leontini and Akragas alone.
8. Diodorus 22.10.
9. Plutarch *Pyrrhus* 22.
10. Plutarch, *Pyrrhus* 22.
11. Polybius 1.56.
12. Justin 23.3.
13. Diodorus 22.10.
14. Diodorus 22.10, 24.1.
15. Diodorus 22.10.
16. Plutarch, *Pyrrhus* 23.
17. Garoufalias, p. 108.
18. Plutarch, *Pyrrhus* 26.
19. Plutarch, *Pyrrhus* 23.
20. Dionysius 20.8.
21. Dionysius 20.8.
22. Plutarch, *Pyrrhus* 23. Most historians follow Plutarch's narrative and place this battle prior to the siege of Lilybauem. Plutarch's text here is, however, muddled. Nor can he be relied upon for accurate chronology. For Pyrrhus to delay the siege of Lilybaeum and march right across the length of Sicily in order to defeat the Mamertines would appear to be unlikely.
23. Plutarch, *Pyrrhus* 23.
24. Zonaras 8.6.
25. Justin 23.3.
26. Justin 23.3.
27. Thucydides 4.64.
28. Plutarch, *Pyrrhus* 23.

Chapter 18

1. Pausanias 6.12.2.
2. Polybius 1.3.

3. Polybius 7.4; Pausanias 6. 12. 3.
4. Diodorus 23.1.
5. Polybius 1.8.
6. Justin 23.4.
7. Polybius 1.8. Probably as a result of the machinations of Dionysius the Elder who had used a similar absentee assembly to have himself voted a bodyguard.
8. Polybius 1.9.
9. Polybius 7.8.
10. Polybius 1.9. Hieron once again emulated Dionysius the Elder who had used a similar ruse to remove fractious mercenaries during the Carthaginian siege of Syracuse.
11. Polybius 1.9.
12. Diodorus 22.13.
13. Livy 7.29.
14 Plutarch, *Pyrrhus* 23. The word means: fit for battle, effective soldiers.
15. Lendon, JE, *Soldiers & Ghosts* (2005) pp. 182–187 argues that the reason that the Romans adopted the manipular formation not for tactical reasons but to encourage this sort of aggressive, individual behaviour.
16. Diodorus 22.13.
17. Diodorus 22.13.
18. Diodorus 22.13.
19. Diodorus 22.13.
20. Justin 23.4. Zonaras (8.6) states that Hieron was; 'not of distinguished family even on his father's side, and on his mother's side actually belonged to the slave class.' Polybius (7.8) agrees with Zonaras, 'having found ready provided for him by fortune neither wealth, fame, nor anything else.' On this occasion it seems best to accept the testimony of Justin and disregard the usual tales surrounding famous men of humble birth and lack of resources.
21. Justin 23.4.
22. Polybius 7.8.
23. Justin 23.4.
24. Polybius 1.10.

Chapter 19

1. Polybius 1.10.
2. Cassius Dio 11.43.
3. Zonaras 8.8.
4. Zonaras 8.9.
5. Polybius 1.11. Polybius account makes no mention of Claudius' initial expedition.
6. Diodorus 22.13.
7. Diodorus 23.1.
8. Zonaras' 8.9.
9. Polybius 1.15.
10. Polybius 1.15.
11. Polybius 1.14. Fabius was a senator who fought in the Second Punic War and wrote a history of Rome from it's foundation to his own times.
12. Diodorus 23.3.
13. Polybius 1.11.

14. Polybius 1.16.
15. Livy, *Periochae* 11, giving the census figures for the year 270.

Chapter 20
1. Polybius 1.17.
2. Polybius 5.84.
3. Polybius (1.18) places the capture of Herbessus prior to Hanno's advance on Akragas. If this is accepted as correct it would, however, make Zonaras' account impossible.
4. Zonaras 8.10.
5. Polybius 1.18.
6. Zonaras 8.10.
7. Zonaras 8.10.
8. Frontinus 2.1.4.
9. Polybius 1.19.
10. Polybius 1.19.
11. Diodorus 23.8.
12. Polybius 1.20.
13. Zonaras 8.11.
14. Polybius 1.20.
15. Grainger, JD, *Hellenistic and Roman Naval Wars 336–31 BC* (Barnsley, 2011), p. *xvi*.
16. Polybius 1.20.

Chapter 21
1. Polybius 1.23.
2. Diodorus 23.10, states that the Carthaginians outnumbered the Romans 200 to 120. Polybius 1.23, records that the Carthaginians had 130 ships and gives no figure for the Romans. Diodorus 22.8, claims that Pyrrhus' flagship was a 'nine'. This may be a different large galley. Ships up to 'sixers' were really larger triremes with up to two men per oar. Larger ships needed were higher, slower to accelerate and difficult to manoeuvre. In effect they were floating fortresses.
3. Diodorus 23.11.
4. Polybius 1.24.
5. Diodorus 23.9.
6. Polybius 1.24.
7. Polybius 1.24.
8. Polybius 1.25.
9. Polybius 1. 26. These numbers are often disbelieved by modern historians. For a defence of Polybius figures, see Goldsworthy, A, *The Punic Wars* (London, 2001), pp. 110–111.
10. Polybius 1.26.
11. Polybius 1.27.
12. Polybius 1.27.
13. Zonaras 8.12.
14. Polybius 1.30–31.
15. Diodorus 23.13.
16. Diodorus 23.12.

17. Polybius 1.32.
18. Polybius 1.34.
19. Diodorus 23.12.
20. Zonaras 8.13; Diodorus 23.16.
21. Polybius 1.36.
22. Diodorus 23.18.
23. Polybius 1.36.
24. Polybius 1.40. Caecilius' tactics were probably copied from those of Dentatus who twenty-four years earlier had routed Pyrrhus' elephants in a similar manner at the battle of Beneventum.
25. Diodorus 23.21 states that only sixty elephants were captured and the Carthaginian defeat was largely the result of drunkenness among its Gaulish mercenaries.
26. Polybius 1.41.
27. Diodorus 24.1.
28. Polybius 1.51.
29. Diodorus 24.2, records a figure of 210 ships for the Roman fleet of which they lost 117.
30. Polybius 1.55.
31. Diodorus (24.11) states that the Roman fleet numbered 300 warships.
32. Polybius 1.61. Diodorus (24.11) records the Carthaginian losses as 117 ships while the Romans lost thirty with another fifty being damaged.
33. Polybius 1.62.
34. Cassius Dio 12.17.

Chapter 22

1. Polybius 1.63
2. Appian, *The Sicilian Wars* 5.3. Translated by H White at: http://www.livius.org/ap-ark/appian/appian_sicily.html
3. Cicero, Verres 2.2.2.
4. Theocraticus, *Idyll* 16. Translated by CS Calverley at: http://www.gutenberg.org/cache/epub/11533/pg11533.txt
5. Polybius 7.8.
6. Polybius (5.88) records this and the other gifts: 'seventy-five silver talents, partly at once and the rest very shortly afterwards, to supply oil in the gymnasium, but dedicated silver cauldrons with their bases and a certain number of water-pitchers, and in addition to this granted ten talents for sacrifices and ten more to qualify new men for citizenship, so as to bring the whole gift up to a hundred talents. They also relieved Rhodian ships trading to their ports from the payment of customs, and presented the city with fifty catapults three cubits long.'
7. Athenaeus, *The Deipnosophists* 5.40–44.
8. Plutarch, *Marcellus* 13.
9. Vitruvius, *On Architecture* 9.10. Translated by J Gwilt at: http://penelope.uchicago.edu/Thayer/E/Roman/Texts/Vitruvius/home.html
10. Rorres C, *The Golden Crown* at: http://www.cs.drexel.edu/~crorres/Archimedes/Crown/CrownIntro.html
11. Polybius 1.67.
12. Polybius 1.70.
13. Polybius 1.83.

14. Polybius 3.28.
15. Polybius 2.13.
16. Polybius 3.14.
17. Goldsworthy, p. 144.
18. Livy 21.8.
19. Polybius 3.13.
20. Polybius 3.11. Livy and Nepos have Hannibal swear to be an active enemy of Rome. Livy 21.1,'he would show himself the enemy of Rome.' Nepos, *Hannibal* 1, 'so cherished in his mind the hatred which his father had borne the Romans.'
21. Livy 21.50.
22. Livy 23.21.
23. Finley, MI, *Ancient Sicily* (London, 1979), p. 120.
24. Livy 24.22.
25. Livy 24.2, also 23.14 and 24.13.
26. Polybius 7.8.

Chapter 23
1. Livy 24.4.
2. Livy 24.4.
3. Livy 24.5.
4. Livy 24.6
5. Livy 24.6.
6. Polybius 7.4.
7. Polybius 7.4.
8. Diodorus 26.15.
9. Polybius 7.7.
10. Livy 24.22
11. Livy 24.23.
12. Livy 24.24.
13. Diodorus 26.15.
14. Livy 24.27.
15. Plutarch, *Marcellus* 13.
16. Livy 24.28.
17. Livy 24.28.
18. Livy 24.29.
19. Livy 24.31.
20. Livy 24.32.
21. Livy 24.32.
22. Plutarch *Marcellus* 23. Polybius 8.3 simply states that they had seized power.
23. Livy 24.33.

Chapter 24
1. Livy 24.34.
2. Livy 24.34
3. Polybius 8.6.
4. Rorres, C & Harris, HG, *A Formidable War Machine: Construction and Operation of Archimedes' Iron Hand*, p. 7. At: http://www.cs.drexel.edu/~crorres/Archimedes/Claw/harris/rorres_harris.pdf

5. Rorres, C & Harris, HG, p. 7.
6. Zonaras 9.4.
7. For a good, concise discussion and further references see: http://www.math. nyu.edu/~crorres/Archimedes/Mirrors/legend/legend.html
8. Polybius 8.7.
9. Polybius 8.7.
10. Plutarch, *Marcellus* 17.
11. Livy 24.36.
12. Livy 24.37.
13. Livy 24.39.
14. Livy 25.23.
15. Livy 25.24.
16. Livy 25.24.
17. Plutarch, *Marcellus* 19.
18. Livy 25.26.
19. Livy 25.26.
20. Livy 25.27.
21. Livy 25.28.
22. Livy 25.30.
23. Livy 25.31.
24. Tzetzes Chiliades. 2.136–49. This is the most entertaining of the various versions of Archimedes death. Others are: Zonaras (9.5), 'He was constructing some figure or other, and hearing that the enemy were at hand, exclaimed: "Let them come at my head, but not at my line!" When a hostile warrior confronted him, he was little disturbed and called out: "Fellow, stand away from my line!" This exasperated the man and he struck him down'; Livy (25.31), 'Amongst many horrible instances of fury and rapacity the fate of Archimedes stands out. It is recorded that amidst all the uproar and terror created by the soldiers who were rushing about the captured city in search of plunder, he was quietly absorbed in some geometrical figures which he had drawn on the sand, and was killed by a soldier who did not know who he was'; Plutarch , *Marcellus* 19, 'but what most of all afflicted Marcellus was the death of Archimedes. For it chanced that he was by himself, working out some problem with the aid of a diagram, and having fixed his thoughts and his eyes as well upon the matter of his study, he was not aware of the incursion of the Romans or of the capture of the city. Suddenly a soldier came upon him and ordered him to go with him to Marcellus. This Archimedes refused to do until he had worked out his problem and established his demonstration, whereupon the soldier flew into a passion, drew his sword, and dispatched him. Others, however, say that the Roman came upon him with drawn sword threatening to kill him at once, and that Archimedes, when he saw him, earnestly besought him to wait a little while, that he might not leave the result that he was seeking incomplete and without demonstration; but the soldier paid no heed to him and made an end of him. There is also a third story, that as Archimedes was carrying to Marcellus some of his mathematical instruments, such as sun-dials and spheres and quadrants, by means of which he made the magnitude of the sun appreciable to the eye, some soldiers fell in with him, and thinking that he was carrying gold in the box, slew him.'
25. Livy 25.40.

26. Plutarch, *Marcellus* 23.
27. The year of the capture of Syracuse is, like so many dates in antiquity, uncertain. It is variously given as 212 or 211. The crucial indication is Marcellus' claim that he had spent 'three years investing Syracuse.' This is often interpreted in the modern sense as lasting for three, from early 214 to early 211. The ancient writers often used such terms to mean over three years, that is 214, 213, 212. I prefer 212 but the siege may have ended early in 211.

Epilogue
1. Plutarch, *Marcellus* 20.
2. Livy 39.51.

Bibliography

Austin, MM, 'Hellenistic kings, War, and the Economy', in *Classical Quarterly* 36 ii (1986).

Berger, S, *Revolution and Society in Greek Sicily and Southern Italy* (Stuttgart, 1997).

Caven, B, *Dionysius I War-lord of Sicily* (New Haven and London, 1990).

Caven, B, *The Punic Wars* (London, 1980).

Champion, J, 'The Causes of the Third Diodoch War 315–311 BC', in *Slingshot*, 213 (2001).

Champion, J, Antigonos' Policy of Freedom for the Greeks, in *Slingshot* 248 (2006).

Champion J, *Pyrrhus of Epirus* (Barnsley (2009).

Champion J, *The Tyrants of Syracuse: War in Ancient Sicily Volume I: 480–367* (Barnsley (2010).

Chaniotis, A, *War in the Hellenistic World* (Malden, 2005).

Crawford, M, *The Roman Republic* 2nd ed. (London, 1992).

De Ste. Croix, GEM, *The Class Struggle in the Ancient World: from the Archaic Age to the Arab Conquests* (London, 1981).

Fields, N, *Roman Conquests: North Africa* (Barnsley, 2010).

Finley, MI, *Ancient Sicily* (London, 1979).

Freeman, EA, *The History of Sicily from the Earliest Times* (Oxford 1891–1894).

Grainger, JD, *Hellenistic and Roman Naval Wars 336–31 BC* (Barnsley, 2011).

Goldsworthy, A, *Roman Warfare* (London, 2000).

Goldsworthy, A, *The Punic Wars* (London, 2001).

Garoufalias, P, *Pyrrhus, King of Epirus* (London, 1979).

Hale, JR, *Lords of the Sea: The Triumph and Tragedy of Ancient Athens* (Gibson Square, 2010).

Hanson, VD, *The Western Way of War: Infantry Battle in Classical Greece* (Oxford, 1988).

Hanson, VD, *The Wars of the Ancient Greeks* (London, 1999).

Harris, WV, *War and Imperialism in Republican Rome 327–70* (Oxford 1987).

Head, D, *The Armies of the Macedonian and Punic Wars* (Goring-by-Sea, 1982).

Kenny A, *An Illustrated Brief History of Western Philosophy*, (Malden, 2006).

Lendon, JE, *Soldiers and Ghosts: A History of Battle in Classical Antiquity* (Yale, 2006).

Lewis, S, editor, *Ancient Tyranny* (Edinburgh, 2006).

Lancel, S, *Carthage: a History* (Oxford, 1995), translated by A Nevill.

Matthew, C, 'When Push Comes to Shove: What was the *Othismos* of Hoplite Combat?', in *Historia* 30 (2009).

Miles, R, *Carthage Must be Destroyed* (2010).

Picard, GC & C, *Carthage* (London, 1968), translated by D Collon.

Porter, WH, *Life of Dion* (New York, 1979).

Salmon, JB, *Wealthy Corinth: a History of the City to 338 BC* (Oxford, 1984).

Sanders, LJ, *Dionysius I of Syracuse and Greek Tyranny* (Beckenham, 1987).

Schwartz, A, *Reinstating the Hoplite* (Stuttgart, 2009).

Scott, M, *From Democrats to Kings* (London, 2009).

Scullard, HH, *The Elephant in the Greek and Roman World* (London, 1974).

Stadter, PA, *Plutarch and the Historical Tradition* (London, 1992).

Talbert, RJA, *Timoleon and the Revival of Greek Sicily*, 344–317 B.C (Cambridge, 1974).

Tillyard, HJW, *Agathocles* (Cambridge, 1908).

van Wees, H, *Greek Warfare: Myths and Realities* (London, 2004).

Westlake, HD, *Timoleon and his Relations with Tyrants* (Manchester, 1952).

Waterfield, R, *Why Socrates Died Dispelling the Myths* (London, 2010).

The following translations of the ancient sources were used:

Aelian, *Varia Historia*, translated by GP Goold (London and Cambridge, Massachusetts, 1997).

Athenaeus, *The Deipnosophists*, translated by CD Yonge, http://www.attalus.org/old/athenaeus11.html

Diodorus, *The Library of History VII*, translated by C L Sherman (London and Cambridge, Massachusetts, 1980).

Diodorus, *The Library of History VIII*, translated by C Bradford Welles (London and Cambridge, Massachusetts, 2003).

Diodorus, *The Library of History IX*, translated by RM Geer (London and Cambridge, Massachusetts, 1984).

Diodorus, *The Library of History X*, translated by RM Geer (London and Cambridge, Massachusetts, 1983).

Diodorus, *The Library of History XI*, translated by RM Geer (London and Cambridge, Massachusetts, 1999).

Dionysius of Halicarnassus, *Roman Antiquities*, translated by E Cary, http.//Penelope.uchicago.edu/Thayer/E/Texts/Dionysius_of_Halicarnassus/home/html

Frontinus, The *Stratagemata*, translated by C E Bennet, http. .//Penelope.uchicago.edu/Thayer/E/Texts/Frontinus/Strategemata/home.html

Justin, *Epitome of the Philippic History of Pompeius Trogus*, translated by J S Watson, http://www.forumromanum.org/literature/justin/english/index.html

Livy, The History of Rome, translated by Rev. C Roberts, http://www2.lib.virginia.edu/etext/index.html

Nepos, *Lives of Eminent Commanders*, translated by the Rev. John Selby Watson, http://www.ccel.org/ccel/pearse/morefathers/files/nepos.htm

Pausanias, *Guide to Greece, volume 2: Southern Greece*, translated by P Levi (Harmondsworth, 1971).

Plato, *The Seventh Letter.* Translated by J Harward at: http://classics.mit.edu/Plato/seventh_letter.html

Plato, *Republic*, translated by B Jowett, http://classics.mit.edu/Plato/republic.9. viii.html

Plato, *Statesman*, translated by B Jowett, http://classics.mit.edu/Plato/stateman.html

Plato, *Timaeus.Critias.Cleitophon.Menexus.Epistles*, translated by RG Bury (London and Cambridge, Massachusetts, 1989).

Plutarch, *Parallel Lives*, translated by B Perrin, http://penelope.uchicago.edu/Thayer/E/Roman/Texts/

Polyaenus, *Stratagems*, translated by R Shepherd, http://www.attalus.org/translate/polyaenus.html

Polybius, *The Histories*, translated by W R Paton, http://penelope.uchicago.edu/Thayer/E/Roman/Texts/Polybius/home.html

Thucydides, *The Landmark Thucydides*, translated by R Crawley (New York, 1998).

Xenophon, *A History of My Times (Hellenica)*, translated by R Warner (Harmondsworth, 1966).

Index